Carolina Currents
Studies in South Carolina Culture

Carolina Currents
Studies in South Carolina Culture
Volume 2. Recovering Lost Stories

   "Understanding for the Common Good"

Carolina Currents is an annual peer-reviewed publication that connects academic research to the lived experiences and practical concerns of South Carolinians

Editor
Christopher D. Johnson, Francis Marion University

Editorial Board
William Bolt, *Francis Marion University*
Eric Crawford, *Coastal Carolina University*
Christopher E. Hendricks, *Georgia Southern University*
Samuel M. Hines, *The Citadel*
Felice F. Knight, *International African American Museum*
Laura L. Morris, *Furman University*
Echol Lee Nix Jr. (1975–2020), *Claflin University*
Mark M. Smith, *University of South Carolina*
Shevaun E. Watson, *University of Wisconsin, Milwaukee*

USC Press Staff
Michael J. McGandy, *Director*; Aurora Bell, *Associate Editorial Director*; Ana Bichanich, *EDP Director*; Cathy Esposito, *Marketing & Sales Director*; Ehren Foley, *Acquisitions Editor*; Jolie Hale, *Publishing Assistant*; Vicki Leach, *Business Manager*; Ashley Mathias, *Digital Publishing Coordinator*; Kemi Ogunji, *Senior Marketing Coordinator/Designer*; Kerri L. Tolan, *Production Editor*; Dianne Wade, *Marketing Assistant*

Copy Editor
Juanita Ruffin Doswell

Published by the University of South Carolina Press in cooperation with Francis Marion University

Carolina Currents
Studies in South Carolina Culture

Volume 2. Recovering Lost Stories

Edited by
Christopher D. Johnson

THE UNIVERSITY OF SOUTH CAROLINA PRESS

Published by the University of South Carolina Press
Columbia, South Carolina 29208

uscpress.com

Printed in the United States of America

Library of Congress Control Number: 2025900984

ISBN: 978-1-64336-572-5 (paperback)
ISBN: 978-1-64336-573-2 (ebook)
DOI: https://doi.org/10.61162/FSYQ1058

The inclusion of this book in the Open Carolina collection is made possible by the generous funding of the University of South Carolina Libraries and Francis Marion University.

Contents

Review Essay

List of Illustrations

Figures

Tables

Society Hill
Adam Houle

One pair of scuffed up sneaks

snug in a mudroom cubby,
the only pair at home, eyelets
like the eyes of meek owls

blinkless blinkless until a soft dusk
settles and headlights splash a wall
or don't. Blinkless past bedtime.

Then, until the social clubs close.
What else is there but hunger?
Who knows who knows.

Adam Houle is the author of *Stray*, a finalist for the Colorado Books Awards. His work has appeared in AGNI, Shenandoah, Post Road, and elsewhere. He is an assistant professor of English at Francis Marion University and co-editor of *Twelve Mile Review*.

Acknowledgments

Carolina Currents would not be possible without the generous support of Francis Marion University (FMU). Dr. Luther F. Carter, president of FMU, and Dr. Alissa Warters, university provost, have provided resources, guidance, and encouragement. My past and current department chairs, Dr. Rebecca Flannagan and Dr. Meredith A. Love, have offered consistent support for the project. The Trustees of FMU have honored me with the designation Research Scholar. The reassigned time associated with that honor has allowed me to devote time and energy toward editing this volume.

Editorial board members have encouraged colleagues to contribute to *Carolina Currents* and have graciously served as reviewers for the many essays we received. Several of my FMU colleagues have also served as reviewers: Lindsey Banister, Adam Houle, Erica Johnson, Scott Kaufman, Jason Kirby, Lorraine de Montluzin, Rachel Spear, and Dillion Stone Tatum. I would also like to thank Professor Bobby J. Donaldson of the University of South Carolina.

Three student workers have helped with production. Leah Tedder worked tirelessly on the bibliographies and notes. She also formatted the book reviews and proofread the final version. Without her good work, the volume would not have been completed on time. Quite unintentionally, Leah seems to have mastered the intricacies of the *Chicago Manual of Style*. Sorry about that, Leah; I'll make it up to you. Gabriel Smith and Anna Floyd also helped with proofreading. My wife, Christine, has listened patiently as I've ruminated about various aspects of the volume. She has also helped proofread the finished version. The good people at the University of South Carolina Press have been, as always, wonderful partners. I would like to acknowledge Michael McGandy, Aurora Bell, and Kerri L. Tolan, all of whom have been exceptionally helpful and patient. The University of South Carolina Libraries have provided vital funding to support the open access version of the volume.

Final thanks must go to the authors who contributed essays and reviews. Without your research, insight, and analysis, there would be no *Carolina Currents*. I am grateful for your skills, wisdom, and perseverance.

Introduction

Christopher D. Johnson

Among the most powerful responses to the attacks of September 11, 2001, is Billy Collins's "The Names." At the beginning of the poem, the speaker spends a rainy night pondering those who died in his home city: "I started with A, with Ackerman, as it happened,/Then Baxter and Calabro,/Davis and Eberling, names falling into place/As droplets fell through the dark."[1] Over the course of the poem, the speaker identifies a victim for each letter of the alphabet and then reaches a somber conclusion: "So many names, there is barely room on the walls of the heart."[2] The power of Collins's poem originates in both its detail and its lack of specificity. On one hand, the poem pulls the victims out of a statistical aggregate and restores their individuality. On the other, it reminds us that the names themselves—"Kelly and Lee,/Medina, Nardella, and O'Connor"—tell us little.[3] We do not know ages, genders, or professions. We do not know who each person left behind, only that they are now gone. In this way, absence defines the loss, and the unanswerable questions raised by the poem show the scope of the vicious assaults. More important, Collins pulls the events of September 11 away from concerns about national security and toward the personal. He reminds us that the victims were people whose lives—perhaps as unremarkable as most lives—had meaning, value, and dignity. The attacks were profound not only in global and national terms but also in human terms. The destruction of the World Trade Center, Collins insists, was more than a national tragedy; it was 2,753 individual tragedies.

Collins never allows the victims to speak, but their silence is resounding. The historian Howard Zinn takes a somewhat different approach. He calls on his readers to awaken the "silent voices of the past, so that we can look behind the silence of the present."[4] For Zinn, history has the power to "untie our minds, our bodies," but only if we acknowledge those who have been left out of the historical record, only if we allow ourselves to hear quieted words.[5] The essays in this volume take up the work of Collins and Zinn. They recover histories that have been forgotten, erased, or appropriated. They challenge us to replace simple narratives with nuanced understandings. Most important, they honor the humanity of the enslaved, the maligned, and the misunderstood.

Several of the essays emerged from a brilliant symposium hosted by the Francis Marion University chapter of Universities Studying Slavery (USS) in February 2023. USS was founded at the University of Virginia in 2016 and currently has over one hundred member institutions, including seven from South Carolina: The Citadel, Clemson University, the College of Charleston, Francis Marion University, Furman University, the University of South Carolina, and Wofford College. The consortium seeks to share "best practices and guiding principles" for individuals and groups engaged in "truth-telling educational projects focused on human bondage and the legacies of racism."[6] The 2023 symposium, organized by a committee ably led by Dr. Erica Johnson, brought together scholars from across the region. It was not, however, a typical academic conference. There were community members, librarians, public historians, archivists, and students, several of whom presented papers and all of whom shared an interest in learning more about their own histories and those of their neighbors. Although much of the research focused on universities' complicity with enslavement, there were also papers on adjacent topics, including the history of slavery at Hobcaw Barony; the development of an African-American historical walking tour in Lake City; the desegregation of Wilson High School in Florence; and archaeological excavations at Jamestown, a postbellum Black community in the Pee Dee.[7] The Center for Civil Rights History and Research at the University of South Carolina provided an expansive exhibit titled "Justice for All: South Carolina and the American Civil Rights Movement." The symposium ended with a splendid walking tour of downtown Florence led by Professor Louis Venters.

For those accustomed to discipline-specific conferences, the USS event was invigorating. Many of the papers were collaborative, often involving undergraduates. Each session was full, and the energy and enthusiasm were palpable. There were abundant questions and a strong sense of common purpose. Community members whose work lies outside the academy used personal remembrance to fill gaps in the historical record. The students, many of whom were making their first scholarly presentations, received guidance from generous scholars eager to encourage a younger generation. At lunch, there seemed to be more sharing and discussion than eating.

The symposium reminded many of us of how meaningful humanities research can be when it connects to people's lived experiences. It also reminded us that collaboration needs to extend beyond academic credentials and disciplinary boundaries. Our communities are filled with experts of serious intention working diligently to recover important histories. These researchers are amateurs, not in the condescending way in which the word is often used but in its original meaning of someone who undertakes a task for love rather than profit. Those of us who are professional scholars need to respect their knowledge and skills. We need to welcome them into our conversations, share what we have learned, and value their perspectives and discoveries. The ivory towers that still exist don't need to be razed, but their doors and stairways need to be opened.

Accessibility, in fact, has never been more essential. Because of funding provided by Francis Marion University, the USS symposium was a free event that was open to the public. Other crucial resources, however, often remain unavailable to those who need them. Scholarly books are notoriously expensive, and journal articles are frequently locked behind paywalls. For those without access to university libraries, vital materials remain unattainable. Many presses are working to address these issues by making their titles available as free, open-access documents. The University of South Carolina Press has been an important leader in these initiatives, especially through the Open Carolina program, which includes all volumes of *Carolina Currents*.[8] Open access, however, is only free to the user. The press still incurs the expenses of production and marketing. The open-access versions of *Carolina Currents*, as well as the affordable paperback volumes, would be impossible without the generous support of Francis Marion University and the University of South Carolina Libraries.

Accessibility, of course, goes beyond cost. To be useful for a wide range of readers, scholarly work needs to be comprehensible, which presents its own challenges. Academic arguments are often complicated and nuanced. They contribute to ongoing dialogues that can be difficult for nonspecialists to understand, and here lies the difficulty: The aims of scholarship cannot be met by simplifying the complex, but the needs of readers cannot be met with indecipherable works. The trick, it seems, is to clarify without dumbing down. The essays in this volume meet this goal. The authors have worked carefully to avoid specialized terms of art, which often appear to be no more than jargon. They have also sought to explain theoretical frameworks in ordinary language. Most important, several of the essays include discussions of methodology. They show not only what was discovered but also how it was discovered. They do so because the authors want to guide those who are undertaking similar work. Collaboration, they recognize, can take place between a text and a reader.

Furthermore, we recognize that some members of our audience use assistive technologies. To make the volume more accessible to them, we adhere to current ebook-conversion best practices. These include clear document structuring and hyperlinking and providing alternative text for all images.

After the introductory materials and Adam Houle's powerful poem, "Society Hill," the volume begins with Aïda Rogers's discussion of Wheeler Hill, a now-gentrified portion of Columbia. In this work of creative nonfiction, Rogers continues the efforts of the USS. She reveals the complicity of the University of South Carolina in destroying an African-American neighborhood and displacing residents whose families had lived in the area for generations. Today, only a few structures from the original Wheeler Hill remain. There are some extant photographs, and, as Rogers records, the memories of a handful of former residents who still worship in the St. James African Methodist Episcopal Church. There are also the paintings of Edmund Yaghjian and the poetry of Dorothy Perry Thompson, particularly *Wheeler Hill and Other Poems*, a collection she wrote for her doctoral dissertation under the direction of James Dickey. These stirring poems, many of which have never been published, provide an artist's recreation of her childhood home. Contextualizing the poems within the history of Wheeler Hill, Rogers shows the power of art to both document injustice and preserve memory.

The next two essays also address the actions of institutions of higher learning. Taylor Diggs and Felice F. Knight reconstruct the biography of Arthur B. Mitchell, a free Black man who served as a musician in the Confederate Army and as a fifer for The Citadel. The essay is an expansion of Diggs's undergraduate thesis, which she completed at The Citadel under Knight's direction. Rich in archival evidence and sound historical analysis, the essay demonstrates the ability of nonprofessionals—in this case, a student—to conduct meaningful original research when given the right direction. Mitchell's story reveals the tenuous position of free Black people in nineteenth-century Charleston. His participation in the Confederate cause seems to have originated in necessity, not ideology. After the war, in fact, he became an officer in the National Guard Service of South Carolina, a militia empowered by Governor Robert K. Scott to suppress insurrection and inhibit violence. As a member of this "Black militia," as it was called, Mitchell had an opportunity to resist the very forces of oppression that he, likely inadvertently, defended. Mary Jo Fairchild engages in similar work as she uncovers the lives of Thomas Peace and his family. Born into slavery, Peace was hired out to the College of Charleston, where he worked on and off until his death in 1887. In the subsequent decades, white Charlestonians appropriated Peace's biography, as they did Arthur Mitchell's, to defend the ideologies of enslavement and segregation and to wash from themselves the stains of oppression. A highly fictionalized and stereotypical version of Peace, for example, appears in a play from the late nineteenth century, showing that art can be an instrument of deception as well as recovery. Through her meticulous archival work, Fairchild introduces the reader to a more accurate, less romanticized, Peace family, whose lives, both ordinary and remarkable, deserve preservation.

Five scholars, all associated with the Belle W. Baruch Center for South Carolina Studies, have been working to identify the enslaved people who lived on the land now known as Hobcaw Barony. In their essay, these scholars describe the difficult, often uncertain, process of tracing the names of the enslaved. Equally important, they discuss their methodology in detail. By providing the tools of discovery, they hope to empower others to engage in similar work, perhaps tracing their own family histories. The seven hundred thirty-one names included in the Appendix acknowledge the humanity of generations of people exploited by white landowners on a small parcel of our state that is now celebrated for its natural beauty and twentieth-century history. Like the names in Collins's poem, the Appendix personalizes the effects of ideologically driven violence. It also reminds us of what has been lost. Many of the enslaved are known only by the Christian names given to them by their captors. Like the young Thomas Peace, they had no surnames. With their authentic identities destroyed, we are left only with ciphers that cannot always be decoded. The sheer volume of names on a relatively tiny piece of land (sixteen thousand acres) underscores the scale of human suffering brought about by chattel slavery. In this way, the essay continues the vital work of the International African American Museum, especially the displays that preserve the African names of those who were enslaved and the Tide Tribute, which honors those who endured the horrors of the Middle Passage.[9]

Michael S. Martin, whose fine book, *Appalachian Pastoral*, is reviewed in this volume, discusses the nineteenth-century poet, novelist, and travel writer Caroline Howard Gilman. In popular works such as *The Poetry of Travelling in the United States* and *Recollections of a Southern Matron*, Gilman defined South Carolina for a wide readership. Her creative portrayals of the South, particularly her treatment of Charleston, emphasize symmetry and balance both geographically and culturally. As Martin shows, Charleston becomes the axis of her vision, and the hierarchical structures that allowed enslavement become the foundation of her imagined social order. In this way, Gilman's evocative poetry and prose not only recorded her understandings of landscape and architecture but also normalized the most toxic aspects of antebellum life. If, as Aïda Rogers argues, Dorothy Perry Thompson's poetry demonstrates how art can resist a dominant culture, Gilman's works show how it can empower forces of persecution and exclusion.

Using the history of experience approach developed by Robert Boddice and Mark M. Smith, Michael Emett offers a conflicting depiction of nineteenth-century Charleston.[10] Recreating the experiences of the abolitionist passengers of the *Oceanus*, who traveled from Brooklyn to Charleston in April 1865, Emett shows how Henry Ward Beecher's theatrical depictions of slave auctions, which were performed predominantly in white northern churches, defined Charleston. Once again, art becomes a powerful force that controls experience, even the visceral reactions the travelers felt when visiting John C. Calhoun's vandalized gravesite.

Lakin Hanna and her professor, Erica Johnson, provide an insightful history of the Lamar Bus Riots, a frequently overlooked event in our state's struggle to desegregate. Using the oral histories of those victimized by the riots, Hanna and Johnson offer a fresh look at the events before and after the violence. Equally important, their research preserves the memories of local residents whose histories and experiences might otherwise be lost. In the volume's final essay, Eli Kibler, Eva Kiser, and Kylie Fisher explore a separate racial history: the establishment of Asian American communities in the upstate. Using a variety of archival materials, the authors show the impact of nineteenth-century missionary work, much of it associated with Furman University. The first Asian arrivals were students seeking a faith-based education that would allow them to continue the work that had shaped their lives. In time, Asian Americans took on faculty roles at Furman. Others settled in the Greenville area and established businesses, some of which continue to operate. Asian immigrants faced many challenges, including racism and prejudice. Still, their stories are happier than those of the enslaved and formerly enslaved. By recovering this important part of South Carolina history, the authors uncover another understudied aspect of the state's rich culture.

The review section begins with an essay by Jo Angela Edwins, who introduces seven new volumes of poetry by South Carolina authors. In some ways, Edwins's work marks a new direction for *Carolina Currents*. She not only provides the first multi-title review; she also focuses exclusively on creative works. This is a deliberate expansion of our previous focus on scholarly works. South Carolina culture, after all, is defined by artists as well as historians, political scientists, and literary scholars, and creative works deserve recognition. Edwins's efforts are joined by those of Landon Houle and Natalie Mahaffey, who review works of fiction and poetry.

The essays and reviews contained in this volume represent thousands of hours of research and analysis. They remind us that many aspects of South Carolina culture are yet to be discovered and that all of us can play a part in unearthing the forgotten stories that make up the state's rich, vibrant, and often tragic past. We are now in an age in which censorship is equated with liberty, in which books are being removed from libraries, and in which teachers fear retribution for acknowledging students' backgrounds and identities. As we hear loud calls to silence voices from the past, to make our history more reassuring than true, we recognize the importance of scholars and artists who will not allow us to retreat into ease and who show us the importance of forgotten names.

Christopher D. Johnson is distinguished professor of English and Trustees' Research Scholar at Francis Marion University. He serves as editor of *Carolina Currents*.

NOTES

1. Billy Collins, "The Names," *New York Times*, September 6, 2002, A23, lines 4–7.
2. Collins, "The Names," line 54.
3. Collins, "The Names," lines 25–26.
4. Howard Zinn, *The Politics of History*, 2nd edition (Champaign: University of Illinois Press, 1990), 54.
5. Zinn, *Politics of History*, 54.
6. "Universities Studying Slavery," *The President's Commission on Slavery and the University*, University of Virginia, https://slavery.virginia.edu/universities-studying-slavery/.
7. This approach is consistent with USS's mission, which includes a commitment to "research, acknowledgement, education, and atonement regarding institutional ties to the slave trade, to enslavement on campus or abroad, and to enduring racism in school history and practice." See "Universities Studying Slavery."
8. For more information about Open Carolina, see "Open Carolina," Columbia: *University of South Carolina Press*, n.d. (https://uscpress.com/Open-Carolina).
9. The International African American Museum is located on Wharfside Street in Charleston, SC. It opened in 2023 and is free for residents of South Carolina and open to the public. For more information, see the International African American Museum, https://iaamuseum.org.
10. For a comprehensive introduction to the history of experience, see Robert Boddice and Mark M. Smith, *Emotion, Sense, and Experience* (Cambridge, England: Cambridge University Press, 2020); see also Mark M. Smith, *A Sensory History Manifesto* (University Park: Penn State University Press, 2021).

WORKS CITED

Boddice, Robert. and Mark M. Smith. *Emotion, Sense, and Experience* (Cambridge, England: Cambridge University Press, 2020)

Collins, Billy. "The Names." *New York Times*, September 6, 2002, A23, lines 4–7.

"Open Carolina." Columbia: *University of South Carolina Press*, 2024. https:// uscpress.com/Open-Carolina.

Smith, Mark M. *A Sensory History Manifesto* (University Park: Penn State University Press, 2021).

"Universities Studying Slavery." *The President's Commission on Slavery and the University,* University of Virginia. https://slavery.virginia.edu/ universities-studying-slavery/.

Zinn, Howard. *The Politics of History*, 2nd ed. (Champaign: University of Illinois Press, 1990), 54.

Side by Side and All with Porches

Columbia's Erased Neighborhoods Were
Rich in Community

Aïda Rogers

It must have been a happy moment—maybe of elation—when the committee tasked with restoring the University of South Carolina's historic Horseshoe realized they had access to free bricks. Their beloved landmark, an expanse of grand trees and architecturally important buildings, was in dramatic need of repair. Free bricks? What a windfall. Brick walls could be built to enhance special gardens. Brick walkways would look so much better, be more historically appropriate, than the asphalt pavement already in place.

Equally convenient, the bricks would be easy to get. They were practically on campus already, the remains of the oldest buildings of the four-acre Booker T. Washington High School. For fifty-eight years, those bricks had held up and held in thousands of students and a devoted faculty. But the Richland County District One School Board had voted. The building was too old; it would cost too much to update or build new somewhere else. The students, teachers, coaches, and counselors would go to newer schools in the district. The bricks would go to the Horseshoe. Elation? Or business as usual? Under pressure to finish their restoration by the country's 1976 bicentennial, the committee acted as any practical, cash-strapped group would: They used what they had. And, as usual, business as usual for white decision-makers created heartbreak and bitterness for the people who loved Booker T. Washington High School, who fought loud and hard to keep it open. The idea of people walking on their school's bricks—essentially walking on them—was too profound a metaphor. In truth, it was sacrilegious. Booker T. Washington High School, with its stellar academics, athletics, and arts, its legion of high-achieving alumni and tirelessly determined faculty, was closed and demolished in 1974. Its bricks were moved in 1975. The committee could meet their 1976 deadline. And "The Great Mother of the Black Community," as science teacher and alumna Frankie B. Outten so accurately put it when she and so many others publicly protested its closure, went quiet.[1]

My mother is driving my sisters and me to Columbia. It's 1968, baby number four is coming, and she has regular obstetrician appointments to keep. For her children, the ride is long and boring until we cross the Broad River into the city. That's when the view gets interesting. A row of houses, side by side and all with porches, cram next to each other on a slope. They look rickety, but I can't look away. I somehow know poor people live there and that they're probably Black, but it seems like a fun way to live—and so different from the carefully spaced, horizontal world of brick ranch houses and grass yards we occupy in our majority-white town.

I figured those small houses were "cabins"—I didn't know the term *shotgun house*—and that the people in them visited each other all the time.[2] I envisioned lots of laughing and hanging over the porches. Fifty-some years later, I learned that I was right. Mrs. Ethel Livingston Pearson, a member of Booker T. Washington High School's last graduating class, smiles when she talks about growing up on "the Hill." Her "Hill" is the Wheeler Hill neighborhood, adjacent to the University of South Carolina. Although Wheeler Hill is not the neighborhood I remember from childhood—that was Arsenal

Figure 1.1. Wheeler Hill children in their play area behind their homes, ca. 1950. From The Joseph E. Winter Photograph Collection, South Caroliniana Library, University of South Carolina, Columbia, SC.

Hill—they were similar. Most of the residents were tenants, Black, and poor.[3]

But poor is a relative term. It can have lots of meanings. You can be poor in money but rich in other ways. Wheeler Hill was rich in community. "We were really neighbors," Mrs. Pearson recalls. "We were close and friendly, and you could reach across the porch and get what you need." Her grandmother and her neighbor would swap yellow and white grits across their porches, she tells me. People would come out in the mornings to greet each other and then back out in the evenings to say good night. Physically close, they were emotionally close too. For the kids, "meeting up" was common practice. "We would meet up to go down the hill to high school or meet up to go up the hill to elementary school," she explains.[4] Wheeler Hill Elementary later was renamed after Florence C. Benson, who taught there. The schools, like the churches, unified the residents. Mrs. Pearson doesn't live on Wheeler Hill anymore. She hasn't for decades, and neither have her friends and neighbors, ever since the university began its slow encroachment into the neighborhood. But does a slow takeover make it any less disruptive? Isn't a tsunami of development—no matter how gradual—still a tsunami?

You can find Mrs. Pearson and other Wheeler Hill old-timers—and some of their descendants—in one of the few places they have left in their cherished neighborhood. St. James African Methodist Episcopal (AME) Church still stands, thanks to Ezra Wheeler, the Ohio doctor who bought land and settled here in the 1870s. Dr. Wheeler sold a plot of it to the church for a dollar, stipulating that it must be used for religious purposes.[5] On Sunday mornings, it's a joyful place to be. When a baby cries, Mrs. Pearson is thrilled. A new baby means a new member.

The truth of it is, nobody should have been surprised that Booker T. Washington closed. The people it served lived in neighborhoods close to the university, and the university needed space. The residents on Wheeler Hill needed only to look west across South Main and Assembly streets and down the Blossom Street hill to see what the university and city of Columbia could do. Their neighbors and classmates in the Ward One community had been scattered years before Booker closed. Their shotgun houses, café, small groceries, and churches were demolished—even their beloved Celia Dial Saxon School—so massive concrete could rise. Exhibit A: The Carolina Coliseum. The 12,401-seat arena, for years the largest in the state, signaled a new skyline for Columbia and the 1968 end of Ward One.

Like Ward One, Wheeler Hill had been self-sufficient. People had everything they needed—a community center, ball fields, churches, a small store,

Figure 1.2. Restaurant on Pickens Street in Wheeler Hill, ca. 1949–51. From the John Hensel Collection, South Caroliniana Library, University of South Carolina, Columbia, SC.

a beauty salon, even a cobbler. Residents were working class, and they obediently kept to themselves. They knew not to cross Wheat Street, which Booker fronted, because they weren't allowed on the university campus on the hill above it—unless they worked there as custodians, groundskeepers, or in food service. Those were the rules until 1963, when the University of South Carolina (USC) admitted its first Black students since Reconstruction.[6]

For its part, the university was in a geographical and financial bind. Like many city-enclosed universities in the United States, post-World War II America meant rapidly growing enrollments. Veterans brought their GI bills; the baby boom brought more students. Those students needed dorms. Gyms. Classrooms. Ballfields. Married housing. USC, having gone from sixty-seven hundred students in 1962 to nineteen thousand five hundred in 1972, was strapped and chafing. Its rescue arrived in a series of midcentury federal urban renewal funds that allowed universities and cities to "fight blight" through "slum clearance."[7] USC was one of many colleges and universities in the country to use those terms and techniques to get the real estate they wanted, and so often, such real estate was owned by absentee landlords. Eminent domain gave the university, through its newly established, nonprofit Carolina Research and Development Foundation, the legal means to buy properties—*acquire* is the word regularly used—and then demolish them for their needs. The result today, in 2024, is dramatic. Ward One, which in 1965 tied with Arsenal Hill as Columbia's most blighted neighborhood, is entirely a university property of behemoth buildings—the Strom Thurmond Wellness and Fitness Center, the Darla Moore School of Business, the Koger Center for the Arts, and its Greek Village for sororities and fraternities. With the opening of the eighteen-thousand-seat Colonial Life Arena in 2002, the Coliseum became practically obsolete.

Wheeler Hill, considered the fourth-most blighted neighborhood, was much slower to change. Now it's mostly residential—a tangle of narrow, winding lanes, large homes, and brick town homes. Vines cover brick walls with wrought-iron gates. Expensive cars front small, manicured yards. The original roads, unpaved, were rerouted. Few signs of shotgun houses here, and certainly no outdoor plumbing. But vestiges of those old communities remain. In Ward One, the long-languishing Palmetto Compress Building, a vast horizontal brick structure where cotton bales were compressed in the early twentieth century, was recently restored into student apartments. Photos of the old neighborhood line the walls, a project of Columbia SC 63, an initiative that recognizes the fiftieth anniversary of the 1963 American Civil Rights Movement.[8] On Wheeler Hill, a few original homes remain, owned by residents who could afford to not sell. And most noticeably, along with the railroad tracks and Benson School, St. James AME.

It was St. James that drew the attention of journalist Janet Kahler, who lived with her family two miles away in the Shandon neighborhood. Driving around Wheeler Hill in the 2000s with her daughter, Sophie, she pointed out the incongruity of an old Black church in a new white neighborhood. When Sophie entered the USC as a history and geography major, she started what became a four-year study of Columbia's old, erased, and redlined neighborhoods. Her curiosity specifically about Wheeler Hill led her to plunder fifteen boxes and cartons of the university's archives and about ten binders of documents and meeting minutes of the Columbia Housing Authority. Her painstaking research resulted first in a nine-page paper published in the January 2020 issue of the *Journal of Historical Geography*. Its headline was as explosive as the letter she uncovered: "'Wipe out the entire slum area': university-led urban renewal in Columbia, South Carolina, 1950–1985."[9] The words came from a letter written by university president Thomas F. Jones to members of Columbia's city council and housing authority. Dated February 22, 1968, Jones put into writing what he and other local power brokers thought, said, and planned: "For many years it has been the goal of the University and the City of Columbia to attempt to wipe out the entire slum area of approximately twelve blocks known as Wheeler Hill."[10] Today, Jones's words sound exceptionally brutal. For the people of Wheeler Hill, they were savage. Forcing people to leave their homes, even if a housing authority says that it will help them find somewhere else to go, is still eviction. Or in the case of a community, exodus.

This word: *slum*. It drags the ear, harms the spirit, insults a community. It's code, Sophie Kahler writes, noting that "by the mid-twentieth century the terms blight and slum were used by government officials as synonyms for African American communities." In Columbia at that time, eighty-one percent of the city's nonwhite residents lived in six areas considered the most blighted. "The desire to wipe out slums, therefore, coincided with a desire to wipe out black communities."[11] Her research has shown that the university, once it had built a gym and athletic fields across from Booker T. Washington High, didn't need the Wheeler Hill property. The land in Ward One was enough. "There are documents where they explicitly say, 'we don't need it for campus but we need it to protect ourselves,'" Kahler said, when I interviewed her for an article about her research.[12] She was particularly struck by how a slow, decades-long development can erode a neighborhood. Her word: *destabilizing*.

As for *slum*, that word is also misleading. Basil Harris, a lifelong member of St. James AME, wants me to know that Wheeler Hill was not that. The Wheeler Hill of his 1970s childhood was more prosperous. Too many people outside the community think that it never changed after the 1930s, he says, when many photos were taken.[13] In actuality, most photos were taken in the 1950s and '60s—at least the ones available for public viewing—when the "Fight Blight" movement hit full gear. Joseph Winter, housing inspector and then-director of the Columbia Rehabilitation Commission, documented those neighborhoods to justify urban renewal and neighborhood demolition. His photos have been collected and digitized by the university's South Caroliniana Library.[14] Winter captured scenes of children working diligently outside, trash piles on the side of their unpaved streets. Did they understand that by "fighting blight" they were helping the effort that eventually would displace them?

Figure 1.3. Booker T. Washington High School, February 26, 1974, the day Richland School District One announced it would close. Photograph by Ed Tilley, *The State.* Richland Library, Columbia, SC.

Basil Harris's family moved to the Eau Claire area north of Main Street. Others headed to neighborhoods on Bluff Road, in the shadow of the university's Williams-Brice Stadium. Like most members of St. James, he hasn't lived on Wheeler Hill in decades. Gentrification made it too expensive. But those are nice cars in the church parking lot on the last Sunday in February, and the sanctuary is spotless and just the right size, recently renovated with electronic screens to read the hymns. Harris, with his three master's degrees from USC, wants me to know that his congregation is one of education. The church helped provide that education, with Sunday school, Vacation Bible School, and Christmas and Easter pageants. His sons have degrees from Claflin University and West Point. The current and past two pastors have doctorates. "*That* is the lineage of Wheeler Hill," he declares.[15]

Harris, who lives in Irmo and works at the State Department of Education, knows his local history, so he knows the name Dorothy Perry Thompson, who grew up here a generation before him. She is the reason people know important things about Wheeler Hill. When Sophie Kahler did her research, Thompson's dissertation was invaluable. In "Wheeler Hill and

Other Poems," Thompson describes her community and the people in it. I'm captivated by her work and irked that her books are out of print.

"I grew up in a calm, dangerous, simple, mysterious place and time," she writes in her introduction, "'Wheeler Hill,' Columbia, South Carolina, 1950–65."[16] What follows are poem after poem about the people who inhabited her neighborhood in her time. They're a colorful crowd—Pink, the bootlegger who "came from Philly/In a sharkskin suit and alligator shoes"; Sister Lakin with her drinking problem and friend Lally who kept her straight; Sonny on the chain gang; Benjamin Jefferson who "whistled in spurts/Of exaggerated life/To the rhythmical pop/Of his shoeshine rag." In "Miss

Figure 1.4. Dr. Dorothy Perry Thompson reading poetry in 1992. Photograph by Joel Nichols. Louise Pettus Archives, Winthrop University.

Juanita's Beauty Salon," Thompson describes how Brother Reese makes sure his Silver Satin wine is hidden inside his coat. He wouldn't want the ladies inside—sisters Fannie Phelps Adams and Celia Phelps Martin—to see him take a drink. "I always turns my back!"[17]

Maybe only a poet can best get across what a lost place was. Her poems reflect childhood impressions and those that came later.

Spend any time learning about Wheeler Hill or Booker T. Washington High and you start recognizing the names. Fannie Phelps Adams and Celia Phelps Martin grew up on the Hill and were respected Booker educators. Their names are engraved on brass plaques on pews at St. James. Brother Reese would be crazy to drink in front of them, or "Miss Jeannette White/ the licensed mid-wife/Who was getting her hair dyed."[18]

Everybody knew everybody, and Dorothy Perry Thompson makes sure we know them too. Some of her "characters" are still on Wheeler Hill; namely, Latrelle Argroe, who'd "have parties for all the children/And make their cos-tumes/For Halloween night." Her husband, Mr. Hump, the plumber, "would fix people's toilets/And let them pay/With what they could."[19] Calm and dangerous, indeed.

Thanks to Thompson's dissertation, we forever have in writing impor-tant facts about midcentury Columbia. She's the one who tells us about the "Keep Out" sign on the wall that divided Wheeler Hill from Myrtle Court, the exclusive white neighborhood next door. From her poems, we learn that people on Wheeler Hill weren't allowed to cross Wheat Street, because Blacks weren't allowed on the university campus then. Her opening poem, "Wheeler Hill," tells us plenty in its first two verses:

It was always there,
Just like us,
subject to the whims and wishes
Of the Almighty Whitey;[20]

Juanita's Beauty Salon is long gone, and Copeland's Corner Store is much changed. A small grocery in Thompson's earlier years, Copeland's eventually became a gourmet grocery called the Purple Cow, distinctive for its large sign outside. Now that building houses DiPrato's Delicatessen, a popular lunch and brunch restaurant. "A country club-type place," Sophie Kahler describes it.[21]

Ethel Livingston Pearson grew up in a house where DiPrato's parking lot is now. At St. James, I ask her if she ever eats there. "Yes," she says, smiling.

She's had lunch there with colleagues. She doesn't tell them she used to live there, but she always looks around and takes a moment to reflect.[22] When I drive by after the service, I notice DiPrato's filling up. It's a beautiful day, one of those faux spring days that come every February. People are sitting at tables outside. They're all white, and like at St. James, new construction is rising around them.

Dorothy Perry Thompson graduated from Booker T. Washington in 1962. She wouldn't have been accepted to the university across the street, so she went to Allen University, a Columbia HBCU. Her 1974 master of arts in teaching, however, came from the USC, which integrated eleven years earlier. By the time she defended her dissertation in 1987, she'd been teaching in high schools for years, all while parenting three children with husband Johnnie Thompson, a Booker classmate. She was the second Black person to earn a PhD in English from USC and the first to do so with a creative writing dissertation. Having watched her Wheeler Hill disintegrate, she had plenty of material. Read her work from her dissertation through her last collection, published in 2001, and you'll realize that while she's reporting on a disappeared place and people, they're ever fresh in her memory. In "Robbie's Spirit at the Purple Cow (*a visit, 40 years later*)," she describes an encounter shopping at the boutique grocery long after Copeland's Corner Store closed:

> I did not know he would be
> in there, among the flavors
> and cellophane,
> . . .
> But up he came to meet me,
> the round, bald head, the ready smile,[23]

The poem continues with a description of how the merchandise is so different: chocolate mints instead of Johnnie cakes, "a kosher row instead of Robbie's/cold cut case." The place is so changed that, in the poem, Thompson tries to keep Robbie's spirit from noticing.

> I did not want him
> to see out through
> the plate glass window,
> the front of the store,
> where the small patch of grass

was dwarfed by a plyboard cut-out,
a life-sized bovine
fading to lilac.[24]

Bobby Donaldson, USC associate professor of history, knows Thompson's work. Director of the university's Center for Civil Rights History and Research, he and his students have studied Ward One and Wheeler Hill and befriended many of those displaced residents. "I think she recognized a responsibility to intervene on her neighborhood's behalf," Donaldson says, "and to tell the truth, it's not an overwhelmingly positive portrait, but multi-dimensional about the characteristics of Wheeler Hill. She tries to set the record straight about a neighborhood that had been largely maligned."[25]

Thompson died in 2002, not long after she'd been promoted to full professor at Winthrop University. She was still in her fifties and a full-blown success, having published three books of poetry and helping establish Winthrop's African American Studies program. Adored by her students, she was "mesmerizing" in the classroom, Donaldson says. Her written work is her legacy. "She uses her life as a window into African American life and culture in Columbia," he asserts. "It is not an objective engagement for her; it's deeply personal. Not only is it a history lesson but she's pulling layers away from her own family. If she had not told the story, it would have been long buried."[26] What a loss that would be. No poems about jukeboxes and fish sandwiches, women working as "pressers" and teens having parties in back yards. Who else has described what living in a shotgun house is like—and as important, getting it published for others to read? "It's a real gift to her neighbors that she's left—a landmark," Donaldson says. "So much is gone, but it lives on in her work, her writing."[27]

And what is writing, particularly poetry, but music? Dot Perry, as her friends would have called her, was a singer, and as a child and teen, she did what my sisters and I did in our back yard, and what our mother and her sister did in theirs, and what girls the world over have done forever: sing and dance and put on a show:

Nobody had the go-go boots
And only Annette could fix her hair
Like the white girls did
. . . But we had the music in our heads
And Stine's back porch
To use as a stage.[28]

In "Hootenanny: The Whitening," Dot and her friends were pretending to be on the popular WIS-TV show of that time. They did the jerk and the monkey, and for the "main attraction," turned a tin tub upside down for one of them to "do /Her dynamite act."[29]

It's the universality of this poem and so many others that win me over, that convinces me her work needs to be collected and reissued. In my writing and editing course, I always assign a young woman to read "Hootenanny" in class. Most of us can relate entirely, until the last three lines:

> The lights dazzled our eyes
> And the applause changed them
> From brown to blue.

Thompson refers to "Hootenanny" as "white dreams" in her dissertation's introduction.[30] But she was serious about her singing. From Booker's 1962 yearbook, we learn that she sang with two school choral groups; her "ambition" was to be a dancer. From Professor Jo Koster, her Winthrop friend and colleague, we learn that Thompson often sang her poems; together, the professors would sing songs by The Marvelettes while walking their office halls.[31]

In high school, Thompson and her friends formed a successful girl group, The Dollettes. When Motown came calling, offering a contract, The Dollettes turned them down, Koster says. College was more important. Learning this, I start fantasizing about more than the publication of Thompson's complete works. What about a Broadway show? A folk opera? Isn't Wheeler Hill as colorful as Catfish Row, its characters as alive as Porgy, Bess, and Sportin' Life? What kid didn't present a coin at a store in exchange for a candy bar? Jo Koster suggests a less ambitious celebration: a reading of her friend's poetry in the Booker T. Washington High auditorium. Thompson's former students, she promises, would love to take part.

The USC campus has changed markedly since 1987, when, in her dissertation's introduction, Thompson described how her grandmother was upset by new dorms obscuring her view. The university built those dorms, Bates House and Bates West, in 1969 and 1974 respectively. They still stand, but are overshadowed by the four-building circa-2023 Campus Village, complete with retail and dining. But what hasn't changed is the geology. You can't get past the hills. Long, tall slopes rise and fall throughout downtown and the USC campus. Railroad tracks cross at the top and bottom. Wheeler Hill, at three hundred one feet above sea level, rises about one hundred feet from Booker T. Washington High on Wheat Street. Before Ezra Wheeler built his house at the top, where a huge water tower now stands, the area was called Pickens Hill. There is no Wheeler Street in this part of Columbia; the "hill" is the top of Pickens Street in that neighborhood. Because of those hills, readers familiar with Columbia can recognize Thompson's settings today.

In "Bo-Shang," written for her brother James Arthur Whaley, she recalls the time his car broke down in the middle of Pickens Street: "not at the bottom where the Black folks live/but up on the hill near the Purple Onion Club/where the white two-stories/are pale, fat and silent."

It wasn't uncommon for poor people to live in hilly neighborhoods, Bobby Donaldson explains, because the terrain made home construction difficult.[32] Arsenal Hill was located far enough away from USC to avoid the university's expansion. But it wasn't immune from city erasure. Now it encompasses the tranquil, shady governor's mansion complex. Of the neighborhoods surrounding USC from that era, only University Hill has remained intact. Populated by whites who owned their homes, University Hill fought off USC's encroachment. And it yielded a resident who, like Dorothy Perry Thompson, left reminders of what Columbia used to be. Edmund Yaghjian wandered Columbia's minority neighborhoods, painting scenes of children playing on porches, housewives chatting, men gathered on corners. His oils, lacquers, and acrylics show them in working-class surroundings—railroad tracks, coal yards, dirt streets. In his circa-1955 *Dumping on Wheat Street*, we see a burn pile in the foreground, with two people and crooked houses crowded behind it.[33] Anyone looking at that painting in the twenty-first century knows that Wheat Street doesn't look anything like that now.

For Yaghjian, born in Armenia in 1905 and raised in Rhode Island from age two, coming to Columbia was risky. He was a nationally exhibited New York artist; he'd graduated with honors from the Rhode Island School of Design. But he was also a grocer's son who grew up in a nineteenth-century clapboard house in a segregated Armenian community in Providence. Columbia's low-income neighborhoods would have been familiar to him, wrote his granddaughter, Robin Waites, in a book dedicated to his work.[34] When Yaghjian accepted the offer from USC to teach in and chair its small art department, he made the most of it, helping establish the Columbia Museum of Art and teaching many students who achieved acclaim. From his arrival in 1945 to his death in 1997, Edmund Yaghjian would have seen those marginalized neighborhoods change or vanish and do his part to preserve them. Who today knows that tall, black "gasometers" rose high behind the church and shotgun houses in Ward One? Yaghjian leaves us that gift with his 1955 *Morning on Huger Street*.[35]

Robin Waites wrote her master's thesis on her grandfather's work. Some of his paintings, those not named by location, reflect a blending of what he saw on his walks along Columbia streets, she says. "Ordinary lives" interested him, Waites wrote in an essay for *Yaghjian*, a book that accompanied a 2007 retrospective of his work at the State Museum. "The ease and honesty with which he portrayed these subjects reveals a willingness to step across boundaries of race and class that were clearly drawn in Columbia in the 1950s."[36]

She too, has helped preserve the city's neighborhoods. In her twenty years as executive director of Historic Columbia, she and Donaldson have collaborated to keep the stories of those neighborhoods alive, conducting and recording oral histories and videos. The Historic Columbia website

Figure 1.5. *Morning on Huger Street,* by Edmund Yaghjian (1903–97), 1955, lacquer on masonite. Greenville County Museum of Art.

includes an impressive array of online tours of African American neighborhoods and heritage sites.[37] One of Donaldson's graduate students, Ashley N. Bouknight, has posted her research online. Titled "And Lest We Forget: Remembering Ward One," it includes a fifteen-minute film with interviews of people who grew up there.[38] Some stories are of happy though crowded times in substandard housing. The film also includes photos from USC yearbooks. I find one from 1967 particularly upsetting: A Black man is pushing a dust mop across a basketball court, students all around. The caption above: "Halftime Entertainment."[39] USC was four years past desegregation by then, one of the last in the South to enroll Black students. Some of the white students had a hard time accepting Black classmates, as evidenced by the 2022 student-produced, award-winning documentary, *The Backbone*, about Black female students at USC. One of them, Gail Bush Diggs, recalled her experience as homecoming queen. She received a crown but not the promised scepter; students threw ice on her when she came back into the stands. It was 1975.[40]

That wouldn't have surprised any of the Booker students. Those who walked to school from other Columbia neighborhoods before 1963 knew they weren't allowed on the USC campus. Donaldson has heard them recall how they either walked long distances out of their way to avoid the campus or ran through it, risking verbal belittlement or getting hit with what university students threw at them. "There were all kinds of indignities hurled at them," he says.[41] But once on the Booker campus, the students were safe.

All that's left of Booker now is its namesake auditorium. Built in 1956, it was in good enough shape for the university to keep and use for other purposes. Now, theater students are among those who use it. Booker's faculty would surely gasp at a poster for a coming play: "*Stupid F*cking Bird*, which is 'kinda based on *The Seagull* by Anton Chekhov.'"[42] But they'd probably approve that it houses USC's Trio program, which helps low-income and first-generation students. The Booker faculty was all about lifting their race. If you walk along the walls and study the large panels that tell the school's history—all in its black-and-gold colors—you'll see the stern faces of principals and teachers. They had impressive credentials and impressed upon their students the need to achieve. Required to visit every child at home, teachers posted their mottos, lesson plans, and goals on their bulletin boards. *The Comet* student newspaper reports alumni and faculty who've gone to Harvard; large photos show the student orchestra with boys in tuxedos and girls in frothy white gowns. Trophies for every sport and basketballs for the years when Booker won the state championship fill glass cases. The list of distinguished scholars, jurists, educators, physicians, and other professionals could fill a book—maybe ten—and so would its opportunities for students. Debate. Carpentry. Cosmetology. "The whole child" was Booker's goal, and they offered night classes for parents, too. At assemblies during his 1932–45 principalship, J. Andrew Simmons, a Charleston native and Fisk University graduate, would recite Florence Earle Coates's poem, "Thank God, a Man Can Grow." The students learned to recite it too.

> THANK God, a man can grow!
> He is not bound
> With earthward gaze to creep along the ground:
> Though his beginnings be but poor and low,
> Thank God, a man can grow!
> The fire upon his altars may burn dim,
> The torch he lighted may in darkness fail,
> And nothing to rekindle it avail,—
> Yet high beyond his dull horizon's rim,
> Arcturus and the Pleiads beckon him.[43]

From its 1916 start in educating students in Grades one through ten, Booker's leaders were ambitious. The school grew steadily over the years, expanding to include a cafeteria, labs, a gym, and an auditorium. It also achieved the rare and coveted accreditation from the Southern Association of Colleges and Secondary Schools. In 1940, the Association of Colleges and Secondary Schools for Negroes identified Booker as one of seventeen of "the most promising high schools" in a national study. Families moved to the city so their children could attend.[44] Parents who lived outside the city sent their children to live with a family member who did, so they could attend such an outstanding school. Who could blame them? Where else could Black children get opportunities as cultured as madrigal singing? Dorothy Perry Thompson sang with them. It was Columbia's only public Black high school until 1949, when C. A. Johnson opened to relieve Booker, by then overcrowded. About seven thousand people graduated from Booker, and for many of them, earning that high school diploma was an achievement about which their forebears could only dream. Just as those who were gifted made names for themselves, those who didn't continue their education contributed to their families, city, and state, Donaldson points out.

In 1970, the state's tricentennial, Booker integrated. White students from Olympia and Dreher High Schools arrived, including Cissie Jones,

Figure 1.6. Booker T. Washington alumni reunion at the Township Auditorium, June 1974. Photograph by Bill Scroggins, *The State*. Richland Library, Columbia, SC.

the daughter of the university president who'd wanted Wheeler Hill transformed.[45] Eventually, friendships developed and grew. Large photos on the school walls show Black and white students in groups, some looking chummy. A year later, an editorial in *The State* newspaper stated that Booker had achieved "a greater degree of understanding and cooperation than some of the other schools."[46]

Booker's last graduation was emotional. It followed a year of tense and angry hearings that faculty and families had with the school board, culminating with Frankie B. Outten's testimonial, calling Booker the "Great Mother of the Black Community." By then, the white students were Booker's children too. "We may not have had a bright modern building, or a new science wing, or a theatre, or wealthy backers and their political influence, but when you've got harmony and togetherness and brotherhood and happiness in your soul, you've got just about everything," valedictorian Bill Canaday, who is white, said that night. "Although our physical home may be torn down, no power on Earth can destroy our love for one another or break our proud spirit of oneness."[47]

When the school's closing was commemorated ten years later, Canaday was back with an equally heartfelt speech. "The older I get, the more convinced I become that the years 1970 through 1974, my Booker T. Washington High School years, were the most important, formative years of my life," he said that night at the Township Auditorium, where graduations were held. "I not only learned how to think, I learned how to feel. . . . We saw the walls of ignorance and hostility come tumbling down."[48] When the news came that Booker wouldn't be rebuilt or moved but closed forever, Assistant Principal Fannie Phelps Adams had to hide her tears so she could comfort angry, crying students. Underclassmen asked where they'd be going next year. Mrs. Adams had her answer ready: "No matter where it is, please go and graduate for me."[49] Margaret N. O'Shea covered the school's reaction for *The State* newspaper that February day. Mrs. Adams told her she'd been "telling the university for years they had 'a laboratory in their lap, but they were interested in the land instead of the people.'"[50]

When I arrived at USC in 1979, I knew nothing of this history. As far as I was concerned, the Coliseum had been there forever. Where else would the journalism school be? Or basketball games? Or concerts and big shows, like the circus? If a neighborhood had been there, it would have been news to me. Same for the Horseshoe. Like so many others, I tripped on those bricks regularly and kept on going, not thinking a thing about it. For me and my friends, there was nothing exceptional about attending the university. I came because I could: It had the state's journalism school, affordable tuition, and, most tellingly, the willingness to accept me with my math SAT score. I should have been more appreciative.

Now I understand how much academic, geographic, and common sense it would have made for the Booker graduates who lived in Ward One and Wheeler Hill to keep on climbing up from their neighborhoods to enter USC. And I recognize that many of Booker's brilliant students had little choice about what to do after graduation. Of course, they'd have to leave the South for other colleges and settle elsewhere. How can that loss be measured? It's a thought Bobby Donaldson has turned over many times. "Here they are at one of the premier African American schools in the state and graduating at the top of their classes and not able to walk across the street and go to school."[51] Dorothy Perry Thompson was just one of them.

I don't remember any racism as a student; in my time at USC, it seemed students from the Middle East were the largest minority. When I returned in 2013 to work for its truly wonderful honors college, I noticed nothing but friendly courtesy between all ages, races, and professions. In my class, I notice how easily some students use the four-letter F-word; to them, the N-word is off limits. After talking to Professor Donaldson, I realized how fast things can change, how ironic life can be. The dorm I lived in my freshman year, up one hill from Booker and another from the Coliseum, was demolished years ago. It was replaced by the new Honors Residence Hall, where I worked at two different times from two different offices. I was back in the very space where I'd lived and from which, Donaldson told me, USC students threw things at Booker students decades before I arrived. Decades later, he says, some of his students made friends with the elderly people who once lived in those erased neighborhoods, attending church services and Bible studies to learn more about that time and place. "Once you chisel the layers," he says, "they find commonality. They're separated by age, by race, by privilege and find things they have in common."[52] It's important to understand, he says, that while the neighborhoods were erased, the people haven't been.

In 1990, USC established the Carolinian Creed. An "aspirational values statement," it includes five promises beginning with "I will." The fourth is "I will discourage bigotry, while striving to learn from differences in people, ideas and opinion."[53] Earlier, it had taken other important steps, such as establishing its Department of African American Studies in 1971. Today, the program has a faculty of fifteen. Among other programs, the university's Office of Access and Opportunity offers classes on stereotyping, which faculty and staff are required to take. Recently, it has taken more conspicuous action, although much of it has come after intense discussions, Donaldson reports. For instance, many university and community members supported renaming the Strom Thurmond Wellness and Fitness Center for Celia Dial Saxon, whose school in Ward One it had acquired and demolished.[54] That didn't happen. Still, in 2022, the board of trustees voted unanimously to name a new dorm, adjacent to Ward One, for her. It's the first and only university building named after a Black person. Born into slavery, Saxon had graduated from the State Normal School on the USC campus during Reconstruction; she died grading papers at home, age seventy-eight.

The university also erected a statue of Richard Greener, Harvard's first Black graduate and the university's first Black professor, whom it fired after Reconstruction.[55] As with Saxon, memorializing Greener came "only after pointed discussions about renaming the Thomas Cooper Library after Greener," Donaldson says.[56] The statue was placed near the library, which retained its original name. A garden commemorating the 1963 desegregation was created near the Horseshoe; a sculpture of the three students who integrated the university was unveiled in April 2024. The university's Presidential Commission of University History, formed in 2019, has recommended that ten of thirteen campus names be changed.[57]

In 2018, Booker T. Washington High was placed on the National Register of Historic Places. In recent years, the university's Center for Civil Rights History and Research has partnered with the African American Civil Rights of the 20th Century Program, administered by the National Park Service, Department of the Interior. To date, more than six million dollars in grants have been secured to complete renovations of the Booker auditorium and exhibit installations about the history of the surrounding African-American neighborhoods. A new building has been proposed for the empty lot beside the Booker Auditorium, an undertaking contingent upon final approval by the USC Board of Trustees and South Carolina Commission on Higher Education—and a successful development campaign, Donaldson says.[58]

Fifty years ago, the Booker students and faculty were "absorbed" into the district. But they held on to their memories and, as their forebears would have appreciated, organized. Its foundation holds reunions and heritage banquets; it awards scholarships named for beloved teachers to descendants of Booker alumni. Its lauded John Work chorus presents concerts.

Then, in 2009, something incredible happened: Reverend Solomon Jackson, class of 1971, won the $259.9 million Powerball. He started sharing his wealth, giving first to Midlands Tech and Morris College, his alma maters. Then he gave $1.7 million to Booker. He'd grown up on Wheeler Hill, the first in his family to graduate high school. To support his wife and eleven children, Jackson's father mowed lawns during the day and, for seventy-five cents an hour, worked as a custodian for USC at night. Numerous improvements were made with Reverend Jackson's gift, including the addition of a special alumni room, which he named for Fannie Phelps Adams. For many, the most gratifying restoration may have been the most obvious. Off came the sand color paint the university had used to make Booker blend in. Then off came the gray-green color under that, the color one university president favored. And there it was—the Booker T. Washington auditorium in its original red brick, straightforward and purposeful as its founders intended.[59]

As for the bricks from the rest of Booker's buildings, the ones that had been transported to the Horseshoe to pave walkways and build walls—that didn't quite work out. For all the excitement about them, the press materials and stories about the Horseshoe renovation with regular mention of the bricks coming from Booker T. Washington High, the result was, to use the restoration committee's language, disappointing.[60] Many of the bricks were too soft. Some had crumbled and flaked. There were requests for silicone repairs. True, USC had also gotten bricks from another of its old buildings and some from Hyatt Park Elementary, which had been demolished by the district. But the university had always trumpeted Booker as the origin of those bricks. In the end, those bricks were turned sideways. It's possible that nobody ever walked on them directly, in a sole-on-soul way.

Did that make the Great Mother of the Black Community laugh? Maybe it was time for her to rest. Maybe her work was done. Imagine the poem Dorothy Perry Thompson could have written about that. Or maybe, she would sing.

Aïda Rogers has worked in publishing for more than forty years. After working as a writer and editor for newspapers and magazines, she created and edited the anthology series *State of the Heart: South Carolina Writers on the Places They Love* (three volumes, USC Press). In 2018, her work on *My Tour through the Asylum: A Southern Integrationist's Memoir* (USC Press) received a silver medal from the Independent Publisher Book Awards. Currently, she writes for the Carolina Family Engagement Center at USC and teaches "Finding Your Voice: Writing and Editing for Life" for the USC Honors College.

NOTES

The Thompson Family has graciously allowed Dorothy Perry Thompson's poetry to appear in this essay.

1. In the unpublished manuscript, Harold Brunton, dean of administration at the University of South Carolina from 1963 to 1983, writes about his friendship with brick mason Ed Stroman: "I got Ed Stroman involved in the messy job of laying brick on the Horseshoe roadway. Once again, I was trying to eliminate asphalt. The Trustees thought the existing asphalt road was fine and that it would cost too much to put brick on top. I finally got approval when I promised we would use surplus brick that we had on hand from tearing down a warehouse on Gadsden Street and brick from a building we tore down at Booker T. Washington High School." See Harold Brunton, *Memoir of the Restoration of the Historic Horseshoe of the University of South Carolina, 2000–2003* (Columbia, SC: South Carolinian Library, 2003). In a published work on that same topic, Brunton notes, "I finally got approval when I promised we could use surplus brick that we had on hand from tearing down old buildings elsewhere on campus." See Brunton, *Renovation & Restoration of the USC Horseshoe: A Memoir* (Columbia: Caroline McKissick Dial Endowment, University of South Carolina, 2002). Frankie B. Outten referred to Booker T. Washington High School as the "Great Mother of the Black Community" while addressing the Richland County School Board on March 12, 1974. See "March Timeline," *South Carolina African American History Calendar* (Columbia: University of South Carolina, 2024).

2. Shotgun houses are narrow structures featuring a one-room-behind-the-other design. They were common in many southern cities and towns beginning in the 1860s. A common belief is they take their name from the idea that someone can

shoot a gun into the front door and the bullet would come straight out the back. Another belief is that "shotgun" is derived from *shogun*, a West African word for "God's house." See Phoebe Tudor, "The Development of the Shotgun House," *New Orleans Preservation in Print* 14, no. 2 (1987): 4–5; and Jay D. Edwards, "Shotgun: The Most Contested House in America," *Buildings & Landscapes: Journal of the Vernacular Architecture Forum* 16, no. 1 (2009): 62–96." Dorothy Perry Thompson wrote poems about growing up in a shotgun house, in particular, "Shotgunning," and "The Middle Room." In the latter, she refers to "Oxner the landlord" placing the sink outside the bathroom door. See Thompson, "Wheeler Hill and Other Poems," PhD dissertation (Columbia: University of South Carolina, 1987).

3. Ethel Livingston Pearson, interview with Aïda Rogers, February 24, 2024.

4. Pearson, interview with Rogers.

5. For a useful history of Wheeler Hill, see Sophie Kahler and Conor Harrison, "'Wipe out the entire slum area': University-led urban renewal in Columbia, South Carolina, 1950–1985." *Journal of Historical Geography* 67 (2020): 61–70.

6. The first Black students since Reconstruction were Henrie D. Monteith, Robert Anderson, and James Solomon, who were admitted on September 11, 1963. See "March Timeline."

7. Kahler and Harrison, "'Wipe out the entire slum,'" 64, 61.

8. Sophie Kahler, "Ward One," *Storymaps*, April 18, 2021; https://storymaps.arcgis .com/stories/dbe13f1e08b345b1b4f02cba73d01fe4.

9. See note 5. Kahler provided additional details in an interview with Aïda Rogers, April 7, 2021.

10. Letter to members of the Columbia City Council and Columbia Housing Authority from Thomas F. Jones, February 22, 1968, Records, Vice President of Operations, South Carolina University Archives, Box 30, 1–2, quoted in Kahler and Harrison, "'Wipe out the entire slum,'" 68.

11. Kahler and Harrison, "'Wipe out the entire slum,'" 65.

12. Sophie Kahler, interview by Aïda Rogers, April 7, 2021.

13. Basil Harris, interview by Ada Rogers, February 24, 2024.

14. Winter, "Joseph E. Winter."

15. Harris, interview by Rogers.

16. Thompson, "Wheeler Hill," iii.

17. Thompson, "Wheeler Hill," 7–8.

18. Thompson, "Miss Jaunita's Beauty Salon," in "Wheeler Hill," 7–8.

19. Thompson, "Pickens Street," in "Wheeler Hill," 3–4.

20. Thompson, "Wheeler Hill," 1.

21. Kahler, interview by Rogers.

22. Pearson, interview with Rogers.

23. Thompson, "Robbie's Spirit," in *priest in aqua boa* (Greenville, SC: Ninety-Six Press, 2001), 20–21.

24. Thompson, "Robbie's Spirit," in *priest in aqua boa*, 20–21.

25. Bobby Donaldson, interview by Aïda Rogers, April 12, 2021.

26. Donaldson, interview by Rogers.

27. Donaldson, interview by Rogers.

28. Thompson, "Hootenanny," in "Wheeler Hill," 23.

29. Thompson, "Hootenanny," in "Wheeler Hill," 23.

30. Thompson, "Introduction," in "Wheeler Hill," vi.

31. Jo Koster, comments during "Tuesday Duets," a regular Facebook poetry pod-cast started and hosted by William Epes. This segment from February 22, 2022, featured a discussion, or "duet," between poet Elizabeth Robin and writer Aïda Rogers about Thompson. See https://www.facebook.com/wm.epes/videos/2103 805816490897. See also Elizabeth Robin and Aïda Rogers, "Following Dorothy in Her Wheeler Hill." In *Ukweli: Searching for Healing Truth, South Carolina Writers and Poets Explore American Racism,* edited by Horace Mungin and Herb Frazier (Charleston, SC: Evening Post Books, 2022), 145–50.

32. Donaldson, interview by Rogers.

33. Edmund Yaghjian, *Dumping on Wheat Street,* ca. 1955; oil on board, collection of Wade Cleveland. See Robin Waites, *Yaghjian: A Retrospective* (Columbia: University of South Carolina Press, 2007), 67.

34. Waites, "Crossing the Boundaries," in *Yaghjian: A Retrospective,* 19.

35. Edmund Yaghjian, *Morning on Huger Street,* ca. 1955, lacquer on board, Greenville County Museum of Art, purchase from the Arthur and Holly Magill Fund. See Waites, *Yaghjian: A Retrospective,* 51.

36. Waites, "Crossing the Boundaries," in *Yaghjan: A Retrospective,* 19.

37. "African American History Tours."

38. Ashley N. Bouknight, "And Lest We Forget: Remembering Ward One," https:// ashleybouknight.com/and-lest-we-forget-remembering-ward-one.

39. Bouknight, "And Lest We Forget."

40. White, *The Backbone,* 1 hr., 11 min., 27 sec.

41. Donaldson, interview by Rogers.

42. Poster on bulletin board at Booker T. Washington auditorium. Written by Aaron Posner, *Stupid Fucking Bird* was directed by Jessica Frances Fichter and performed February 9–24, 2024, on the Thigpen Mainstage of the Trustus Theatre in Columbia, SC.

43. "Thank God a Man Can Grow!," panel with photo of Principal J. Andrew Simmon, Booker T. Washington auditorium. The actual title of Florence Earle Coates's poem is "Per Aspera," a shortened version of the Latin phrase *per asperia ad astra*: through hardship to the stars. The poem was published in a two-volume edition of Coates's work, *Poems* (New York: Houghton Mifflin, 1916).

44. Neville Patterson, "Era Ends For BTW Grads," *The Columbia Record,* May 29, 1974, 20-C. https://infoweb.newsbank.com.

45. A photo of Cissie Jones, class of 1973, is on a wall panel at the Booker T. Washington auditorium. On the panel, Jones is identified as the daughter of USC President Thomas Jones. A message from Cissie Jones is on a "stone" on the Booker T. Washington Commemorative Tree. It reads: "When you get to where you're going remember where you came from."

46. "Difficult Test Passed," *The State,* May 7, 1971, 24. https://infoweb.newsbank .com.

47. Bill Canaday, "Booker T. Washington High means love, tolerance, hope," *The Columbia Record,* June 23, 1984, 8, https://infoweb.newsbank.com. This was an excerpt of Canaday's speech delivered June 17, 1984, at the Township Auditorium,

which commemorated the tenth anniversary of the school's closing. In his speech, Canady comments from his 1974 valedictory address.

48. Canaday, "Booker T. Washington," 8.
49. Margaret N. O'Shea, "Demise Notice Brings Frustration, Anger At BTW," *The State*, February 28, 1974, 12-A.
50. O'Shea, "Demise Notice Brings Frustration, Anger At BTW," 12-A.
51. Donaldson, interview by Rogers.
52. Donaldson, interview by Rogers.
53. "The Carolinian Creed."
54. Westbrook, "USC names residence hall."
55. Horn, "Larger than Life," interview with Katherine Chaddock, retired USC professor of education. See also Katherine Chaddock, *Uncompromising Activist: Richard Greener, First Black Graduate of Harvard College* (Baltimore: Johns Hopkins University Press, 2017).
56. Donaldson, interview by Rogers.
57. See "Final Report—Executive Summary."
58. Donaldson, interview by Rogers. See also Alexis Watts, "National Parks Service partnership advances UofSC's role in telling civil rights history," University of South Carolina, September 27, 2022; https://sc.edu/uofsc/posts/2022/09/crc_nps.php."
59. For more on Reverend Jackson's generosity, see Marian Wright Edelman, "Reverend Solomon Jackson, Jr.: Blessed to be a Blessing," *Huffpost*, November 1, 2010; https://www.huffpost.com/entry/reverend-solomon-jackson_b_776879."
60. See Brunton, *Renovation & Restoration*, 86: "Before long we ran into a problem that I should have anticipated. W. S. Turbeville, our director of physical plant, showed me some bricks from which pieces were beginning to flake off. He said, 'Some of these are soft brick. Many of them are not usable.' We put a couple of men to work on the piles of brick, trying to sort out the soft ones. Then we decided to lay brick on their sides rather than flat which we thought would give more strength. Finally, we coated the finished product with silicone sealer. This project sounds simple, but consider this: most masons lay brick vertically. In paving the Horseshoe, all the brick-laying was horizontal. Looking back now with the wisdom of 25 years of detachment, I must honestly admit we probably didn't save any money using the surplus brick. By the time we paid workers to sort out soft brick and then paid for the additional labor to lay brick on their sides, we probably could have bought new hard brick. But there is another aspect. Even though we weren't successful in culling out all the soft brick and occasionally one will crumble, (for which I apologize to today's physical plant people who have inherited a problem I inadvertently created), it nevertheless does my heart good when I walk on the uneven pavement and hear some visitors saying, 'Isn't it exciting? I guess this brick road has been here for more than 100 years.'"

WORKS CITED

"African American History Tours," Historic Columbia. https://www.historic columbia.org/tours/african-american-history.

Bouknight, Ashley N. "And Lest We Forget: Remembering Ward One." https://ashleybouknight.com/and-lest-we-forget-remembering-ward-one.

Brunton, Harold. *Memoir of the restoration of the historic Horseshoe of the University of South Carolina, 2000–2003.* MMS ID: 99101264437970568. South Carolinian Library. Columbia, SC, 2003.

Brunton, Harold. *Renovation & Restoration of the USC Horseshoe: A Memoir.* Columbia: Caroline McKissick Dial Endowment, University of South Carolina, 2002.

"The Carolinian Creed." Columbia: Student Affairs and Academic Support, University of South Carolina. https://sc.edu/about/offices_and_divisions/student_affairs/our_initiatives/involvement_and_leadership/carolinian_creed/index.php.

Chaddock, Katherine. *Uncompromising Activist: Richard Greener, First Black Graduate of Harvard College.* Baltimore: Johns Hopkins University Press, 2017.

Coates, Florence Earle. "Per Aspera." In *Poems* (2 vols.). New York: Houghton Mifflin, 1916.

Edwards, Jay D. "Shotgun: The Most Contested House in America." *Buildings & Landscapes: Journal of the Vernacular Architecture Forum* 16, no. 1 (2009): 62–96.

Edelman, Marian Wright. "Reverend Solomon Jackson, Jr.: Blessed to be a Blessing." *Huffpost*, November 1, 2010 [updated May 25, 2011]. https://www.huffpost.com/entry/reverend-solomon-jackson_b_776879.

Epes, William, host, Tuesday Duets, February 22, 2022. Podcast, 1 hr., 27 min., 40 sec. https://www.facebook.com/wm.epes/videos/2103805816490897.

"Final Report—Executive Summary." *University History.* Columbia: University of South Carolina, July 16, 2021. https://sc.edu/about/our_history/university_history/presidential_commission/commission_reports/final_report/index.php.

Horn, Chris, host, "Larger than Life, Richard T. Greener," Remembering the Days, January 27, 2021. Podcast, 7 min., 15 sec. https://sc.edu/uofsc/posts/2021/01/episode_20_remembering_the_days.php.

Jones, Thomas F. Letter to members of the Columbia City Council and Columbia Housing Authority from Thomas F. Jones, February 22, 1968, Records, Vice President of Operations, South Carolina University Archives, Box 30, 1–2.

Kahler, Sophie. "Ward One." *Storymaps.* April 18, 2021. https://storymaps.arcgis.com/stories/dbe13f1e08b345b1b4f02cba73d01fe4.

Kahler, Sophie, and Conor Harrison. "'Wipe out the entire slum area': University-led urban renewal in Columbia, South Carolina, 1950–1985." *Journal of Historical Geography* 67 (2020): 61–70.

"March Timeline." *South Carolina African American History Calendar.* Columbia: University of South Carolina, 2024. https://scafricanamerican.com/march-timeline.

Posner, Aaron. "Stupid Fucking Bird." New York: Dramatists Play Service, 2016. https://www.dramatists.com/previews/5075.pdf.

Robin, Elizabeth, and Aïda Rogers, "Following Dorothy in Her Wheeler Hill." In *Ukweli: Searching for Healing Truth, South Carolina Writers and Poets Explore American Racism*, edited by Horace Mungin and Herb Frazier, (Charleston, SC: Evening Post Books, 2022), 145–50.

Thompson, Dorothy Perry. *priest in aqua boa.* Greenville, SC: Ninety-Six Press, 2001.

Thompson, Dorothy Perry. "Wheeler Hill and Other Poems." PhD dissertation. Columbia: University of South Carolina, 1987.

"Timeline." *University History,* University of South Carolina, 2021. https://sc.edu/about/our_history/university_history/timeline.

Tudor, Phoebe. "The Development of the Shotgun House," *New Orleans Preservation in Print* 14, no. 2 (1987): 4–5.

Waites, Robin. *Yaghjian: A Retrospective.* Columbia: University of South Carolina Press, 2007.

Watts, Alexis. "National Parks Service partnership advances UofSC's role in telling civil rights history." University of South Carolina. September 27, 2022. https://sc.edu/uofsc/posts/2022/09/crc_nps.php.

Westbrook, Thad H. "USC names residence hall for renowned African American educator Celia Dial Saxon." Columbia: University of South Carolina, October 11, 2023. https://sc.edu/uofsc/posts/2023/10/residence-hall-named-celia-dial-saxon.php.

White, Hannah Joy, director. *The Backbone.* Columbia: University of South Carolina, 2022. 1 hr, 27 min. https://linktr.ee/thebackbonefilm.

Winter, Joseph E. "Joseph E. Winter (1920–1992) Collection." Columbia: Digital Collections, University of South Carolina Libraries, 2008. https://digital.library.sc.edu/collections/the-joseph-e-winter-1920-1992-collection/.

The Untold Story of Arthur B. Mitchell

The Citadel's Fifer

Taylor Diggs and Felice F. Knight

Peter Filene writes in the *Joy of Teaching*, "When you teach you are *engaging in a relationship* with your students."[1] During my career as a history professor, I was blessed to engage in many meaningful teaching relationships with students. But one relationship stands out in my mind: working with Taylor Diggs, a student enrolled in The Citadel's Summer Undergraduate Research Experience (SURE). During the summer and fall of 2020, I guided Taylor, then a junior honors student, through a rigorous and rewarding journey to uncover the story of one of The Citadel's earliest known black workers, Arthur B. Mitchell.

The significance of Mitchell, a free Black man who worked as the fifer for the Corps of Cadets from 1844 through his death in 1893, cannot be overstated. Established in 1842 on the site of an arsenal created by South Carolina legislators to protect white Charlestonians in the wake of a failed slave insurrection, The Citadel was not a welcoming place for African Americans. During the nineteenth century, a Black person typically did not set foot on the school's campus unless they worked there. And if they worked there, they were not well paid—if they were paid at all. Most Black workers were enslaved and leased to the institution by their enslavers, who pocketed any money received for their labor.[2] Free at a time when Charleston had fewer than two-thousand free Black people, Arthur B. Mitchell is an exception to that story.[3] It is unclear how much The Citadel paid for his services, but records indicate that Mitchell relied upon his wages to support his family. The 1860 census lists him as the head of a household that comprised his wife and a daughter.[4] Furthermore, the 1870 census lists his wife as "keeping house," indicating that she did not work outside of the home.[5]

Mitchell's role as the single income generator for his family appears to be the driving force behind a series of decisions he made during the time of the Civil War—decisions that may both surprise and confuse the modern reader. From 1861 to 1863, Mitchell appears several times in the Confederate Army's muster rolls. Each time he is listed as "chief musician."[6] After 1863, he is described as "deserted," a term that implies that he left the service of his own accord and without permission.[7] He is then found listed in other records, such as a roster of free Black Charleston firefighters, as a fireman and a cooper.[8] He likely took on each of these jobs—whether he wanted to or not—to support his family.

Without Taylor Diggs's research, these and other details of Arthur B. Mitchell's life would have remained lost to posterity. I am very proud of Taylor. Not only did she write a comprehensive honors thesis based on her research, but she also presented her research at various forums conducted by SURE. Additionally, her work constituted an invaluable contribution to The Citadel's Universities Studying Slavery Project, a multiyear research initiative, begun in 2017 by faculty and administrators in the Department of History and Daniel Library. Since then, the project has grown to include several members across various departments and campus entities and has produced additional student research projects as well as contributions to The Citadel's President's Task Force on Race, Diversity, and Inclusion.[9] I am confident that readers will share my enthusiasm for Taylor's meticulous research as she presents it in the following essay, which is a slightly revised version of her honors thesis.

Her work points to two crucial ideas. First, it underscores the importance of recovering the stories of people—especially African Americans—whose experiences have been overlooked or erased from the historical records. In this way, Taylor's work contributes to essential efforts of scholars and institutions, such as the recently opened International African American Museum, where I serve as director of education. Without memory, there can be no hope of reconciliation. Second, it reminds readers, especially those who work in higher education, of the importance of undergraduate research. With guidance from faculty mentors, students can not only begin their scholarly careers but can also make meaningful contributions to our understandings of our culture and the forces that created it. In an age when the humanities seem to be under constant scrutiny and attack, Taylor's work demonstrates the need for critical inquiry and the vital vibrancy that defines the liberal arts.

The Untold Story of Arthur B. Mitchell, The Citadel's Fifer

In recent years, The Citadel has increased its commitment to understanding its complicated relationship with the Black community. In *The Story of The Citadel*, Oliver J. Bond briefly mentions a Black employee who worked for The Citadel in the mid-nineteenth century. Bond describes the man, named

Mitchell, as the "colored fifer" for the Corps of Cadets. Bond states that Mitchell was such an integral part of cadet life that Citadel cadets attended his funeral, a sign of respect not often extended by white Americans, at that time, to African Americans.[10] Bond's account is corroborated by a funeral notice in the *News and Courier.* The notice, likely written by his family or church, provides some information about Mitchell's private life. It states that Mitchell was a husband and father, member of Calvary Baptist Church, and major of the First Regiment N.G. of South Carolina.[11] An article in the same edition of the paper, titled "His Last Tattoo," states that Mitchell began his employment at The Citadel in 1844 and even went "to the front" during the "great struggle."[12] One sentence in this article catches the modern reader's eye: "There is not a colored man in Charleston who stands higher with his white friends."[13] This statement causes the modern reader to wonder: Who was Arthur B. Mitchell? Was he enslaved or free? Why did the white authors speak laudably of him during a period in which race relations were strained at best? Which group in The Civil War did Mitchell support and why? This research project sets out to answer these questions and uncover the story of one of The Citadel's earliest Black employees, a man who worked for an overtly Confederate institution during a period of enslavement and national conflict and who likely risked his life on the battlefield wearing the uniform of the people who deprived him of freedom. Through an examination of public records, such as census documents, death certificates, and financial records, my research uncovers important details about Arthur Mitchell's life, including the fact that Mitchell was a freeman. Contextualizing these details through the historical frameworks provided by Bernard E. Powers Jr.'s *Black Charlestonians* and Kevin M. Levin's *Searching for Black Confederates,* I seek to provide a broader understanding of the life of a Black man in Charleston during the antebellum period.

Powers provides a crucial understanding of the city which Arthur Mitchell inhabited. We can be certain that Mitchell's vocation as a military fifer was low paying and that he was not among the very few affluent Blacks in antebellum Charleston. Instead, he was part of a subjugated workforce, both enslaved and free, who were maligned and mistreated, even though their labor was integral to Charleston's success. Enslaved people, Powers demonstrates, were involved in thirty-eight occupations, which included coopers, musicians, carpenters, bakers, plasterers, and other skill-based tasks.[14] Powers depicts Charleston as a bustling city in which free Black people and enslaved people lived closely together and were involved in all aspects of a labor-central economy. Although unable to vote or hold office, Black residents remained engaged in the civic life of their city. One contemporary observer cited by Powers estimated that ten percent of political rally attendees were Black.[15]

Still, white leaders afforded Black residents few freedoms, and the decades preceding emancipation became a time of increased oppression. In fact, as the Civil War approached, white South Carolinians increased their efforts to restrict Black people and maintain a strict social hierarchy based on race. In 1820, South Carolina enacted a law that required legislative approval to emancipate any enslaved person.[16] In large part, the law was intended to curtail the growth of the free Black population.[17] To circumvent these laws, some free Black people purchased enslaved family members. For example, a free man named James Patterson, unable to purchase their freedom, instead purchased both his wife and daughter.[18] In 1822, the legislature passed another law that required free Black migrants to pay special taxes and to have a designated white guardian.[19] In 1841, the state effectively outlawed the emancipation of any enslaved person.[20] White leaders also sought to preserve social stratifications by restricting Black wages. For example, the Charleston City Council limited the amount a free Black person could earn in one day to just one dollar.[21]

Even the creation of The Citadel in 1842 was in response to white fears of Black advancement, particularly anxiety about violent rebellion after the Denmark Vesey plot of 1822.[22] The struggle for social and economic freedom persisted long after the Emancipation Proclamation. After the Civil War, white leaders instituted Black codes, which defined African Americans as inferior by law and greatly restricted basic civil rights. Under the provisions of these codes, any white person could arrest a Black person if they witnessed them committing a crime. Black people who aspired to own businesses had to meet "certain criteria" established and enforced by white officials, and special courts were created to hear cases against Black individuals.[23] During Arthur Mitchell's time, Charleston had a large number of free Black people, and there were many opportunities for employment. However, the city's culture was predicated on race; specifically, the assumption of white supremacy and persistent efforts to enforce oppressive racial hierarchies. Mitchell's life, as we will see, illustrates both the highs and lows for a Black man attempting to provide for himself and his family during this period.

Arthur B. Mitchell first appears in census records in 1860, where he is included among the "free inhabitants" of Charleston. This record provides concrete evidence that Mitchell was a free Black man before the Civil War. The census document also mentions two family members: Martha Mitchell,

Arthur's wife, and Mary Mitchell, his young daughter. At this time, Arthur is listed as being thirty-six years old and his wife as twenty-eight.

Significantly, in the census document, Mitchell is designated as "B" for Black. The other options of classification were mulatto and white. The distinction of color was an important component in Charleston society and communicated status. White people were at the top of a social hierarchy, and the lower ranks were composed of levels of Blackness. Black slaves were at the bottom, whereas biracial people (mulattoes, in nineteenth-century terms) were caught between Black and white.[24] As a darker skinned free man, Mitchell would have been excluded from the upper echelons of the free Black society. He almost assuredly faced discrimination not only from powerful whites but also from fellow African Americans with lighter skin tones.

By the spring of 1861, the Civil War had begun after the Confederate bombardment of Fort Sumter on April 12. As the first state to secede, South Carolina and all its inhabitants were thrown into the conflict. The almost panegyric obituary "His Last Tattoo," referenced earlier, celebrates Mitchell's support of the Confederate army. For modern readers, the claim may seem implausible. In fact, it may seem like an example of Lost Cause propaganda, an effort to erase a history of violence by making the oppressed willing accomplices of their oppressors.[25] In *Searching for Black Confederates*, Kevin L. Levin addresses claims that Black people served in the Confederate Army. There was a group of free Black men residing in New Orleans who attempted to create a militia called the Native Guard to assist the South, but the Confederate Army refused their assistance.[26] Levin argues that slaves did not serve as soldiers in the Confederate ranks and that this belief is strictly fiction.[27] He does acknowledge, however, that free Black men did assist the Confederacy. Those whose names appear on muster rolls, he says, were paid service workers.[28] Further, Levin argues that allowing Black men to serve as combat soldiers would have created practical and ideological risks, because a man who learns to fight one enemy is well prepared to fight another. Moreover, placing Black soldiers in roles that required quick thinking, bravery, and honesty would have exposed the lie of white supremacy. To support this claim, he offers the words of Confederate Secretary of War James Seddon: "If slaves make soldiers, our whole theory of slavery is wrong."[29]

Mitchell's experiences both support and complicate Levin's claims. An early twentieth-century historical text, *South Carolina Troops in Confederate Service*, by A. S. Salley Jr., reports that Mitchell enlisted in October of 1861 and was given the title chief musician.[30] Mitchell then seems to disappear from regimental muster rolls until 1862, when he enlisted again in Suffolk, Virginia, and was once again listed as a musician, not a combat soldier. He appears in muster rolls for several months until February 1863, when he is designated AWOL. By April of the same year, Mitchell had returned to Charleston and was officially designated a deserter.[31] Salley's account partially refutes Levin's claim about Black members of the Confederate army. Mitchell was clearly more than a "paid service worker." He enlisted twice in the Confederate Army and was listed as a deserter when he failed to report for duty. These details affirm that he was military personnel, not a civilian (or enslaved) worker. Still, there is no record that he was ever assigned a regular military rank, nor that he underwent any sort of basic training. Mitchell seems to have a sort of hybrid position, both in and out of the Confederate military.

Salley's historical record also casts doubt on other reports of Mitchell's service during the Civil War. Oliver Bond states that Mitchell served The Citadel, "until 1861, when he became the body servant of General Maxcy Gregg, and afterwards General Colquitt."[32] The historical records, however, indicate that Mitchell served as a musician, not a servant. It is also difficult to determine when Mitchell could have entered either man's service. Colquitt joined the Confederate Army in May of 1861.[33] Gregg joined the Confederate cause immediately after secession and was tasked with organizing the first group of volunteers.[34] It is unlikely that Mitchell joined their service at the start of the war, because records indicate that Mitchell did not become employed by the Confederate Army until October 1861, several months after the conflict had begun. More important, the records indicate that Mitchell enlisted in the Confederate Army, something that would not have been necessary for a personal servant.

During the spring of 1862, Gregg's regiment was sent to Virginia, which corresponds to Mitchell's second enlistment.[35] During the spring and summer of the same year, Colquitt also spent considerable time in Virginia.[36] It is possible, then, that Mitchell met both men in 1862 when all three were in Virginia. Curiously, like Mitchell, Colquitt returned to South Carolina in 1863.[37] Still, there is no reason to conclude that Mitchell worked as Colquitt's servant. Had he returned to South Carolina in Colquitt's service, he would not have been designated a deserter. We may never know all of the roles Mitchell served during the war, nor his motivations for deserting his post. By 1863, the war had gone on for two long years, and as the Confederacy inched closer to Union territory, Mitchell would have found himself in a dangerous environment, far from home. It seems unlikely, however, that

Mitchell returned to Charleston because he was in the service of a Confederate officer.

The assumption that Mitchell served as a body servant to highly respected Confederate generals, however, very likely contributed to the favorable treatment he received in *The Story of The Citadel* and "His Last Tattoo." In the decades after the war, former body servants and camp workers were often visible at veteran reunions and were used to support the Lost Cause narrative of the "loyal slave."[38] Levin reports that some African Americans even made careers for themselves by performing the parts of loyal slaves. For example, a man named Steve Perry attended reunions using the name Uncle Steve Eberhart. His stage name appeared frequently in newspapers across the South, and white audiences no doubt enjoyed hearing his narratives of willing service to Confederate officers. The tales he told, however, were not true.[39] Another former camp slave, William Mack Lee, gained so much notoriety at Confederate reunions that he was asked to testify before the Georgia House of Representatives. To that group, Lee acknowledged "his perfect faith in the white man of the South doing the right thing for his race."[40] Like Steve Perry, Lee was comfortable fabricating events, no doubt with a view toward personal gain. He often told tales that placed him in close proximity with Robert E. Lee. In an autobiographical pamphlet, he even stated that the two men were "real friends."[41] An article published by the Confederate Veteran magazine challenged that claim, noting that Robert E. Lee was unlikely to make anyone a confidant and would never "have revealed himself to a negro servant."[42]

There is no evidence that Mitchell fabricated any details of his service. It is, however, entirely possible that others may have given him a fictitious past. For those invested in the Lost Cause ideology, a faithful Black servant would have been more reassuring than a brave Black fifer. Mitchell may have crossed the paths of Gregg and Colquitt, but it remains unclear, even doubtful, that he served as a body servant to either man. It is, however, very likely that Mitchell's support of the Confederate cause in whatever capacity helped him gain respect amongst white Charlestonians later in life.

Mitchell appears in public records again in 1864 within a document titled, "A Descriptive List of Free Negroes Belonging to City Engine No. 7," indicating that he was serving as a fireman, although that was not his primary job.[43] The document lists thirty men and includes details about age, height, occupation, and residence. Mitchell's occupation is designated as a cooper, not a musician, which suggests that he was working as a tradesman when he returned to Charleston.[44] As has been previously established, both free and enslaved Black men worked in thirty-eight occupations in Charleston before the end of slavery—with cooper being one of them. Furthermore, considering the need for additional tradesmen during the Civil War, it was likely easier for Mitchell to get a job as a cooper than as a musician.

As a husband and father, Mitchell must have felt immense pressure to provide for his wife and young daughter. In some limited ways, it was becoming easier for free Black people to control their own finances. On March 3, 1865, President Lincoln signed into law an act that established the Freedman's Savings and Trust Company.[45] The Trust Company gave free Black people access to regular banking services and provided an important pathway to financial independence.[46] In 1866, Mitchell established an account with the Trust Company.[47] Mitchell's banking records provide crucial biographical information but also raise new questions. The bank required customers to identify their previous masters. Mitchell's records provide no such information and identify him as "Free," substantiating that he was not enslaved before the Emancipation Proclamation. Also, the document lists the names of Mitchell's brother, sister, mother, and father and reports that, by 1866, both Mitchell's father and sister had died. His mother and brother were still alive and living in Charleston. Consistent with the 1860 census, the banking records identify Mary as Mitchell's daughter, but it lists Mitchell's wife's name as Dorcus. Given the fact that both the 1860 census and the 1870 census lists Mitchell's wife name as Martha, it is unlikely that Mitchell had remarried in 1866 but, rather, that Martha had more than one name. Perhaps Dorcus was her first name and Martha her middle name. In either case, the banking document also mentions an "unnamed" baby boy as a member of the Mitchell household. The Mitchells may have had another child, but neither the 1880 census nor Mitchell's funeral notice in the *News and Courier* reference a son. Perhaps tragedy struck the household after the banking document was recorded, and the baby boy died.

Along with thousands of other African Americans, Mitchell no doubt hoped that the Freedmen's Bureau Bank would provide a safe depository for his savings. By 1873, however, customers seem to have lost confidence in the bank, and there were runs on several branches. The following year, the bank closed and with it the hopes of economic enfranchisement for many Black people. In the nineteenth century, the federal government did not ensure deposits. As a result, some depositors lost all their money. Others were "lucky" enough to recover three-fifths of their account balance.[48] We do not know how the Mitchells fared through these difficult events.

The 1870 census provides little new evidence about Mitchell's life and adds to the uncertainty of his age. In this document, Mitchell is recorded as forty years old. Four years earlier, however, Mitchell's bank records also indicated that he was forty years old. To add to the uncertainty, the 1880 census states that Mitchell was forty-five years old and that his wife Martha was one year younger than him.[49] Twenty years earlier, the 1860 census stated that Martha was eight years younger than Mitchell. The contradictions in the public documents make it virtually impossible to determine Martha and Arthur's actual ages and suggest that they may have been unaware of their birthdates.

Mitchell's experiences as a soldier and musician after the Civil War, however, are well documented. Although "His Last Tattoo" does not reference Mitchell's military rank, the funeral notice in the *News and Courier* refers to him as "Major of the 1st Regiment N.G. of S.C.," indicating that he was a high-ranking officer in the National Guard of South Carolina. If Mitchell's earlier enlistments in the Confederate Army made him an accomplice, however reluctantly or unintentionally, to the horrors of enslavement, his role in the National Guard may have allowed him to work against the forces of segregation, disenfranchisement, and white supremacy. During Reconstruction, white southerners resisted change and worked to maintain their hegemony. Before the war, voting was a singularly white privilege. The influx of Black voters after the war changed the political power structure seemingly overnight. In 1865, South Carolina's provisional governor, Benjamin Franklin Perry, expressed great disdain at the thought of "negro suffrage" and even stated, "they [the Republican Party] forget that this is a white man's government, and intended for white men only."[50] Perry's overtly racist statement seems somewhat surprising and demonstrates the depth of racism in white southern culture. In 1851, Perry founded the *Southern Patriot*, which promoted the Union cause. Although he supported the Confederacy after succession, he was appointed to the office of provisional governor by Andrew Johnson and charged with implementing a new state constitution. President Johnson entrusted him to ensure Black enfranchisement, but the forces of white supremacy overrode his earlier Union sympathies. It was under Perry's direction that South Carolina instituted the unconstitutional Black codes designed to hinder Black voters.[51] These initial efforts, however, were not entirely successful. In 1870, Black voters in South Carolina surpassed white voters by over twenty-six thousand.[52] White southerners subsequently used violence and intimidation to restrict Black political power.

The Ku Klux Klan, particularly in upstate counties, terrorized Black communities with seeming impunity. In October 1868, the Klan murdered Benjamin Randolph, a Black minister, educator, Union veteran, and politician. The assassination took place in broad daylight in Hodges, South Carolina, while Randolph campaigned for state office.[53] These horrific efforts proved successful. After Klan intimidation, Black voting declined significantly. In 1868, Abbeville County recorded thirty-three percent Black voter turnout, Laurens County recorded forty-six percent, and Anderson County recorded only fifty percent.[54] The decrease in Black voter turnout boosted the Democratic Party's prospects in these counties. The violent actions used to intimidate Black voters created mayhem.

To put an end to the violence, Governor Robert K. Scott signed the South Carolina Militia Law of 1869, sometimes called the National Guard Service of South Carolina. The legislation allowed men of any color from ages eighteen to forty-five to enlist in militia forces deployed to suppress insurrection and prevent violence.[55] Many whites refused to serve in these desegregated units, which caused the militias to be identified as "Black militias."

These militias allowed Black men to bear arms and fight against white violence. They proved somewhat effective in restoring Black participation in elections. Democrats still carried the elections of 1868, but after the implementation of the "Black militias," Democrat candidates received only forty-three percent of the vote in twelve upstate counties.[56] Unsurprisingly, white residents attempted to disarm the Black militias, and several Republicans were killed in the violence.[57] Mitchell's involvement in the militia is especially notable. If his military career began as an almost certainly reluctant participant in the Confederate cause, it ended with him serving as an officer in units intended to protect Black lives, property, and political enfranchisement.

Federal legislation also sought to protect Black civil rights. In 1870, Massachusetts senator Charles Sumner introduced the Civil Rights Act as an amendment to a bill to grant immunity to former Confederate soldiers. The Act sought to protect access to accommodations, including theaters, churches, and public schools. It was eventually passed in 1875, but as the history of Jim Crow demonstrates, it was never effectively enforced.[58] The Enforcement Act of 1871, also known as the Ku Klux Klan Act, empowered the president to suspend the writ of habeas corpus to suppress terrorist activity, especially the actions of the Klan. Despite these efforts, the Klan and its allies continued to steer South Carolina politics. By the spring and summer of 1871, some Black militias disbanded, Republican voters had been thoroughly intimidated, and many Republican officials lost their seats.[59] In Charleston, many Black people could not find work unless they provided evidence that they had voted for Democratic candidates.[60] Racial terror destroyed the rights of Black citizens and undoubtedly defined the lives of Arthur Mitchell and his family.

The final public record for Mitchell is a certificate of death, dated November 2, 1893.[61] It reports that at the age of sixty-seven, Mitchell succumbed to typhus malaria in the comfort of his home. His last residence was on Reed Street in Charleston's Ninth Ward. During the fifty years of his life that can be documented, Mitchell and his family moved homes four times. This movement likely reflects Mitchell's quest for survival, to provide for his family, and to serve. His last occupation was musician, specifically a fifer for The Citadel. One hopes that music provided not only sustenance for his family but also joy both in his early and later years.

There are, of course, many unanswered questions about Arthur Mitchell's life. Census records prove that he was free before the war, but it is unclear whether he was born free. The journey to freedom for enslaved people was complicated and could follow many paths. Records from Mitchell's early life are scant, and it is all but impossible to discover details concerning his wife, Martha, and their marriage. The struggles of the enslaved have been extensively studied and have found their way into popular culture and literature. The stories of working-class free Black men have received much less attention. In presenting a more complete understanding of Arthur B. Mitchell's life, this paper hopes to shed light on a remarkable man who demonstrated resourcefulness and resilience as he sought to make a life for himself and his loved ones during times of enslavement, violence, and oppression. The brief historical accounts of Oliver J. Bond and others do not fully capture the mental, social, and economic challenges a Black individual faced during the precarious period before and after the Civil War. The author of "His Last Tattoo" attempted to define the meaning of Mitchell's life by indicating that he was respected by white peers. The claim is almost certainly true, but so too is the fact that the author appropriated Mitchell's life to mitigate, if not erase, the horrors of white supremacy. Mitchell's life is meaningful because he was a husband, father, and friend. If we want to assign a larger meaning, it should not be that of Confederate ally or Lost Cause sympathizer. Rather, we should view Arthur Mitchell's life as an allegory of the struggle that African Americans faced in the years before and after the Civil War in their quest to secure the full benefits of American citizenship.

A Note from the Author

My mother's maiden name is Mitchell. We believe it comes from her ancestors' time as enslaved people in Mitchell County, Georgia. During my research, I often wondered if Arthur B. Mitchell was a distant maternal relative. Although the thought created a sense of familiarity, it also evoked a feeling of loss. The legacy of white supremacy and American chattel slavery is the continued loss of history. At a time when politicians across the South ask us to forget and move on, descendants of the enslaved, like myself, continue to dream of the day when we can open the archives and tell our families' truths. For this reason, it has been an honor to pursue the truth behind the man we spotted in the archives.

As I reflect on my experience researching the life of Arthur B. Mitchell, I am struck by the notion that understanding Mitchell is inextricably linked to understanding his oppressors. To tell Mitchell's story, I first needed to understand the pervasiveness of white supremacy and racism in ante- and postbellum South Carolina. Although Arthur B. Mitchell was a free man, his worth was determined by his proximity to whites and the value *they* placed on his skills as a musician, cooper, and fireman. As I wrote "The Untold Story of Arthur B. Mitchell," I continued to reflect on why it was untold. I struggled to find primary sources because Black people in America were relegated to a lesser status, not entirely erased, but largely excluded from public records for much of the antebellum period. For this reason, I have only grasped at part of Mitchell's story.

It is not lost on me that I stand on the shoulders of the perseverance and resilience of Black Americans of the past. As I complete my studies at Harvard Law School, I will go forward with the understanding that white supremacy was codified into law in more ways than I ever could have imagined. However, because of this research, I have gained the skill to see beyond the law written on a page and always question how our legal system affects the most vulnerable.

Researching Black history and emphasizing the humanity of African Americans of the past is an act of resistance against white supremacy. I am grateful to teachers and mentors like Dr. Felice F. Knight, who instills in younger generations the skills to think critically and to search for truth.

Taylor Diggs holds a bachelor of arts degree in political science from The Citadel, where she pursued research on the antebellum and postbellum periods. She is currently a juris doctor (law degree) candidate at Harvard Law

School, where she is an editor on the *Civil Rights – Civil Liberties Law Review* and continues to pursue her interest in American history.

Felice F. Knight is director of education at the International African American Museum in Charleston, SC. A recognized scholar of race, slavery, and the African-American experience, she applies her extensive track record in academia to support nonprofit and educational organizations as they build community engagement, motivate teams, and optimize project management.

NOTES

1. Peter Filene, *The Joy of Teaching: A Practical Guide for New College Instructors* (Chapel Hill: The University of North Carolina Press, 2009), 75; emphasis original.
2. "Slavery and Universities LibGuide" (Charleston, SC: Daniel Library, The Citadel), 2021.
3. Mitchell was likely born in the 1820s and according to census records in 1820, Charleston had a free Black population of 1,475, an enslaved Black population of 12,652 and a white population of 10,743. See Bernard Edward Powers Jr., *Black Charlestonians: A Social History, 1822–1885* (Fayetteville: University of Arkansas Press, 1994), 267.
4. *United States Census, 1860*, database with images, *FamilySearch*, https://www.familysearch.org.
5. *United States Census, 1870*, database with images; *FamilySearch*, https://www.familysearch.org.
6. A. S. Salley, *South Carolina Troops in Confederate Service*, vol. 1 (Columbia, SC: The R. L. Bryan Co., 1913), 218.
7. Salley, *South Carolina Troops*, 378.
8. "Descriptive List of Free Negroes Belonging to City Engine No. 7 [Copy 2]." Lowcountry Digital Library. The Charleston Museum Archives, 1864.
9. For examples of student research projects connected with The Citadel's Universities Studying Slavery project, see "Slavery and Universities." Information about The President's Task Force on Race, Diversity, and Inclusion—on which the authors served—may be found at *President's Task Force on Race, Diversity and Inclusion*, The Citadel, https://www.citadel.edu/rdi-task-force/.
10. Oliver J. Bond, *The Story of The Citadel* (Greenville, SC: Southern Historical Press, 1989), 136.
11. "Funeral Notices," *News and Courier*, November 4, 1893.
12. "Funeral Notices." See also Bond, *Story of The Citadel*, 136. A military tattoo is a musical performance, such as would be led by a fifer.
13. "His Last Tattoo," *News and Courier*, November 4, 1893.
14. Powers, *Black Charlestonians*, 10.
15. Powers, *Black Charlestonians*, 16.
16. Powers, *Black Charlestonians*, 38–39. For a useful discussion of this and other laws restricting emancipation and the courts' efforts to reverse those laws, see Smiddy, "Judicial Nullification," 655.

17. Powers, *Black Charlestonians*, 38–39.

18. Powers, *Black Charlestonians*, 39.

19. Powers, *Black Charlestonians*, 32.

20. Powers, *Black Charlestonians*, 39.

21. Powers, *Black Charlestonians*, 44.

22. Denmark Vesey was a free Black man who helped establish the Mother Emanuel African Methodist Episcopal Church. He plotted a slave revolt in Charleston and was publicly hanged along with his co-conspirators. His actions caused great fear among white South Carolinians and caused the state legislature to create and staff a municipal arsenal at Marion Square. In 1842, the state established the South Carolina Military Academy, now The Citadel, on that site. For a brief of these events, see "Denmark Vesey," National Park Service, https://www.nps.gov/people/denmark-vesey.htm.

23. Powers, *Black Charlestonians*, 81.

24. Powers, *Black Charlestonians*, 56. See also Kathy Russell, Midge Wilson, and Ronald Miller, *The Color Complex: The Politics of Skin Color Among African Americans* (New York: Anchor Books, 1993).

25. For accessible essays concerning Lost Cause propaganda, see Alan T. Nolan and Gary W. Gallagher, eds., *Myth of the Lost Cause and Civil War History* (Bloomington: Indiana University Press, 2000).

26. Kevin M. Levin, *Searching for Black Confederates*, 45.

27. Levin, *Searching for Black Confederates*, 45.

28. Levin, *Searching for Black Confederates*, 46.

29. Quoted in Levin, *Searching for Black Confederates*, 61.

30. Salley, *South Carolina Troops*, 218.

31. Salley, *South Carolina Troops*, 378.

32. Bond, *The Story of The Citadel*, 136.

33. Myler, "Alfred H. Colquitt (1824–1894)." In *New Georgia Encyclopedia*, March 3, 2006.

34. Ouzts, "Maxcy Gregg and His Brigade of South Carolinians at the Battle of Fredericksburg." *The South Carolina Historical Magazine* 95, no. 1 (1994), 8.

35. Ouzts, "Maxcy Gregg," 8.

36. Ouzts, "Maxcy Gregg," 8.

37. Myler, "Alfred H. Colquitt."

38. Levin, *Searching for Black Confederates*, 92.

39. Levin, *Searching for Black Confederates*, 94.

40. Quoted in Levin, *Searching for Black Confederates*, 94.

41. Quoted in Levin, *Searching for Black Confederates*, 94.

42. Quoted in Levin, *Searching for Black Confederates*, 94.

43. "Descriptive List of Free Negroes."

44. "Descriptive List of Free Negroes."

45. For a detailed discussion of the Freedman's Savings and Trust Company and its importance for researching the history of African American families, see Reginald Washington, "Freedman's Savings and Trust Company and African American Genealogical Research." *Federal Records and African American History* 29, no, 2 (Summer 1997).

46. Washington, "Freedman's Savings and Trust." Access to banking services has been an ongoing problem for African Americans. In the 1930s, W. E. B. Du Bois wrote that "economic enfranchisement" was high on Black people's priority list but would not be possible until African Americans had access to secure savings and reasonable loans. For additional information on Charleston's Freedman's Savings and Trust, see Powers, *Black Charlestonians*, 100. While he was enlisted in the Confederate Army, Mitchell would have had access to another bank: the Military Savings Bank, which was established in 1864 by General Rufus Saxton for African American soldiers and civilians serving the Confederate cause. The bank was later named the South Carolina Freedmen's Savings Banks. See Washington, "Freedman's Savings and Trust."

47. "Registers of Signatures of Depositors, 1865–1874, Roll 21: Charleston, South Carolina; December 19, 1865–December 2, 1869," database with images, *Ancestry*, https://www.ancestry.com.

48. Washington, "Freedman's Savings and Trust."

49. "Year: 1880; Census Place: Charleston, Charleston, South Carolina; Roll 1222; Page 338A; Enumeration District: 068," database with images, *Ancestry*, https://www. ancestry.com.

50. Kevin J. Dougherty and Robert J. Pauly, *American Nation-Building Case Studies from Reconstruction to Afghanistan* (Jefferson, NC: McFarland & Company, 2017), 72.

51. See Perry's biography as recorded on *SCIWay: South Carolina's Information Highway*, https://www.sciway.net/hist/governors/perry.html. "Black codes" were laws enacted after the Civil War to restrict African Americans. These codes denied basic rights, limited wages, mandated harsh working conditions, and imposed harsh penalties for vagrancy. For a useful discussion of Black Codes and the establishment of Jim Crow, see Novak, *Wheel of Servitude*.

52. Dougherty and Pauly, *American Nation-Building*, 74.

53. For a comprehensive discussion of this event and other acts of violence during Reconstruction, see Zuczek, *State of Rebellion*.

54. Dougherty and Pauly, *American Nation-Building*, 76.

55. Dougherty and Pauly, *American Nation-Building*, 75. See also Lou Falkner Williams, *The Great South Carolina Ku Klux Klan Trials, 1871–1872* (Athens: University of Georgia Press, 1996).

56. Dougherty and Pauly, *American Nation-Building*, 77.

57. Dougherty and Pauly, *American Nation-Building*, 77–78.

58. See "Landmark Legislation: The Civil Rights Act of 1875," US Senate.

59. Dougherty and Pauly, *American Nation-Building*, 79–80.

60. Powers, *Black Charlestonians*, 114.

61. South Carolina Death Records, South Carolina Department of Archives and History; Columbia, SC.

WORKS CITED

1880 US Federal Census. Ancestry. http://www.ancestry.com.

"Benjamin Franklin Perry." *SCIWay: South Carolina's Information Highway.* 2024. https://www.sciway.net/hist/governors/perry.html.

Bond, Oliver J. *The Story of The Citadel.* Greenville, SC: Southern Historical Press, 1989.

"The Citadel." *Voices: Stories of Change.* https://www.africanamericancharleston .com/places/the-citadel.

"Descriptive List of Free Negroes Belonging to City Engine No. 7 [Copy 2]." Lowcountry Digital Library. The Charleston Museum Archives, 1864. https://lcdl .library.cofc.edu/lcdl/catalog/lcdl:27199.

Dougherty, Kevin J., and Robert J. Pauly. *American Nation-Building Case Studies from Reconstruction to Afghanistan.* Jefferson, NC: McFarland & Company, 2017.

Filene, Peter. *The Joy of Teaching: A Practical Guide for New College Instructors.* Chapel Hill: The University of North Carolina Press, 2009, Kindle.

"Universities Studying Slavery." *Inclusive Excellence.* Charleston, SC: The Citadel, 2004. https://www.citadel.edu/inclusive-excellence/ universities-studying-slavery/.

"Landmark Legislation: The Civil Rights Act of 1875." US Senate. https://www .senate.gov/artandhistory/history/common/generic/CivilRightsAct1875.htm.

Levin, Kevin M. *Searching for Black Confederates: The Civil War's Most Persistent Myth.* Chapel Hill: The University of North Carolina Press, 2019.

Myler, Barton. "Alfred H. Colquitt (1824–1894)." In *New Georgia Encyclopedia,* March 3, 2006 [last edited April 14, 2016]. https://www.georgiaencyclopedia .org/articles/government-politics/alfred-h-colquitt-1824-1894/.

Nolan, Alan T., and Gary W. Gallagher, eds. *The Myth of the Lost Cause and Civil War History.* Bloomington: Indiana University Press, 2000.

Novak, Daniel A. *The Wheel of Servitude: Black Forced Labor After Slavery.* Lexington: University of Kentucky Press, 2014.

Ouzts, Clay. "Maxcy Gregg and His Brigade of South Carolinians at the Battle of Fredericksburg." *The South Carolina Historical Magazine* 95, no. 1 (1994): 6–26.

Powers, Bernard Edward Jr. *Black Charlestonians: A Social History, 1822–1885.* Fayetteville: University of Arkansas Press, 1994.

"Registers of Signatures of Depositors, 1865–1874. Roll 21: Charleston, SC; December 19,1865–December 2, 1869." *Ancestry.* https://www.ancestry.com.

Russell, Kathy, Midge Wilson, and Ronald Miller. *The Color Complex: The Politics of Skin Color Among African Americans.* New York: Anchor Books, 1993.

Salley, A. S. *South Carolina Troops in Confederate Service,* vol. 1. Columbia, SC: The R. L. Bryan Co., 1913.

"Slavery and Universities LibGuide." Charleston, SC: Daniel Library, The Citadel, 2021. https://library.citadel.edu/c.php?g=43078&p=9573643.

Smiddy, Linda O. "Judicial Nullification and State Statutes Restricting the Emancipation of Slaves: A Court's Call for Reform." *South Carolina Law Review* 42, no. 3 (1991): 590–655.

South Carolina Death Records; Year Range: 1875–1899; Death County or Certificate Range: Charleston. South Carolina Department of Archives and History. Columbia, SC.

"United States Census, 1860." *FamilySearch.* https://familysearch.org.

"United States Census, 1870." *FamilySearch*. https://familysearch.org.

"U.S., Freedman's Bank Records, 1865–1874." *Ancestry*. https://www.ancestry.com.

Washington, Reginald. "The Freedman's Savings and Trust Company and African American Genealogical Research." *Federal Records and African American History* 29, no, 2 (Summer 1997). https://www.archives.gov/publications/prologue/1997/summer/freedmans-savings-and-trust.html.

Williams, Lou Falkner. *The Great South Carolina Ku Klux Klan Trials, 1871–1872*. Athens: University of Georgia Press, 1996.

"Year: 1880; Census Place: Charleston, Charleston, South Carolina; Roll: 1222; Page: 338A; Enumeration District: 068." *Ancestry*. https://www.ancestry.com.

Zuczek, Richard. *State of Rebellion: Reconstruction in South Carolina*. Columbia: University of South Carolina Press, 1996.

The Peace Family

Legacies of Slavery and Dispossession at the College of Charleston

Mary Jo Fairchild

Memory work is not just about remembering the past, but about reckoning with it—that is, establishing facts, acknowledging, apologizing, . . . and repairing the harm that was done through both material and immaterial forms of reparation.

> —Doria Johnson, Jarrett Drake, and Michelle Caswell, "From Cape Town to Chicago to Colombo and Back Again"

And although many institutions are still unclear about the relationship between reparations and institutional transformation, the possibility for creative responses to this question has rarely been more alive than it is today.

> —Leslie M. Harris, "Higher Education's Reckoning with Slavery"

In a State, even a democracy, where power is hierarchic, how can you prevent the storage of information from becoming yet another source of power to the powerful—another piston in the great machine?

> —Ursula K. LeGuin, *Always Coming Home*

On April 27, 1887, the *Charleston News and Courier* published an obituary for Thomas Peace, a long-serving employee of the College of Charleston:

Thomas Peace, for many years before was janitor of the Charleston College and as such, well known and remembered by hundreds of matriculates and alumni of that institution, died yesterday. 'Old Tom' was loved by the collegians, and later in life, as sexton of the Huguenot Church and janitor of the South Carolina Loan and Trust Company, won the kindly regards of all with whom he came in contact. He boasted that, like Randolph of Roanoke, and the Butler family of this State, he had Indian blood in his veins and his physiognomy justified the claim. In 'The Collegiad' the production

44

of a student, now a prominent city theologian, Peace is thus mentioned in the closing lines: 'Mysterious truth! Unknown to Ancient Rome, Where Peace prevails and dark Nero his home.'[1]

From these words, one senses that Peace was a trusted and beloved member of the college community. The pejorative nickname "Old Tom" and casual reference to "Indian blood," however, suggest something entirely different: that Thomas Peace, a Black man who had worked at the college since the time of enslavement, was always an outsider. He was within the community but never a part of it, and certainly never an equal to his white employers, despite the celebratory depiction offered in the obituary and an earlier student essay. More important, as in all obituaries, the words in the *Charleston News and Courier* not only record but also define a life. In this case, the laudatory memorial, almost certainly written by someone associated with the college, appropriates Thomas Peace's biography for ideological reasons.[2] With just a few sentences, "Old Tom" is reduced to a friendly subservient perfectly content living amid oppressive social hierarchies. Presenting his life through the lens of white authority, the author erases Thomas Peace and offers, instead, an avatar to defend the worst aspects of nineteenth-century Charleston culture.

This essay has three related purposes. First, through extensive primary research, it seeks to recover the lives of Thomas Peace; his wife, Isabella; and their children. Second, it demonstrates the severe limitations of archival resources and suggests strategies for recovering information about marginalized people and communities. Third, it shows the College of Charleston's participation in systems of enslavement, oppression, and segregation. In this way, the essay interrogates the unexplored and intertwined roles of dispossession and slavery in the development of the college from the late eighteenth century through the middle of the twentieth century.

Thomas Peace worked at the College of Charleston on and off beginning in the late 1820s, until his death almost sixty years later. At first, he worked while enslaved. After emancipation, he served as "janitor," "porter," and courier at the college.[3] From various sources, including the minutes of the College of Charleston Board of Trustees, treasurer's records, City of Charleston capitation tax records, Charleston city directories, census data, newspaper articles, and Freedmen's Bureau records, we can piece together a rough outline of Peace's life, but the records are always incomplete, and Peace always remains in their background. Black feminist historians and scholars such as Tiya Miles, Marisa J. Fuentes, Deborah Gray White, and

Saidiya Hartman have established that archives are rife with problems, not the least of which is the erasure of the experiences of disenfranchised and oppressed people. Peace's biography substantiates their claims. For Miles, the fragmented historical record creates an urgent need for new scholarly skills. "It is a worthwhile practice," she contends, "to learn the skill of valuing what has previously been voided. For here, in the space of loss and longing that the enslaved knew too well, we can choose an abundant approach to history, resisting the default in which historical gaps feed contemporary forgetfulness."[4] This essay seeks to challenge the "contemporary forgetfulness" that erased the harsh realities of Peace's life and elided the college's complicity in his mistreatment.

Who Was Thomas Peace?

The traditional narrative of the history of the College of Charleston includes caricatured descriptions of a man called "Tom" or "Thomas" Peace. The first reference to include both his first and last names occurs in 1855, on a receipt that he signed for his pay, but there are numerous earlier references to a "Tom" or "Thomas" who is almost certainly the same person.[5] The fact that Peace signed for his wages might suggest that he was legally free at that time, but this is almost certainly not the case. After the passage of Act No. 2236 in 1820, it was impossible for an enslaved person to be freed without an act by the South Carolina Legislature, and no such record is extant.[6] The earlier records, as we will see, indicate strongly that he was enslaved when he began working for the college in 1829, and there is no reason to believe that he was officially emancipated before 1863. The records also indicate that Peace and his family were removed from their home in 1855, when the college began construction on new facilities. From city records, we learn that Peace married a free Black woman, Isabella, and that they had five children, three of whom survived into adulthood: Rebecca, St. Julien, and Eugene.[7] Additionally, Thomas and Isabella had at least seven grandchildren and at least three great-grandchildren. Census records indicate that their descendants lived in Detroit, Boston, Chicago, and Charleston.

A funeral notice published in the *Charleston News and Courier* by members of the Unity and Friendship Society, a prominent African-American burial society in Charleston, reports that Thomas Peace died three years to the month after Isabella.[8] In that notice, N. T. Spencer, secretary of the Unity and Friendship Society, summoned members "to attend the funeral of [their] late brother Thomas Peace."[9] Peace was buried at the Unity and Friendship

Society cemetery located on Cunnington Avenue adjacent to several other large burial grounds such as the Friendly Union, Humane and Friendly, Magnolia, Bethany, and Lawrence cemeteries.[10] The cemetery—maintained by the Brown Fellowship Society, another prominent African-American burial society—also relocated to this area after remaining members sold the Society's lots to the Catholic Diocese of Charleston for the expansion of Bishop England High School in 1945. Since 2005, this same hallowed ground has been occupied by the College of Charleston's Marlene and Nathan Addlestone Library.[11]

One year after Peace's death, his eldest daughter, Rebecca, wrote a beautiful, poetic tribute to her father:

> The death of this good and true man has left a void not only in the home circle but in the community where he lived and labored for four score years, filling responsible positions with honor and retaining the confidence of those reposing trust in him. His courtesy endeared him to all with whom he came in contact and his entire demeanor stamped him an honest man. Devotion to duty was his Polar star from which he never severed. A consistent Christian for half a century, he adorned his profession by an exemplary life. The loss of his beloved wife cast a gloom over the evening of his days, which was intensified by the sad taking of his son without a moment's warning. Alas, the beautiful rod broken, and the state of his declining days removed, nature succumbed and his buoyant spirits gave way under the shock. Solaced by the care and affection of a devoted daughter, he gently passed away to be forever with the Lord.[12]

This memorial is very different from the recollections offered in the earlier obituary. It is more personal, loving, and exceedingly tender. It mentions the tragedies of losing his wife, Isabella, in 1883 and his son St. Julian in 1886, citing these as reasons for his decline. Rebecca's words affirm many of the personal characteristics mentioned in the earlier memorial, but they also call attention to the strength of Peace's faith and his devotion to his family. No longer the caricature "Old Tom," Peace becomes a recognizable man, someone whose worth and purpose exceed the service he provided for his employer.

Few other facts about Thomas Peace's life are extant. As slavery scholar Saidiya Hartman poignantly notes, "the archive yields no exhaustive account" of the lives of enslaved and marginalized people such as Thomas and Isabella Peace.[13] There are no birth records, no childhood addresses, and few clues about extended family. Still an honest and repair-driven effort to reconstruct the Peace story is possible if using a Black feminist epistemological approach alongside critical theory and more traditional historical research methods. At times, these approaches provide evidence that is more probable than certain. These limitations notwithstanding, careful analysis of the historical record, however scant, yields a fuller picture of Thomas Peace and his family. It also documents his relationship with the College of Charleston.

College records establish that starting in January 1829, the treasurer, Charles Fraser, paid a woman named Ann Wagner twenty-four dollars "for Tom's wages, 3 months."[14] According to a city directory published in 1831, Ann Wagner resided at 52 St. Philip Street at the heart of campus in the antebellum era.[15] Tom was hired to "ring the bell, keep every part of the college clean together with the yard, cut the wood and make fires in the winter, keep the philosophical apparatus clean, and be in constant attendance when not otherwise engaged to do the duties of a messenger."[16] In April 1829, the college increased the payment to include two dollars per month for "Tom's lodging," suggesting that Wagner may have rented accommodations for Tom and that the college reimbursed her for those expenses. Thereafter, Wagner received ten dollars per month, paid in quarterly installments of thirty dollars for Tom's labors and lodging through 1838.[17] In 1838, the College transitioned from a private to a municipal entity. Subsequent changes in accounting and budgeting operations likely explain why receipts from Tom's wages were no longer recorded. However, in March of that year, members of the board of trustees, which now included the city council, reauthorized administrators to "engage Mrs. Wagner's boy, Tom, for the use of the College."[18] These records demonstrate that the college employed at least one enslaved person, Tom, whose wages were paid to his enslaver. Further evidence suggests strongly that this enslaved person, identified only as "Tom," is Thomas Peace.

At the time of his death, Peace was said to be at least seventy-five years old, which would make him at least seventeen years old in 1829, certainly old enough to be hired out for a job that required a measure of self-sufficiency.[19] We can also be certain that Thomas Peace was enslaved during the early decades of the nineteenth century. Had Peace been free, his name, age, occupation, and other demographic information would have been recorded in capitation records, which the city used to collect taxes on free Black persons.[20] Capitation taxes essentially penalized free Black people for earning wages for labor that would otherwise have been unpaid. In this way, the taxes reinforced the racial subjugation of individuals who occupied what historian Bernard Powers calls an anomalous status "dictated by the region's commitment to slavery."[21] The city had financial and ideological incentives to keep capitation records current and complete. The absence of Thomas Peace's name provides strong evidence of his enslavement and reinforces the speculation that Ann Wagner hired out his services to the College of Charleston. As Tiya Miles points out "endeavoring to reconstruct any history, but especially the histories of the marginalized, requires an attentiveness to absence as well as presence."[22] In this case, his absence in tax records evidences his enslaved status.

The minutes of the College of Charleston's board of trustees provide additional evidence. In 1843, those documents note not only that Tom was working at the college but also that he needed housing.[23] Ann Wagner, it should be noted, died in 1843. As we will see, she left considerable debt, and her estate was liquidated shortly after her death. The evidence suggests that Tom remained the property of the Wagner family until her death. The fact that his living arrangements became unstable at the same time as Wagner's home was sold provides compelling evidence that the enslaved Tom, whose labor was sold beginning in 1829, is the same man who needed housing in 1843.

Furthermore, in the course of campus expansion and construction in 1855, the college removed Thomas and Isabella Peace, along with their children, from their home. The fact that the Peace family was living until that time in housing located on the campus of the college further substantiates that Thomas Peace had once been enslaved by Ann Wagner. The college assented to Tom's living on campus at her death only to revoke the arrangement twelve years later. Cumulatively, the evidence makes it all but certain that the Thomas Peace who died in 1887 was the same person who began working at the college in 1829.

Municipal and archival records allow us to fill in more gaps. Because Thomas Peace was enslaved during most of his life, there is little documentary evidence of his ancestry. According to capitation tax records, however, his wife, Isabella Peace, was a free woman of color living in Charleston as early as 1843. Contrary to the common white and patriarchal custom of women taking the surnames of their husbands upon marriage, Tom, a man born into slavery and possessing a first name only, with no generational wealth and property to convey, chose to adopt the family name of Isabella and her ancestors, all free women of color making their lives in Charleston.

There were at least six free women of color bearing the last name "Peace" living and working in Charleston from as early as 1790 up until the 1860s.[24] Given their ages and the proximity of their dwellings listed in capitation tax records, it is likely these women were grandmothers, aunts, sisters, and perhaps even mother to Isabella Peace. There is, of course, an abundance of records for Ann Wagner, and these provide important insights for Peace's life. If, as historian Stephanie McCurry holds, "historical visibility is everywhere related to social power," locating Thomas Peace outside of the institutional archives of the College of Charleston requires investigating documentary footprints left by members of the elite white family that enslaved him.[25]

The widow of a wealthy lawyer and planter, Ann Wagner (née Hrabowski) became the head of household while her three sons were minors. As a result, she played a significant role in negotiating her family's business affairs, which included publicly buying and selling enslaved people and conducting real estate transactions for dwellings located near the college campus. Wagner was born in St. Augustine, Florida, on October 2, 1769, and died in Charleston on March 5, 1843.[26] In 1788, she married George Wagner, and the couple had at least four children: John, George Jr., Effingham, and States. Like many white families in the antebellum South, the Wagners accumulated wealth through the systematic oppression and enslavement of Indigenous and African-descended people.

George Wagner died in 1808, leaving Ann to manage the family's affairs until her sons came of age. For a time, Ann maintained the family residence located at 101 Broad Street, a relatively affluent section of Charleston. Ann also retained significant status, as evidenced by the label "planter" assigned to her in the 1809 *Directory for the District of Charleston, Comprising the Places of Residence and Occupation of the White Inhabitants*. It was uncommon for a woman to be designated "planter," and she almost certainly inherited the title from her recently departed husband. The designation "planter" also served the interests of her brother Richard Hrabowski, the compiler and publisher of the city directory for the year 1809.[27]

In 1814 and 1818, Ann Wagner corresponded with her family, most often, her son Effingham, while traveling up and down the eastern seaboard visiting family and friends. She wrote of attending parties, enjoying elaborate dinners, and visiting friends at their country homes, noting in one letter, "I have not had time [to write more often] for the very great attention of my friends are such that we are not allowed to have one hour to spare." Her days, she further noted, were "spent in one continuous roar of laughter and good humor."[28] Wagner's 1814 trip took her to Petersburg, Virginia; Providence,

Rhode Island; Boston, Massachusetts; and parts of New York. She shared
news of family and friends, social outings, and experiences. However, the
family was experiencing financial pressures. Wagner wrote to Effingham,
who by this time had taken on responsibility for the family's finances, asking whether he had "sold the rice," collected income from rental properties,
and, most significantly, received wages for the services of people the Wagner
family enslaved.[29] Wagner also wrote that "it gives me some uneasiness to
know that you have so much trouble with my business but I hope you will be
able to make out." From her rooms in Boston, she lamented: "I see so many
things here that I should like but fear my limited funds will not hold out."[30]
Hoping that Effingham would "be able to make [her] a remittance soon,"
Ann turned to discussing not only the wages of the people she enslaved
but also Effingham's management and supervision of those people. She felt
"great pleasure to hear they behave so well" and asked Effingham to "tell
Paul I will bring him a handsome present and he shall be rewarded for his
good behavior." Wagner closed her letter by instructing Effingham to also
tell "the rest of them," the enslaved people, how "pleased" she was "to hear
they behave so well." In a postscript to this letter, she singled out an enslaved
person named Thomas, writing "I hope Thomas is a good boy. If he is, I will
bring him a new hat."[31] This brief mention very likely provides the earliest
reference to Thomas Peace. Although whites often applied the term "boy"
to any enslaved man regardless of age, here it seems probable that "Thomas"
actually was a child at the time. Wagner's promise of a gift suggests that
she may have had some fondness for young Thomas and saw him as being
somewhat different, apart, or exceptional from other enslaved people in the
household. On the basis of his estimated age at his death, Thomas Peace was
likely born in or a few years before 1812, which would make him a toddler or
young boy in 1814.[32]

Wagner's financial struggles culminated in a significant liquidation of
her assets in 1816. According to the Charleston *City Directories*, she sold her
posh residence at 101 Broad Street and relocated to St. Philip Street, a more
working-class neighborhood near the college.[33] In February of that year, a
bill of sale recorded in Charleston District indicated that Wagner and her
two eldest sons, John and George Jr., sold fifty-three enslaved people to
one Henry McAlpin.[34] If her earlier correspondence suggested a somewhat
benevolent relationship with her "servants," this action demonstrates her
willingness to participate in the cruelty of chattel slavery. Wagner used the
profit from the sale, nearly twenty-two thousand dollars ($21,857.14), "for
myself and as guardian for Caroline, Emeline, Clara, and Eugenia Wagner,

Henry Coming, and Effingham Wagner."[35] The names of the people sold were Jack, Nanny, Sampson, Susan, Diane, Jack, Betsy, Emba, Nelly, Paris, [Fortimor], Hector, Jenny, Caesar, Marian, William, Tom, Hester, Bob, Robin, April, Hetty, Venus, Juba, Bella, Binah, Peter, Joe, Johnny, Harriot, Nanny, Jupiter, Sarah, Hercules, November, Chloe, Will, Eve, Cindy, Jimmy, Philis, Judy, Dinah, Esoph, Dick, Loena, Dick, July, Frank, [Fortimor], Philis, Comba, and Old Lady.[36]

In 1818, Ann Wagner traveled to Fishkill, New York, to attend the wedding of her eldest son, John, who was working at West Point Academy. During her visit, she wrote separate letters to her other two sons, Effingham and George Jr., inquiring about the possibility of gifting John and his new wife, Lydia, "two or three thousand dollars out of the principal of my estate" to "make a beginning in his profession and life."[37] During this trip, Wagner also visited New York, Philadelphia, and Providence. Again, she frequently inquired about the "conduct" of the people enslaved by the Wagner family as well as their wages. In a letter written from New York City in May of 1818, Wagner expressed "hope that all things go on well and that the servants are obedient and give no trouble for I shall be much hurt if they do."[38] Her words express the inherent contradictions of enslavers. To raise money, Wagner willingly sold enslaved people, not only treating them as commodities but also undoubtedly separating family members and friends. In her correspondence, she projects a personal relationship with the same people she considered property. In the following months, Wagner repeated her inquiries about the "servants'" obedience and the collection of their wages. From Fishkill, Wagner wrote, "I hope the negroes conduct well and you received their wages punctually"; from Providence, she remarked, "I hope the servant's wages have been punctually paid and that they give you as little trouble as possible."[39]

Ann Wagner died at the age of seventy-three from apoplexy in March of 1843.[40] Her estate inventory listed household goods and furniture in great detail, and every item she owned was sold to pay debts attached to her estate. Column after column enumerated chairs, clocks, plates, pots, silver cutlery, and more.[41] There is not a last will and testament on record for Ann Wagner; she likely died intestate. These circumstances make it difficult to know exactly what became of "Tom" or Thomas. The record in the board of trustees' minutes referring to Thomas needing a home in 1843 strongly suggests that he was still associated with both Ann Wagner, or at least the Wagner family, and the college at the time of her death.[42]

Documents related to Ann Wagner's oldest son, Dr. John Wagner, provide more evidence of Tom's possible whereabouts in the late 1830s and early 1840s. John Wagner graduated from Yale University and studied medicine in New York, Britain, and France before returning to South Carolina to set up a medical practice.[43] In Charleston, Wagner was a well-known surgeon. In 1829, he was appointed assistant chair of pathological and surgical anatomy at the South Carolina Medical College. Several years later in 1832, he was promoted to full chair of surgery, a position he occupied until his death from an enlarged liver in 1841.[44] In this role, Wagner participated in the inhumane practice of using enslaved people's bodies to demonstrate surgical techniques. In her research on "medicalizing blackness," historian Rana Hogarth has discovered several advertisements published by Dr. John Wagner in Charleston newspapers soliciting the patronage of "slaves and coloured persons, laboring under surgical diseases and accidents." Hogarth demonstrates that the "unfortunate slave patient who went to Wagner's infirmary was not a recipient of care but rather a teaching apparatus."[45]

This inherently depraved practice, not uncommon among physicians in the English-speaking Atlantic World, did not lead to Wagner's success. His death, most likely due to alcoholism, left his wife, Lydia, and six children destitute. In May of 1842, Wagner's widow petitioned the Court of Equity of the State of South Carolina for authorization to sell Wagner's pew at St. Michael's Church, as his other assets, with the exception of "some house servants," had already been sold to reduce his sizable debts. His principal liabilities were owed to his own brother, Effingham. Lydia Wagner's petition indicated that the "house servants" were already mortgaged to her brother-in-law and, therefore, she "pray[ed] to be authorized to sell the pew and apply the proceeds to the payment of her late husband's debts."[46]

John Wagner's estate appraisal was not recorded until May of 1843, just after his mother's death. It is probable that Effingham Wagner balanced the family budget in 1843, consolidating assets and debts from his mother and brother at the same time. Whatever the case, when it was eventually inventoried and appraised, John Wagner's estate included seven enslaved people, quite possibly the "house slaves" to whom Lydia Wagner referred in her petition. Included in the list is "Thomas."[47] If this person is Thomas Peace, he was likely engaged by both Ann and her son, John Wagner, at different intervals in addition to his duties at the college.

Several months later, in December 1843, seven enslaved people from the Wagner estate were sold at public auction. Multiple creditors traded in the bonds they held over John Wagner's estate for ownership of Abraham, Phoebe, Harriette, Hannah, Betsey, James, and Thomas.[48] One creditor, F. W. Capers, purchased Thomas for two hundred twenty dollars. At the time, Capers had just resigned as a member of the faculty at the College of Charleston to join that of The Citadel Academy. Capers was an alumnus and valedictorian of the College of Charleston's class of 1840.[49] As a student, Capers may have interacted with the man known as "Tom, the janitor."

As mentioned earlier, from 1838 to 1855, the college's cash receipt ledger ceased to document expenses such as salaries and wages. The quarterly funds paid for Tom's labor vanished from those records, but his association with the college continued. On October 14, 1844, the board of trustees "resolved that Thomas the Janitor of the College be allowed to occupy the building on the premises during the pleasure of the Trustees-he repairing it and making it habitable, at his own expense."[50] At this point, Thomas had worked at the college, perhaps with concurrent duties in Wagner family households, for fifteen years. It was in the college's best interest to provide a solution to the housing instability that Peace experienced. It is also likely that as he aged and his tenure at the college lengthened, Peace edged away from the status he occupied as a younger person—that of an enslaved person—and closer to that of a free person of color. This trend is well established by scholars of free Black urban life in nineteenth-century South Carolina. Marina Wikramanayake, for example, argues that the "conditions in the city of Charleston yielded a peculiar class of blacks who operated in a . . . state of limbo, neither slave nor free. As increasing urbanization offered more opportunities for employment, it had been the practice of slaveholders in the cities to allow slaves to 'hire their own time.' . . . Such slaves were afforded a higher degree of laxity than the usual and often lived away from their owners."[51] Whatever autonomy Thomas Peace enjoyed was tied to his labors at the College of Charleston.

The precarity of Peace's provisional freedom and living conditions eventually led to crisis. In 1855, the college displaced Thomas Peace and his young family from their home at the center of campus to make way for what would become the institution's first freestanding library on the grounds of the iconic greenspace colloquially referred to as "The Cistern." The development of that area of campus was part of a large expansion that had begun before the Civil War. The primary classroom building, now known as Randolph Hall, was enlarged and expanded from 1850 to 1851. At the same time, the college constructed the building known as "Porter's Lodge," designed by architect Edward Brickell White, along George Street to "aggrandize" the new south-facing entrance to campus.[52] Several years later, on January 20, 1855, the college embarked on efforts to construct a new library building located on the west side of the modern day "Cistern" known as "College Green."[53] It is likely that the Peace family was displaced in this early stage of the construction. The library was formally opened on July 24, 1856.[54] Because the Peace family home stood in the path of these changes, the college demolished it without ceremony.

In October 1856, Peace submitted a petition to the Charleston City Council requesting two hundred dollars for the loss of the home he had "fitted up at his own expense." According to city council proceedings, the removal of the house took place without Peace's consent and was "detrimental to his pecuniary interests."[55] A subcommittee of the city council denied Peace's request. Noting only that Peace "derived the benefit of his expenditure from the occupancy of the building," the committee members disregarded the labor and money that Thomas and Isabella Peace had invested in their home. The affluent (and all-white) council members also ignored the fact that such a loss for someone like Thomas Peace, with a young family straddling the limits of slavery and freedom, would be a cruel hardship. Instead, the committee stated that Peace should be "regarded in no other light than as a tenant at will."[56] Outside of the significant harm the College perpetrated in displacing Peace and his family in 1855, we cannot say exactly when, where, and by whom he was treated fairly or unfairly. However, it is very likely that his bodily autonomy became increasingly attached to his role at the College of Charleston and connections to the elite white administrators, faculty, and students there. Again, as a Black man living in the tenuous space between slavery and freedom, finding alternative employment would have been difficult for Peace before legal emancipation.

Although conditions have changed, new iterations of the same restrictions on job opportunities persist at the College of Charleston. In her 2008 investigation of working conditions and experiences of Black service workers at the college, Kaylee Rogers conducted interviews that document how persistent this precarity is for many Black employees. The past, regrettably, is present. As one worker explained, "A lot of people are not getting paid what they should . . . not getting paid what they're worth . . . brought in because they can't get a job nowhere else . . . [They] get stuck in the system."[57]

The Peace Family

Thomas Peace spent his life and made a family with his wife, Isabella, a free woman of color who was born around 1830 and worked as a seamstress and mantua maker.[58] The process of uncovering more about Isabella's early life and lineage—including determining at what point her ancestors became free—is both similar to and different from that of reconstructing Thomas Peace's early life. Traditional records rarely document the lives and experiences of nonwhite, marginalized, and oppressed people such as Thomas and Isabella Peace. As Marisa J. Fuentes notes, an incomplete archive, dependent on the "conditions under which our subjects lived," greatly limits "our ability to recount."[59] Michel-Rolph Trouillout extends the point by demonstrating how social power structures create "silences" around marginalized populations that persist throughout "the process of historical production."[60] The limitations of the archive, many of which stem from the unequal distribution of power, render it wholly inadequate for preserving records of marginalized lives. For this reason, Fuentes urges historians to "resist the authority of the traditional archive that legitimates structures built on racial and gendered subjugation."[61] Yet without the archival materials preserved by the very people who enslaved and oppressed the Peaces, it would be even more difficult to reconstruct their lives. One can resist the authority of the flawed archive while deriving benefit from its contents. In the case of Isabella Peace, state-produced records such as capitation tax rolls and municipal birth and death records both document and erase her life.

Isabella was almost certainly born free. In the eighteenth century as Amrita Chakrabarti Myers demonstrates there were a number ways Black women could emancipate themselves and their families, including purchasing themselves and their kin, filing affidavits with the courts, drafting wills, engaging in extralegal trusts, and building alliances with persons who could help them on their "quest for liberty."[62] Many manumissions, however, remain untraceable because "owners and laborers alike believed it was unnecessary to formalize such deeds."[63] By the time Isabella was born in 1829, these opportunities had almost entirely vanished. In the early nineteenth century, white fears became especially acute, in large measure because of uprisings in so-called "slave societies," such as Haiti, Jamaica, and Virginia. An explosive growth in Charleston's free Black community—from five hundred eighty-six people in 1790 to fourteen hundred seventy-four people by 1820—further fueled these fears.[64] Most significantly, the state legislature passed the Act of 1820, which made manumission possible only by an act of law. The Act also prohibited migrations of free persons of color into and out of the state.[65] Black children, however, could still be born free under the doctrine of *partus sequitur ventrem*, or "the offspring follows the belly." This doctrine, originally established in 1662 by the Virginia Assembly, ensured the enslavement of children born to enslaved mothers. It also "incentivized the rape of enslaved Black women by their white enslavers."[66] Although intended to subjugate Black people, it could also provide for their freedom. Isabella's mother, the evidence suggests, must have been a free Black person, and that freedom transferred to her daughter at birth, as it would later to Isabella's children.

Isabella Peace paid capitation taxes from 1843 until 1864, which is to say from the time she was fourteen until she was thirty-five. The records for these taxes document that she lived on Wentworth and Society Streets in 1843 and 1844, respectively. From 1845 to 1851, she lived on St. Philip Street. It was during this time that she likely began a relationship with Thomas Peace, who was living on the campus of the college. In the capitation tax book dating to 1852, Isabella Peace is listed as living at the corner of College and George Streets.[67] In 1855 and 1857 (there is no extant capitation tax book for 1856) Isabella Peace was living at 24 Laurens Street, which coincides with the Peace family's displacement from their campus home in early 1855 as a result of the construction of the new library.[68]

In her book on marriages between enslaved and free Black people, historian Tera W. Hunter notes that women "made up a greater percentage of free black populations" because they were "manumitted more often than men." Because of this demographic imbalance, free Black women were "forced to seek spouses outside their cohort, including among the enslaved."[69] As was the case with Thomas Peace, "slaves able to hire themselves out and live independent of their masters were most likely to be in positions to marry or engage in intimate arrangements with free blacks."[70] This "uneven achievement of freedom meant that many blacks found themselves related to or married to unfree people," in what Hunter calls "mixed-status marriages," which were part of a "larger pattern of irregular marriages . . . among slaves, quasi-free people, and poor populations across the color line."[71]

Isabella established herself as a successful mantua maker and seamstress. She also apprenticed several enslaved women. In an 1855 letter to his daughter, a local attorney named David Lewis Wardlaw reported that he had "placed" two enslaved women, Lizzy and Martha, with Isabel Peace, whom he described as a "colored mantua-maker, wife of Reverend Peace, colored janitor of the Charleston College."[72] It is likely that, in addition to having the help of Lizzy and Martha, Isabella Peace also took pains to teach them the seamstress trade in Charleston.

The fact that Isabella established and expanded her own business is remarkable. As Tera Hunter points out, antebellum culture restricted free

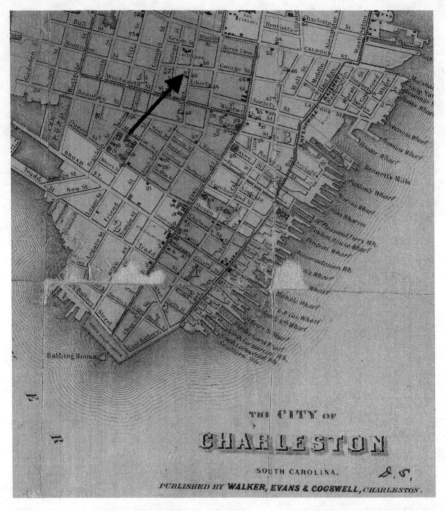

Figure 3.1. Nineteenth-century map of Charleston published by Walker, Evans and Cogswell showing the proximate location of Isabella Peace's home on St. Philip's Street. Special Collections, College of Charleston.

Black women largely to "domestic labor in private homes."[73] White women had opportunities to work in shops and factories producing "candy, clothing, textiles, paper boxes" and other commodities, but the "range of job opportunities for black women" was even "more narrow than for black men."[74] Isabella Peace and her descendants were part of a small segment of the population able to move away from domestic work and into more desirable, and presumably lucrative, jobs in the needle trade and later, as we will see, in the classroom.

Because the first recorded generation of free Black Peace family members in Charleston straddles the eighteenth and nineteenth centuries, it will be helpful to outline the number of ways in which Black people came to occupy this so-called "free" status during the age of slavery. Although sparse, records for members of the free Black Peace family go back as early as 1827 and include death certificates for two women in the same generation. This first generation of free Black Peace family members included a woman called Pender Peace, who was born in Charleston in the year 1737 and died on September 2, 1827, of "old age."[75] Another woman called Molly Peace was born in 1743 and died on September 13, 1831.[76] These women lived to be ninety and eighty-eight years old, respectively.

Barbara Peace, who was born in 1790 and died sixty years later in 1850, is the sole member of the second generation of the free Black Peace family documented in the extant historical record.[77] Four women, Julia, Emily M., Sarah G., and Isabella, belonged to the third generation of the free Black Peace family in Charleston. Isabella Peace was born in 1829 and lived to be almost fifty-five years old, passing away in 1883.[78] One young man, Joe Peace, was also part of this third generation. Born in 1829, Joe Peace was enslaved by Molly Peace. He died at the age of eleven in 1831. He was buried at the Bethel Graveyard.[79] Given his age and the common circumstances under which free Black people often kept their families—consisting of both enslaved and free people—together, it is very likely that Joe Peace was Molly's grandson, nephew, or another such relation. The fourth generation consisted of Thomas and Isabella Peace's five children: Rebecca, Thomas Jr., Eugene, Isabella, and St. Julian. Two of their children, Thomas Jr. and Isabella, did not survive childhood. Death records indicate that Thomas Jr. died on February 25, 1860, at the age of seven from tonsillitis. He was buried at the First Baptist Colored Cemetery. Young Isabella died on May 10, 1862, from whooping cough. She was only one month old and was buried at St. Patrick's Cemetery.[80]

Except for Rebecca, who was born between 1853 and 1855, all the Peace children were born during the Civil War. A note adjacent to Rebecca's name in the 1870 census indicates that she attended school and was able to read and write. Rebecca attended the Avery Normal Institute, which was located on St. Philip's Street, in the same neighborhood where Thomas and Isabella Peace started their family. The school, originally named the Saxton School, was founded in October 1865, during the Reconstruction era by the American Missionary Association and led by Francis L. Cardozo. It became the

Avery Normal Institute on May 5, 1868. At its inception, the school served one thousand children, nearly a quarter of Charleston's Black school-aged population.[81] Rebecca and her siblings were among the first students to matriculate at the school. Rebecca graduated in 1873 and according to notes jotted in the margins of the commencement program, her teachers and administrators "hope[d] she may teach in this school soon."[82]

In 1876, the twenty-six-year-old Rebecca married Benjamin Hurlong of Alabama. The young couple lived with members of their extended family at 12 Nassau Street in Charleston. Other members of the household included Thomas Peace, who worked as a porter at South Carolina Loan and Trust, Isabella Peace, Julian Peace, and Eugene Peace. Both Julian and Eugene worked as barbers.[83] According to the 1878 and 1879 city directories, Rebecca was a teacher and Benjamin was a barber at the posh Pavilion Hotel.[84] Tera Hunter notes that "few black women were able to escape common labor and enter professions such as teachers."[85] Rebecca's accomplishments were remarkable and would not have been possible without the education she received at the Avery Normal Institute and her parents' encouragement and direction.

Rebecca's teaching career, however, did not last long. From 1878 to 1879, she taught at a school "named for the antislavery Union colonel Robert Gould Shaw and leased to the City of Charleston by its trustees on the condition that it employ at least some black teachers."[86] She may have stopped teaching to care for her four children: Isabelle, Raymond, Granville, and Ada, all of whom grew up in Charleston. Benjamin Hurlong died in 1900, when their youngest child, Ada, was eight years old and attending school with her brother Granville.[87] At this time, Rebecca began working as a seamstress using skills she learned from her mother. As both a teacher and seamstress, Rebecca, like Isabella, was among the growing ranks of Black women laboring outside domestic service. Opportunities for Black women, however, were still severely limited, and progress, although real, was slow. In the city of Atlanta, for example, "the proportion of black women in domestic work dropped from 92 to 84 percent" between 1900 and 1910.[88] Rebecca died in 1935.

Thomas and Isabella's second child, Eugene Peace, was born in 1861. According to the census taken of Charleston residents in 1861, the Peaces then lived at 40 Coming Street.[89] Like other members of his family, Eugene worked as a barber. According to city directories, in 1878 and 1879, he worked for J. W. Aveilhe, and from 1881 to 1883, he worked with Black barber George A. Lord at 484 King Street.[90] He married Elizabeth "Bettie" Tomlinson around 1882.

Both were literate.[91] By 1889, Eugene and Bettie had relocated to Philadel-phia. A baptismal record for a son, Harold St. Julian Peace, was recorded at the Crucifixion Episcopal Church on August 31, 1889.[92] Eugene and Bet-tie had two more sons while living in Philadelphia: Eugene LeRoy (called LeRoy), born October 1892, and Robert Tucker (called Tucker), born in 1898. Sometime during the first decade of the twentieth century, Eugene Peace's family relocated to New York City. Eugene died sometime around 1909. The 1910 census indicates that Bettie was a forty-eight-year-old widow who had been married for twenty-seven years. Their sons, Harold, LeRoy, and Tucker, lived with their mother in an apartment located at 125 West 133rd Street in Manhattan. Bettie worked as a trained nurse in a private home. At age twenty, Harold worked in the card room at a club. Seventeen-year-old LeRoy worked in the cloakroom of a club, perhaps the same one as his brother. Young Robert, twelve years old, was likely still in school.[93]

St. Julien Peace, Thomas and Isabella's third child, was born in July of 1863 and likely attended the Avery School along with his sister, Rebecca, and brother Eugene. By the age fifteen, he was working as a barber with his brother-in-law, Benjamin Hurlong, at the Pavilion Hotel.[94] An advertise-ment in the 1877 city directory claimed that the Pavilion was a "first-class hotel . . . situated on Meeting Street on one of the widest, handsomest, and busiest thoroughfares of the city within steps of the largest wholesale houses and connected by street railway with the Railroad Depots, Post Office, Banks, etc." The advertisement boasted that the clerks were "competent and polite," and the servants were "quick and attentive."[95]

Tragically, St. Julian Peace died of an accidental gunshot wound early in the morning on March 6, 1886, at the Pavilion Hotel. He was only twenty-three years old. Preparing for the day, hotel workers were startled by the sound of a pistol coming from the engine room of the hotel. The *Charleston News and Courier* reported that co-workers found St. Julian Peace "lying on the floor with his head in a pool of blood, unconscious but still living."[96] A doctor did "all in his power to relieve the wounded boy, but in vain." Witnesses overheard a conversation between engineer A. T. Doyle and porter Peter White over the "respective abilities of Buffalo Bill and Dr. Carver as marksmen." White summoned his friend St. Julian Peace, and the two men engaged in a friendly tussle. Peace playfully brandished a razor, placing the back of the blade toward White's throat. White then "put his hand in his pocket and pulled out his pistol." Moments later, witnesses heard the shot and saw Peace fall to the ground. In the aftermath, "White seemed more affected by grief at having slain his friend than by any fear of consequences to himself."[97] St. Julian Peace was buried at the Unity and Friendship Cemetery.

Mythologized Historical Narratives and the Legacy of Slavery

Without question, Thomas Peace left a favorable impression on many faculty members and students. Alumnus James De Bow includes "Tom" in a sentimental reflection of his college days:

> In the old campus, and under the shady mulberries how often met to discourse on many a theme pertaining more to aught else in the world than the coming recitation or lecture till Tom, whose fame belongs to the college, and shall descend as an heirloom when his ghostly shadow only may glide through those halls, sounded from his belfry, and the noisy tread of feet told of a new shuffle of classes and of our hour.[98]

De Bow's representation seems mostly innocent and charitable. Tom remains in the background of his description, almost a part of the scenery, but his well-deserved fame, De Bow assures the reader, will endure long after his death.

Other depictions of Thomas Peace are far more sinister. They either erase Peace or distort the nature of his relationship with the college. As a result of institutional and cultural colonialism and the collective legacies of slavery, the actual Peace family story disappears from the published histories of the College of Charleston.[99] Until recently, in fact, highly mythologized historical narratives that champion the accomplishments of faculty, students, and administrators, most of whom were white and male, occupy the bulk of the institution's historical imagination. As discussed at the beginning of the essay, the obituary published in the *Charleston News and Courier* hid the college's exploitive behavior and normalized oppressive racial hierarchies under a panegyric veneer. This was far from the only attempt to appropriate Peace's life for disreputable purposes.

James H. Easterby's 1930 history of the college, for example, omits the fact that "Tom's" wages were not paid directly to him but, instead, to his enslaver. In this foundational history of the College of Charleston, Easterby writes "with the erection of the 'new College edifice' (Randolph Hall) in 1828 the trustees had thought seriously of purchasing a 'servant,' but the idea seems to have been forestalled by Mr. Adams. A short time later he reported that he had hired a janitor at $100 per annum."[100] Easterby holds that "it is not improbable that [this janitor] was the Tom Peace whose faithful services were still winning the approbation of the faculty and students in the early [eighteen] fifties."[101] Using the common euphemism "servant," Easterby first obscures the college's participation with enslavement and then misrepresents Peace's biography to support his claim.

A few years later, a highly fictionalized Thomas Peace appears as a character in Emmett Robinson's play, *Lewis Gibbes—A Legend for Tomorrow*. To celebrate the centennial anniversary of the college's conversion from a private to a municipal institution, a large cast of students, alumni, and community members enacted the play "on the evening of May 10, 1937."[102] The play centers on Gibbes, who served as professor of mathematics, astronomy, and chemistry from 1837 until 1892. The preface acknowledges that the story was a "legend based on certain incidents taken from the life of Lewis Reeves Gibbes and the history of the College of Charleston."[103] The author also admits to taking liberties with some aspects of the plot where "securing the exact picture of the period" would be impossible. In the absence of direct evidence, Robinson was "guided by [his] own imagination" and "let the ideals of the theme carry through to achieve a dramatic result."[104] The play celebrates a romanticized southern past, repeatedly referring to Charleston as the "Athens of the South," which is to say an exclusive arena dominated by the intellectual pursuits of white men such as Lewis Gibbes and Charles Fraser. When Gibbes arrives in Charleston to begin his academic career, Charles Fraser's character muses, "[Y]ou see, Lewis, it is for such men as ourselves to see that our city becomes an example of well-rounded community life. It is our duty to emulate the noble Greeks in our love for our native city. We must cause her to put on the beautiful garments of literature and science."[105]

Tom Peace's character opens the play. The scene takes place on a street near the Cooper River and depicts Black workers preparing for the arrival of a passenger ship, "scattered about in small groups singing a work-spiritual."[106] Peace's character, portrayed by Willam H. Grimball Jr., enters the stage, carrying a letter, and speaks in Gullah dialect with a dock worker named Sam. Stage directions scribbled in the margin of the typescript call for "Negro spirituals being sung at [curtain] rise."[107] The racial division could not be clearer. Literature, science, and the classical heritage belong to white intellectuals. Hard work and presumed comforts of spiritual music belong to Blacks. Each, as depicted in this play, knows their place, and each benefits from the separation of spheres. During the early to middle parts of the twentieth century, many white writers and singers in Charleston performed similar versions of Black life to reinforce the white supremacist norms of the antebellum era. By appropriating Black music and language, all-white groups such as the Society for the Preservation of Spirituals, reinscribed racist ideas and policies while glorifying life and culture during a bygone era.[108] Emmett Robinson appropriates Thomas Peace's life for exactly this purpose.

Robinson, however, goes further than many of his contemporaries. The play not only offers Black characters functioning as happy subservients but also stokes racial fears by presenting a subplot that includes a rebellion of enslaved people. The same actors who played the parts of Tom Peace and Sam also played the parts of the "first and second negro insurrectionists."[109] This doubling of roles no doubt reduced production costs. It also reinforced white constructions of Blackness. Under white control, Black people serve as happy, docile workers; outside that control, they threaten social order. Having the same actor play Peace and a violent insurrectionist, the organizers of the play suggested that Thomas Peace's civility and purpose originated in white social structures. The fictionalized Thomas Peace promotes the very ideology that oppressed the real Thomas Peace and his family.

The mistreatment and misrepresentation of Thomas Peace did not end in the 1930s. In a 1961 news article, John G. Leland repeats Easterby's falsehoods and introduces another: that the building now known as Porter's Lodge served as a "residence for the janitor."[110] Leland writes, that Peace was hired at the salary of one hundred dollars per year by Jasper Adams, president of the college, in 1828, after Adams "refused to go along with a proposal by the trustees to 'purchase a servant' for the college."[111] Leland further tells his readers that Adams "was a member of the well-known New England Adams family and was opposed to slavery."[112] His claims are misleading on two accounts. First, Leland perpetuated a fabricated notion that Peace lived in Porter's Lodge when, in fact, we know that Peace and his family occupied a smaller building that was demolished not long after Porter's Lodge was constructed in the 1850s. Second, according to the minutes of the board of trustees discussed earlier, it was Adams who went to the board to request purchase of a "servant." Much like the five leaders who came before him (Bishop Robert Smith, Thomas Bee Jr., George Buist, Elijah Ratoone, and Nathaniel Bowen), Adams participated in the buying, selling, and hiring out of enslaved laborers. In fact, two bills of sale show Adams purchasing and selling enslaved people. In 1829, Adams purchased "a female slave Nancy and her girl child Sarah Ann" for three hundred sixty dollars from Elizabeth Adcock. In 1838, Adams sold an enslaved family—Peter; his wife, Sillah; and their children, Sulley and Peter—to George A. Eggleston for fifteen hundred dollars.[113] Adams was certainly not opposed to slavery. Leland simply whitewashes his participation in systemic oppression and makes the college appear more innocent than it was. In a 1968 article, Leland reiterated these falsehoods, again referencing Jasper Adams' antislavery leanings and Peace's salary (which the historical record proves went directly to his enslaver, Ann Wagner) with a "fringe benefit" of living in Porter's Lodge beginning in 1828.[114]

Biased twentieth-century narrators, such as Robinson and Leland, obscure the actual historical record, which reflects racial, gender, and socio-economic inequities and lend credence to cruel power structures. At the same time, they make the College of Charleston into something it was not. Uncovering the actual lives of Thomas and Isabella Peace and their descendants reveals how the accepted historical record so often contradicts itself, eroding its own claims to legitimacy while calling for a more expansive use of information that exists outside of traditionally accepted source materials.

Conclusion

At times, the silences and omissions of the historical record leave us with more questions than answers. Historians must mine evidence from the past, including that which exists "along the bias grain," to demonstrate how institutions such as the College of Charleston would not exist in their current forms without the contributions of people who were historically marginalized.[115] Moreover, had the labors of men and women such as Thomas and Isabella Peace been properly acknowledged, compensated, and valued, they may not have been erased from the institution's historical memory. It is time to mark their names and publicly acknowledge the contributions of the people whose labor, forced and then stolen, constructed and shaped this institution.

This research, and that of a growing number of scholars on campuses around the world, interrogates historical evidence and sources using a lens that centers the experiences of historically marginalized and oppressed people. Subsequent discoveries and conclusions must be leveraged to support restorative justice dialogue and efforts to reconcile ourselves with the persistent legacies of slavery and dispossession in our communities. As a leading scholar of the role that higher education played in perpetuating slavery and racism, Leslie Harris argues that while "these histories are not a complete answer to the sometimes confounding racial situations in which colleges and universities find themselves, uncovering them goes a long way toward making clear how embedded issues of race and racism are in our institutions—and how covering them up has done no one any favors."[116] Expanding dialogue and narratives around the past through critical evaluation of archival evidence—troubling the archive, we might say—must inform substantive changes in structural power dynamics rooted in white supremacy.

Mary Jo Fairchild oversees all research, access, and instruction services for Special Collections and Archives at the College of Charleston Libraries. Fairchild holds master's degrees in history and in library and information science, and she is a certified archivist. Her research interests revolve around archival public services, access and representation in archives and cultural heritage spaces, and critical pedagogy using primary sources in archives and special collections.

NOTES

1. "Peace to His Ashes," *Charleston News and Courier*, April 27, 1887, 12.
2. In 1887, the board of trustees paid tribute to "Old Tom, the janitor," using the same language found in the *Charleston News and Courier*, including the words "boasted that he had Indian blood in his veins and his physiognomy justified the claim." College of Charleston Board of Trustees Minutes, Volume IV, 602, College of Charleston Archives: Historical Records, Mss 202.00, College of Charleston Libraries, Charleston, SC.
3. College of Charleston Board of Trustees Minutes, Volumes II, III, and IV, College of Charleston Archives: Historical Records, Mss 202.00, College of Charleston Libraries, Charleston, SC.
4. Tiya Miles, *All That She Carried: The Journey of Ashley's Sack, A Black Family's Keepsake* (New York: Random House, 2021), 89.
5. Cash Receipt Book, 1855–1859, College of Charleston Archives: Historical Records, Mss 202.00, College of Charleston Libraries, Charleston, SC On October 2, 1855, the treasurer of the college wrote a receipt for thirty dollars in wages for three months of work The receipt is signed "Thomas Peace," in a different hand Thereafter, Peace signed receipts for his wages on a monthly ($10) basis through April 1857 Thomas Peace's name did not appear in cash receipt books again until 1871 From February 1871 to March of 1874, the treasurer of the college recorded three receipts, totaling twenty dollars, signed by Thomas Peace for "services rendered in carrying summonses, notices, etc for the Board."
6. Act No 2236, "An Act to restrain the emancipation of slaves, and to prevent free persons of color from entering into this state, and for other purposes," ratified on December 20, 1820, See David J McCord, *Statutes at Large of South Carolina*; Edited Under Authority of the Legislature, vol 7 (Columbia, SC: A S Johnston, 1840), 459–60.
7. "United States, Freedman's Bank Records, 1865–1874," database with images, *FamilySearch*, https://www.familysearch.org.

8. The Unity and Friendship Society was established in 1844 and provided sick and burial insurance to members See Kimberley Martin, "Community and Place: A Study of Four African American Benevolent Societies and Their Cemeteries." Master's thesis, Clemson University, 2010 https://open.clemson.edu/2014.html 17–18, 40, 42.

9. "Peace," *Charleston News and Courier*, April 27, 1887, 12.

10. Martin, "Community and Place," 17–18, 40, 42.

11. J W Joseph, "Of Sterling Worth and Good Qualities": Status and Domesticity in Nineteenth-Century Middle Class Charleston: Archaeological Investigations at Site 38CH1871, Marlene & Nathan Addlestone Library, College of Charleston (Stone Mountain, GA: New South Associates, 2004), 16.

12. "Peace," *Charleston News and Courier*, April 26, 1888, 8.

13. Saidiya Hartman, "Venus in Two Acts," *Small Axe: A Journal of Criticism* 12, no 2 (2008): 10.

14. College of Charleston Board of Trustees Minutes, Volume II, p 313, College of Charleston Archives: Historical Records, Mss 202.00, College of Charleston Libraries, Charleston, SC.

15. Morris Goldsmith, *Directory and Strangers' Guide for the City of Charleston and Its Vicinity* (Charleston, SC: Printed at the Office of The Irishman, 1831), 116.

16. Kaylee Rogers documents the persistent overrepresentation of African Americans in the service sector at the College of Charleston and "consequently how racial hierarchies are reproduced within the local labor market." In an anonymized interview, one worker told Rogers "They walk by us like we don't exist We're invisible. We are overworked, and underpaid." See Kaylee Rogers, "Overworked and Underpaid: 'Black' Work at the College of Charleston," *Chrestomathy: Annual Review of Undergraduate Research* 7 (2008), 227–47. In her National Book Award–winning work that tells the stories of enslaved women and their descendants in South Carolina using material culture as the primary evidence, scholar Tiya Miles points out that "endeavoring to reconstruct any history, but especially the histories of the marginalized, requires an attentiveness to absence as well as presence." See Miles, *All That She Carried*, 302. There are no birth records for Thomas and Isabella Peace We learn about Thomas and Isabella Peace from institutional archives, letters of enslavers, municipal tax collectors, and newspaper publishers.

17. College of Charleston Board of Trustees Minutes, Volume IV, p 602, College of Charleston Archives: Historical Records, Mss 202.00, College of Charleston Libraries, Charleston, SC.

18. College of Charleston Board of Trustees Minutes, Volume II, 313, College of Charleston Archives: Historical Records, Mss 202.00, College of Charleston Libraries, Charleston, SC.

19. College of Charleston Board of Trustees Minutes, Volume IV, 602, College of Charleston Archives: Historical Records, Mss 202.00, College of Charleston Libraries, Charleston, SC Sadly, enslavers hired out people they enslaved at very young ages See also Jonathan D Martin, *Divided Mastery: Slave Hiring in the American South* (Cambridge, MA: Harvard University Press, 2004), 64–65.

20. See Judith M Brimelow and Michael E Stevens, *State Free Negro Capitation Tax Books, Charleston, South Carolina, ca 1811–1860* (Charleston, SC: Department of Archives and History, 1983).

21. Bernard Edward Powers Jr., *Black Charlestonians: A Social History, 1822–1885*, 36–37.

22. Miles, *All That She Carried*, 302.

23. College of Charleston Board of Trustees Minutes, Volume III, 32, College of Charleston Archives: Historical Records, Mss 202.00, College of Charleston Libraries, Charleston, SC.

24. "South Carolina Deaths and Burials, 1816–1990," database with images, *Family-Search*, https://www.familysearch.org.

25. McCurry, *Masters of Small Worlds: Yeoman Households, Gender Relations, and the Political Culture of the Antebellum South Carolina Low Country* Oxford, England: Oxford University Press, 1995, 37.

26. Biographical and Historical Research on the Wagner family, Vertical File 30–01 South Carolina Historical Society.

27. Richard Hrabowski, Directory for the District of Charleston, Comprising the Places of Residence and Occupation of the White Inhabitants (Printed by John Hoff, for Richard Hrabowski, 1809).

28. Ann Wagner to Effingham Wagner, Fishkill, New York, 1 June 1818, Cheves and Wagner Family Papers #147, Southern Historical Collection, The Wilson Library, University of North Carolina at Chapel Hill.

29. Ann Wagner to Effingham Wagner, Providence, June 20, 1814, Cheves and Wagner Family Papers #147.

30. Ann Wagner to Effingham Wagner, Boston, July 17, 1814, Cheves and Wagner Family Papers #147.

31. Ann Wagner to Effingham Wagner, Boston, July 17, 1814, Cheves and Wagner Family Papers #147.

32. Ann Wagner to Effingham Wagner, Boston, July 17, 1814, Cheves and Wagner Family Papers #147.

33. Abraham Motte, *Charleston Directory and Strangers' Guide for the Year 1816 Including the Neck to the Six Mile House* Charleston, SC: Printed for the purchaser, 1816.

34. "South Carolina, Charleston District, Bill of sales of Negro slaves, 1774–1872," database with images, *FamilySearch*, https://www.familysearch.org.

35. "South Carolina, Charleston District, Bill of sales of Negro slaves, 1774–1872," database with images, *FamilySearch*, https://www.familysearch.org.

36. "South Carolina, Charleston District, Bill of sales of Negro slaves, 1774–1872," database with images, *FamilySearch*, https://www.familysearch.org.

37. Ann Wagner to George Wagner, Fishkill Landing, New York, 1 June 1818, Cheves and Wagner Family Papers #147.

38. Ann Wagner to Effingham Wagner, New York, 13 May 1818, Cheves and Wagner Family Papers #147.

39. Ann Wagner to Effingham Wagner, Fishkill, New York, June 1, 1818, Cheves and Wagner Family Papers #147; Ann Wagner to Effingham Wagner, Providence, RI, August 15, 1818, Cheves and Wagner Family Papers #147.

40. [Death Record for Ann Wagner, March 1843], Charleston City Death Records, 1821–1926, database with images, *FamilySearch*, https://www.familysearch.

41. "South Carolina, Charleston District, Estate inventories, 1732–1844," database with images, *FamilySearch*, https://www.familysearch.or.

42. College of Charleston Board of Trustees Minutes, Volume III, 32, College of Charleston Archives: Historical Records, Mss 202.00, Charleston, SC: College of Charleston Libraries.

43. Joseph Ioor Waring, *A History of Medicine in South Carolina, 1825–1900* (Columbia, SC: R L Bryan Co., 1967), 313.

44. Nathan Smith Davis, Contributions to the History of Medical Education And Medical Institutions In the United States of America, 1776–1876: Special Report (Washington: Government Printing Office, 1877), 32; [Death Record for John Wagner, 1841], Charleston City Death Records, 1821–1926 Department of Archives and History, Columbia, database with images, *FamilySearch*, https://www.familysearch.org.

45. Rana A Hogarth, *Medicalizing Blackness: Making Racial Difference in the Atlantic World, 1780–1840* (Chapel Hill: University of North Carolina Press, 2017), 181–84.

46. "Petition of Lydia Wagner, May 31, 1842," database with images, *Race and Slavery Petitions Project*, https://dlas.uncg.edu.

47. "South Carolina Probate Records, Bound Volumes, 1671–1977," database with images, *FamilySearch*, https://www.familysearch.org.

48. "Inventory of the Estate of John Wagner," South Carolina Probate Records, Bound Volumes, 1671–1977, Charleston Inventories, Appraisements, and Sales, 1839–1844, Vol A, 548 Columbia: South Carolina Department of Archives and History.

49. James H Easterby, *A History of the College of Charleston, Founded 1770* (Charleston, SC: College of Charleston, 1935), 101; Salley, "Captain William Capers and Some of His Descendants," *The South Carolina Historical and Genealogical Magazine 2, no 4 (1901)*," 288.

50. College of Charleston Board of Trustees Minutes, Volume III, 32, College of Charleston Archives: Historical Records, Mss 202.00, College of Charleston Libraries, Charleston, SC.

51. Wikramanayake, *World in Shadow: The Free Black in Antebellum South Carolina* (Columbia: University of South Carolina Press, 1973), 11 See also E Horace Fitchett, "Status of the Free Negro," The Status of the Free Negro in Charleston, South Carolina, and His Descendants in Modern Society: Statement of the Problem." *Journal of Negro History* 32, no 4 (1947): 430–51; Fitchett, "The Origin and Growth of the Free Negro Population of Charleston, South Carolina," *Journal of Negro History* 26, no 4 (1941): 421–37; Richard C Wade, *Slavery in the Cities: the South, 1820–1860* (Oxford, England: Oxford University Press, 1967); and Amrita Chakrabarti Myers, *Forging Freedom: Black Women in Antebellum Charleston* (Chapel Hill: University of North Carolina Press, 2011).

52. Robert P Stockton, *Historic College of Charleston Buildings and Structures: An Evolutionary History* (Charleston, SC, 2006), 26–27.

53. Stockton, *Historic College of Charleston*, 25.

54. Stockton, *Historic College of Charleston*, 26–27.

55. "Abstract of the Proceedings of Council," *Charleston Mercury*, October 29, 1856, 1. In the petition, Thomas Peace is referred to as "a free colored man." Wikramanayake holds that the "conditions in the city of Charleston yielded a peculiar class of blacks who operated in a state of limbo, neither slave nor free. See Wikramanayake, *World in Shadow*, 11. Because of financial and leadership challenges, the College of Charleston transitioned from a private to a municipal institution in 1837. As a result, the mayor and city aldermen became members of the college's board of trustees. The college remained under municipal governance until 1949 when administrators sold the public charter to a private board of trustees for a nominal fee to avoid integration. See Easterby, *History of the College of Charleston*, 90–95, and Nan Morrison, *History of the College of Charleston, 1936–2008* (Columbia: University of South Carolina Press, 2011), 60.

56. "Committee on Public Institutions, Buildings and Grounds," *Charleston Daily Courier*, November 13, 1856, 4.

57. Rogers, "Overworked and Underpaid," 233–34.

58. The 1883 death certificate for Isabella Peace indicates she died at the age of fifty-five, which would mean she was born in 1828 or 1829.

59. Marisa J Fuentes, *Dispossessed Lives: Enslaved Women, Violence, and the Archive* (Philadelphia: University of Pennsylvania Press, 2016), 7.

60. Michel-Rolph Trouillot, *Silencing the Past: Power and the Production of History* (Boston: Beacon Press, 1995), 26.

61. Fuentes, *Dispossessed Lives*, 12.

62. Myers, *Forging Freedom*, 40.

63. Myers, *Forging Freedom*, 41–42; see also Robert Olwell, *Masters, Slaves & Subjects: The Culture of Power in the South Carolina Low Country, 1740–1790* (Ithaca, NY: Cornell University Press, 1998).

64. Charleston, SC, City Council, H William De Saussure, and J L Dawson *Census of the City of Charleston, South Carolina, for the Year 1848, Exhibiting the Condition and Prospects of the City, Illustrated by Many Statistical Details* (Charleston, SC: J B Nixon, 1849), 3–4.

65. For a discussion of the events leading up to the Act of 1820 and its immediate aftermath, see Myers, *Forging Freedom*, 60–61 For a discussion of white Charlestonian's fears of insurrection due to influence of people coming from the Caribbean, especially Haiti, during this time see Powers, "Denmark Vesey," 17–37; and "The Act of 1820," in McCord, *Statutes at Large*, vol 7, 459–60.

66. Roberts, "Race," 38, 50 See also Hunter, *Bound in Wedlock*, 65.

67. "South Carolina, Charleston, Free Negro Capitation Books, 1811–1860" (Columbia: South Carolina Department of Archives and History, 2022)

68. "South Carolina, Charleston, Free Negro Capitation Books, 1811–1860" (Columbia: South Carolina Department of Archives and History, 2022).

69. Hunter, *Bound in Wedlock*, 92.

70. Hunter, *Bound in Wedlock*, 92.

71. Hunter, *Bound in Wedlock*, 91.

72. David Lewis Wardlaw and Sarah Margaret Wardlaw Smith, Letter to Sally Wardlaw, Charleston, South Carolina, 1855 (Columbia: South Caroliniana Library,

University of South Carolina) This is the only known reference to Thomas Peace as a reverend.

73. Tera W Hunter, *To 'Joy My Freedom: Southern Black Women's Lives and Labors After the Civil War* (Cambridge, MA: Harvard University Press, 1997), 26.

74. Hunter, *To 'Joy My Freedom*, 26.

75. "South Carolina Deaths and Burials, 1816–1990," database with images, *FamilySearch*, https://www.familysearch.org.

76. "South Carolina Deaths and Burials, 1816–1990," database with images, *FamilySearch*, https://www.familysearch.org, Molly Peace, 1831.

77. "South Carolina Deaths and Burials, 1816–1990," database with images, *FamilySearch*, https://www.familysearch.org, Barbara Peace, 1850.

78. "South Carolina Deaths and Burials, 1816–1990," database with images, *FamilySearch*, https://www.familysearch.org, Isabella E Peace, 1883.

79. "South Carolina Deaths and Burials, 1816–1990," database with images, *FamilySearch*, https://www.familysearch.org, Joe Peace, 1831.

80. "South Carolina Deaths and Burials, 1816–1990," database with images, *FamilySearch*, https://www.familysearch.org, Isabella Peace, 1862; Thomas Peace, 1860.

81. Edmund L Drago and Marvin Dulaney, *Charleston's Avery Center: From Education and Civil Rights to Preserving the African American Experience* (Charleston, SC: History Press, 2006), 49, 58.

82. Drago and Dulaney, *Charleston's Avery Center*, 58.

83. A E Sholes, *Sholes' Directory of the City of Charleston* (Charleston, SC: Walker Evans & Cogswell, 1879), 190.

84. Sholes, *Sholes' Directory*, 1879, 408.

85. Hunter, *To 'Joy My Freedom*, 26.

86. Blain Roberts and Ethan J Kyrtle, *Denmark Vesey's Garden*, 156.

87. United States of America, Bureau of the Census, *Twelfth Census of the United States, 1900* (Washington, DC: National Archives and Records Administration, 1900).

88. Hunter, *To 'Joy My Freedom*, 111.

89. Census of the City of Charleston, South Carolina, For the Year 1861 Illustrated by Statistical Tables Prepared under the Authority of the City Council by Frederick A Ford (Charleston, SC: Steam-Power Presses of Evans & Cogswell, 1861), 71.

90. Sholes, *Sholes' Directory*, 189, 190; A E Sholes, *Sholes' Directory*,1883, 520.

91. According to census data, Eugene and Elizabeth "Bettie" had been married for eighteen years in 1900 This would mean they married in 1882, probably in Charleston They both could read and write.

92. "Pennsylvania, Philadelphia City Births, 1860–1906," database with images, *FamilySearch*, https://www.familysearch.org.

93. United States of America, Bureau of the Census, *Thirteenth Census of the United States, 1910* (Washington, DC: National Archives and Records Administration, 1910).

94. Sholes, *Sholes' Directory*, 1877, 190.

95. Sholes, *Sholes' Directory*, 1877, 96.

96. "Razor and Revolver," *Charleston News and Courier*, March 7, 1886, 8.

97. "Razor and Revolver, 8."

98. De Bow, "The Light of Other Days," *Debow's Review, Agricultural, Commercial, Industrial Progress and Resources* 6, no 3 (1848): 237 According to College records, James De Bow graduated in 1843 with honors.
99. These include Easterby's *History of the College of Charleston* and Morrison's *History of the College of Charleston*.
100. Easterby, *History of the College of Charleston*, 140.
101. Easterby, *History of the College of Charleston*, 140.
102. Emmett Robinson, "Lewis Gibbes—A Legend for Tomorrow," Lewis R Gibbes papers, Mss 0020 (Charleston, SC: College of Charleston Libraries, 1937), 12 In 1837, the College of Charleston was "revived and placed under the patronage of the city government."
103. See biographical note for Lewis R Gibbes, College of Charleston Special Collections, http://findingaids.library.cofc.edu/repositories/2/resources/86.
104. Robinson, *Lewis Gibbes*, preface.
105. Robinson, *Lewis Gibbes*, 13.
106. Robinson, *Lewis Gibbes*, 1.
107. Robinson, *Lewis Gibbes*, 1.
108. See Kyrtle and Roberts, *Denmark Vesey's Garden*, 196–224; Ibram X Kendi, *Stamped from the Beginning: The Definitive History of Racist Ideas in America* (New York: Nation Books, 2016), 1–11.
109. "Students and Alumni Give College Play This Evening," *Charleston News and Courier*, May 10, 1937, 5.
110. John G Leland, "The College of Charleston Lodge to Link Old and New," *Charleston News and Courier*, January 9, 1961, 9.
111. Leland, "College of Charleston."
112. Leland, "College of Charleston."
113. "South Carolina, Charleston District, Bill of Sales of Negro Slaves, 1774–1872," Jasper Adams, February 2, 1829, and July 13, 1838; Records of The Secretary Of State, Recorded Instruments, Miscellaneous Records (Main Series), Bills Of Sale Volumes, 436, (Columbia: South Carolina Department of Archives and History).
114. John G Leland, "Coeds Conquer College Bastion," *Evening Post*, October 24, 1968, 13.
115. Fuentes, *Dispossessed Lives*, 78.
116. Leslie M Harris, "Higher Education's Reckoning with Slavery" (Washington, DC: American Association of University Professors, 2020) https://www.aaup.org/article/.

WORKS CITED

Brimelow, Judith M., and Michael E. Stevens. *State Free Negro Capitation Tax Books, Charleston, South Carolina, ca. 1811–1860*. Charleston, SC: Department of Archives and History, 1983.

Charleston, SC, City Council, H. William De Saussure, and J. L. Dawson. *Census of the City of Charleston, South Carolina, for the Year 1848, Exhibiting the Condition* and Prospects of the City, Illustrated by Many Statistical Details. Charleston, SC: J. B. Nixon, 1849.

Charleston, SC, City Council, and F. A. Ford. *Census of the City of Charleston, South Carolina, for the Year 1861*. Charleston, SC: Evans & Cogswell, 1861.

The Charleston City Directory, 1782–1870, Microfilm Reel One, 1782–1838; Reel Two, 1840–1870. Charleston, SC: Charleston Library Society, 1951.

Cheves and Wagner family papers, #147. Southern Historical Collection, The Wilson Library, University of North Carolina at Chapel Hill.

College of Charleston Archives: Historical Records, Mss 202.00, Charleston, SC: College of Charleston Libraries. http://findingaids.library.cofc.edu/repositories/2/resources/554.

"Committee on Public Institutions, Buildings and Grounds," *Charleston Daily Courier*, November 13, 1856.

De Bow, James. "The Light of Other Days." *Debow's Review, Agricultural, Commercial, Industrial Progress and Resources* 6, no. 3 (1848): 236–40.

Drago, Edmond L., and Marvin Dulaney. *Charleston's Avery Center: From Education and Civil Rights to Preserving the African American Experience*. Charleston, SC: History Press, 2006.

Easterby, James H. *A History of the College of Charleston, Founded 1770*. Charleston, SC: College of Charleston, 1935.

Fay, Thomas C. *Charleston Directory, and Strangers' Guide, for 1840 and 1841: Embracing the Names of Heads of Families; Firms and the Individuals Composing Them; Together With All Persons in Business, and Their Residences, Alphabetically Arranged: Also, Each Street, and Numbers Where Practicable, With the Names of the Occupants Respectively Noted-Thereby Answering the Purpose of a Cross Index*. Charleston, SC: T. C. Fay, 1840.

Fick, Sarah and Julia Eichelberger, "A History of St. Philip Street," *Discovering Our Past: College of Charleston Histories*. https://discovering.cofc.edu/items/show/12.

Fitchett, E. Horace. "The Origin and Growth of the Free Negro Population of Charleston, South Carolina." *Journal of Negro History* 26, no. 4 (1941): 421–37.

Fitchett, E. Horace. "The Status of the Free Negro in Charleston, South Carolina, and His Descendants in Modern Society: Statement of the Problem." *Journal of Negro History* 32, no. 4 (1947): 430–51.

Fuentes, Marisa J. *Dispossessed Lives: Enslaved Women, Violence, and the Archive*. Philadelphia: University of Pennsylvania Press, 2016.

Goldsmith, Morris. *Directory and Strangers' Guide for the City of Charleston and Its Vicinity*. Charleston, SC: Printed at the Office of The Irishman, 1831.

Harris, Leslie M. "Higher Education's Reckoning with Slavery." Washington, DC: American Association of University Professors, 2020. https://www.aaup.org/article/higher-education%E2%80%99s-reckoning-slavery.

Hartman, Saidiya. "Venus in Two Acts." *Small Axe: A Journal of Criticism* 12, no. 2 (2008): 1–14.

Hogarth, Rana A. *Medicalizing Blackness: Making Racial Difference in the Atlantic World, 1780–1840*. Chapel Hill: University of North Carolina Press, 2017.

Hunter, Tera W. *Bound in Wedlock: Slave and Free Black Marriage in the Nineteenth Century.* Cambridge, MA: Harvard University Press, 2017.

Hunter, Tera W. *To 'Joy My Freedom: Southern Black Women's Lives and Labors After the Civil War.* Cambridge, MA: Harvard University Press, 1997.

Kendi, Ibram X. *Stamped from the Beginning: The Definitive History of Racist Ideas in America.* New York: Nation Books, 2016.

Kennedy, Cynthia M. *Braided Relations, Entwined Lives: The Women of Charleston's Urban Slave Society.* Bloomington: Indiana University Press, 2005.

Johnson, Doria, Jarrett Drake, and Michelle Caswell, "From Cape Town to Chicago to Colombo and Back Again: Towards a Liberation Theology for Memory Work," *Reflections from the 2016 Mandela Dialogues.* Houghton, South Africa: Nelson Mandela Foundation, 2017. https://www.nelsonmandela.org/news/entry/reflections-from-the-2016-mandela-dialogues.

Joseph, J. W. "Of Sterling Worth and Good Qualities": Status and Domesticity in Nineteenth-Century Middle Class Charleston: Archaeological Investigations at Site 38CH1871, Marlene & Nathan Addlestone Library, College of Charleston. Stone Mountain, GA: New South Associates, 2004.

Le Guin, Ursula K. "Pandora Converses with the Archivist of the Library of the Madrone Lodge at Wakwaha-na." In *Always Coming Home,* edited by Todd Barton, 314–317. New York: Library of America, 2019.

Martin, Kimberley. "Community and Place: A Study of Four African American Benevolent Societies and Their Cemeteries." Master's thesis, Clemson University, 2010. https://oatd.org/.

Mazyck, Arthur. *Guide to Charleston Illustrated: Being a Sketch of the History of Charleston, S. C. with Some Account of Its Present Condition, with Numerous Engravings.* Charleston, SC: Walker, Evans & Cogswell, 1875.

McCurry, Stephanie. *Masters of Small Worlds: Yeoman Households, Gender Relations, and the Political Culture of the Antebellum South Carolina Low Country.* Oxford, England: Oxford University Press, 1995.

Mears, Leonard, and James Turnbull. *The Charleston Directory: Containing the Names of the Inhabitants, a Subscriber's Business Directory, Street Map of the City, and an Appendix, of Much Useful Information.* Charleston, SC: Walker and Evans, 1859.

Miles, Tiya. *All That She Carried: The Journey of Ashley's Sack, A Black Family's Keepsake.* New York: Random House, 2021.

Morrison, Nan. *A History of the College of Charleston, 1936–2008.* Columbia: University of South Carolina Press, 2011.

Motte, Abraham. *Charleston Directory and Strangers' Guide for the Year 1816 Including the Neck to the Six Mile House.* Charleston, SC: Printed for the purchaser, 1816.

Myers, Amrita Chakrabarti. *Forging Freedom: Black Women in Antebellum Charleston.* Chapel Hill: University of North Carolina Press, 2011.

Olwell, Robert. *Masters, Slaves & Subjects: The Culture of Power in the South Carolina Low Country, 1740–1790.* Ithaca, NY: Cornell University Press, 1998.

Powers, Bernard Edward Jr. *Black Charlestonians: A Social History, 1822–1885.* Fayetteville: University of Arkansas Press, 1994.

Powers, Bernard Edward. "Denmark Vesey, South Carolina, and Haiti." In *Fugitive Movements: Commemorating the Denmark Vesey Affair and Black Radical Anti-Slavery in the Atlantic World*, edited by James O'Neil Spady, 17–37. Columbia: University of South Carolina Press, 2022.

Purse, R. S. *Charleston City Directory and Strangers Guide for 1856*. New York: J. F. Trow, 1856.

"Razor and Revolver," *Charleston News and Courier*, March 7, 1886.

Roberts, Blain, and Ethan J. Kyrtle. *Denmark Vesey's Garden: Slavery and Memory in the Cradle of the Confederacy*. New York: The New Press, 2018.

Roberts, Dorothy. "Race." In *The 1619 Project: A New Origin Story*, edited by Nikole Hannah-Jones, Caitlin Roper, Ilena Silverman, and Jake Silverstein, 45–61. The New York Times Company, 2021.

Robinson, Emmett. "Lewis Gibbes—A Legend for Tomorrow," Lewis R. Gibbes papers, Mss 0020. Charleston, SC: College of Charleston Libraries, 1937.

Rogers, Kaylee. "Overworked and Underpaid: "Black" Work at the College of Charleston." *Chrestomathy: Annual Review of Undergraduate Research* 7 (2008): 227–47.

Salley, A. S. "Captain William Capers and Some of His Descendants." *The South Carolina Historical and Genealogical Magazine* 2, no. 4 (1901): 273–98. http://www.jstor.org/stable/27574968.

Sholes, A. E. *Sholes' Directory of the City of Charleston*. Charleston, SC: Walker Evans & Cogswell, 1879.

Sholes, A. E. *Sholes' Directory of the City of Charleston*. Charleston, SC: Walker Evans & Cogswell, 1883.

Sholes A. E. *Sholes' Directory of the City of Charleston for 1877-'78: Containing a List of the Inhabitants Their Residence and Occupation; a Classified Commercial Directory; a Complete Record of City Officers Churches Courts Secret Societies Military Organizations &c.; Also a Full and Complete List of Officers of the State and National Governments*. Charleston, SC: Walker Evans & Cogswell, 1877.

Sinha, Manisha. *The Counter-revolution of Slavery: Politics and Ideology in Antebellum South Carolina*. Chapel Hill: University of North Carolina Press, 2000.

South Carolina, Charleston City Death Records, 1821–1926. Database. *Family-Search*. Columbia: South Carolina Department of Archives and History, 2024. https://FamilySearch.org.

South Carolina, Charleston City Death Records, 1875–1899. Database. *Family-Search*. Columbia: South Carolina Department of Archives and History, 2024. https://FamilySearch.org.

"South Carolina, Charleston, Free Negro Capitation Books, 1811–1860." Database with images. *FamilySearch*. Columbia: South Carolina Department of Archives and History, 2024. https://FamilySearch.org.

Stockton, Robert P. *Historic College of Charleston Buildings and Structures: An Evolutionary History*. Charleston, SC, 2006.

"Students and Alumni Give College Play This Evening," *Charleston News and Courier*, May 10, 1937.

Trouillot, Michel-Rolph. *Silencing the Past: Power and the Production of History*. Boston: Beacon Press, 1995.

US, Delayed Birth Records, 1766–1900, and City of Charleston, South Carolina, US, Birth Records, 1877–1901. Columbia: South Carolina Department of Archives and History, 2024 https://FamilySearch.org.

"United States, Freedman's Bank Records, 1865–1874," Roll 21, December 19, 1865–Dec 2, 1869, accounts 1–319, 2151–3824 (image 432 of 697), NARA microfilm publication M816. Washington, DC: National Archives and Records Administration, 1970.

Wade, Richard C. *Slavery in the Cities: the South, 1820–1860.* Oxford, England: Oxford University Press, 1967.

Wardlaw, David Lewis, and Sarah Margaret Wardlaw Smith. Letter to Sally Wardlaw, Charleston, South Carolina. 1855. Columbia: South Caroliniana Library, University of South Carolina.

Waring, Joseph Ioor. *A History of Medicine in South Carolina, 1825–1900.* Columbia, SC: R. L. Bryan Co., 1967.

White, Deborah Gray. "Ar'n't I a Woman? and the Changing Historical Archive." Panel presentation at the Different Archives, Different Histories conference, University of Illinois Chicago, Institute for the Humanities, October 30, 2020. https://huminst.uic.edu/conferences-2/different-archives-different-histories/.

Wikramanayake, Marina. *A World in Shadow: The Free Black in Antebellum South Carolina.* Columbia: University of South Carolina Press, 1973.

Naming the Enslaved of Hobcaw Barony

Steven C. Sims-Brewton, Lynn Hanson, Madison Cates,
Adam Houle, Richard A. Almeida, Greg Garvan,
Patti Burns, and Megan Hammeke

In 1776, within the colony of South Carolina, Charles Cogdell was one of Georgetown District's more fortunate residents, living on a rice plantation carved from cypress swamps by enslaved Africans. The plantation that bore his name was part of a former land grant called Hobcaw Barony, established by the king of England to reward a loyal supporter.[1] Nearing his death, Cogdell requested in his last will and testament to leave "12 Negroes, one Feather Bed, two Pillows and a Bolster" to a nephew.[2] For readers in the twenty-first century, the words in the will are shocking. Equating people with objects, Cogdell erases the humanity of the twelve enslaved individuals. Treating them as a fungible commodity whose worth is measured by quantity rather than particularity, the will resembles many other antebellum documents in which the enslaved are presented as aggregate numbers, not individual people. The callousness manifested in documents such as Charles Cogdell's will signifies both the urgency and challenges of our scholarly project, which seeks to recover the names of enslaved people living on the sixteen thousand acres that constituted the king's land grant. Sold and subdivided numerous times over two centuries, most of the original Hobcaw Barony tract is now unified again, owned and managed by the Belle W. Baruch Foundation in Georgetown, South Carolina.

Our work is urgent not only because it helps establish a more complete history of the region but also because it helps individual families—many of whom have remained in the area since the time of enslavement—understand their own histories. The work of finding those names, however, remains difficult, and the results, as discussed in the following text, sometimes balance speculation with certainty. In its discussion of our ongoing work, this essay has two purposes. First and most important, it documents the names of seven hundred thirty-one enslaved people and provides information on where they lived and who enslaved them. Second, it narrates our research process. In doing so, the essay provides practical guidance to those undertaking similar work. Our hope is that the project will fill some gaps in the history of the Hobcaw Barony and the Waccamaw Neck region while also providing guidance to other researchers working to recover the identities of people whose stories remain unknown.

Who We Are and Where We Work

Francis Marion University, like other universities in South Carolina and throughout the South, is built on a former plantation. The university also is a founding partner with Coastal Carolina University of the Belle Baruch Institute for South Carolina Studies, a research center for the humanities and social sciences based at Hobcaw Barony, where rice plantations and enslaved people once contributed to the region's phenomenal wealth. The forced labor of enslaved communities, in fact, generated much of the wealth that made Georgetown District the second richest in the state, per capita, by 1860.[3] These geographic locations create an imperative for Francis Marion University's participation in the Universities Studying Slavery initiative and motivate our research on the history of slavery on the property where our institute is based (Figure 4.1).

Now a stunningly beautiful research reserve, Hobcaw Barony is owned and operated by the Belle W. Baruch Foundation near Georgetown, South

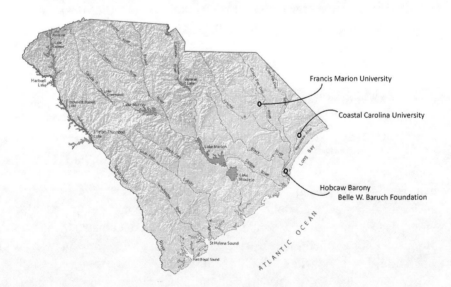

Figure 4.1. Map of South Carolina showing principal locations for Belle Baruch Institute for South Carolina Studies. "South Carolina Lakes and Rivers Map," GIS-Geography.com, https://gisgeography.com/south-Carolina-lakes-rivers-map/.

Carolina. As the daughter of financier and presidential adviser Bernard Baruch, Belle established the Foundation in 1964 to manage her property for environmental research and protection.[4] The Foundation's mission includes conserving the natural and cultural resources of Hobcaw Barony, encouraging research, and providing educational programs.[5]

In accord with its mission, the Belle W. Baruch Foundation provides tours and public programs to showcase its coastal environment and historical significance. Although scholars have pursued a range of studies on Hobcaw's history from Native American activities through the 1960s, the greatest historical attention on the Foundation's tours often goes to Bernard M. Baruch, most famous for his role in advising US presidents during both World Wars.[6] In 1905, Bernard Baruch began purchasing the former rice plantations that previously subdivided the original Hobcaw Barony land grant. By 1956, his daughter Belle Baruch had purchased the entire acreage from him to maintain its coastline, marshes, and forests as she had enjoyed them throughout her life.[7]

In contrast to the property's twentieth-century significance, the African and African-American influences on Hobcaw Barony during previous centuries have not been as well explored. Few artifacts and little documentation are available regarding the enslaved people who lived and worked on Hobcaw's former rice plantations.[8] Although the Foundation's tours include remnants of the remaining villages where the enslaved lived, until recently, the names of only a few former enslaved people from the property were known, even to locals knowledgeable about Hobcaw Barony and the broader area.

Under the auspices of the Belle Baruch Institute for South Carolina Studies, our research group—which comprised academics, librarians, student interns, and public historians—has been working to recover the names of enslaved people on the property. Our goal is to promote a more comprehensive historical perspective of the region and the lives of the enslaved people who lived there. We hope that this work will help provide resources for families, genealogists, and scholars and help them to unpack the full measure of the Barony's past and gain insights into the lives of the enslaved on the Waccamaw Neck.

Obstacles to the Research

Every day in South Carolina, we live, work, and walk on land where enslaved Africans and African Americans were once held against their will, legally declared property, and forced to endure involuntary labor and dehumanizing conditions. These realities make acknowledging our full history painful. In addition, historical records of those who lived outside the public eye are often scarce, incomplete, or inaccessible. Going further back in time compounds the challenges. People move from place to place, and sometimes their names change. Families begin, merge, split, and sometimes end. Over time, the names of places themselves often change. Even a shallow dive into genealogical research can quickly reveal that the pool hides many perils. Tracing the history of the enslaved at Hobcaw Barony reflects these challenges.

According to reports from the *Low Country Digital Library*, many enslaved Africans were imported because of their skills in cultivating rice, coming from the Angola (40.0%), Senegambia (19.5%), Windward Coast (16.3%), and the Gold Coast (13.3%), as well as other countries in smaller percentages.[9] The cultural and regional names that identified them in their home countries were denied them when they were kidnapped.[10] Even before their arrival in South Carolina, merchant and shipping records inventoried the enslaved only by gender and age brackets, rarely mentioning names. Imprisoned in plantation labor camps, the enslaved used cultural names and family names only in private and among themselves.[11]

The usual difficulties of tracing enslaved people's movements and places of origin are exacerbated by their dehumanized position in the American colonies. As property, enslaved people had value, but not as persons. For the 1850 federal census, population records named only "free inhabitants," tallying enslaved men and women in separate slave schedules, in much the same way as the agricultural records tallied cattle, horses, sheep, and chickens.[12] The identities and humanity of the enslaved were systematically disregarded, marginalized, and neglected. Even the occasional records that do mention names reflect this devaluation, often only noting their tasks as laborers or their estimated age and market value. Furthermore, in the eighteenth and nineteenth centuries, recordkeeping was haphazard and literacy rates lower. Not all vital records were committed in writing, and much of what was written down has been inevitably and irretrievably lost. Births, deaths, and other important events were only recorded sporadically, if at all.

To know someone's name, and to say that name, is to acknowledge their existence—their right to be known. In this project to recover the names of any formerly enslaved people, we make a first step toward rediscovering and honoring those names—the names signifying those lives.

The Imperfect Process for Discovery

Whereas those with privilege and power have always had the means to record their struggles and accomplishments, accounts describing enslaved individuals and their contributions are few and far between. Authors such as Frederick Douglass and Harriet Jacobs are among comparatively few exceptions.[13] Tiya Miles's recent study, *All That She Carried*, reveals both the challenges and importance of researching the lives of enslaved African Americans. Miles chronicles the difficulties of tracing an African-American family's history when little has been recorded and much has been erased. "Archives," she notes, "do not faithfully reveal or honor the enslaved."[14] Important details remain unrecoverable, and accounts are always incomplete. Still, seemingly inconsequential items and records can provide vitally important information, as Miles shows through her heart-rending account of Ashley, a nine-year-old girl sold away from her mother, Rose, in the 1850s. Using the only items that Rose could give her daughter before parting—a simple cloth sack holding an old worn dress, several pecans, a lock of hair, and "my Love always"—Miles adds layers of research about the material life of the enslaved, the harsh conditions that women especially endured, the systems that imprisoned them, and the environments surrounding them.[15] Through her meticulous research and thoughtful contextualization, Miles shows the significance of the ostensibly trivial. She uses each artifact, the handmade sack, the worn dress, the meagre pecans, and the lock of Rose's hair, as a series of lenses through which the reader can see, however faintly, the profound horrors of enslavement and some of the contours of Rose and Ashley's lives. Acknowledging both her limitations and purpose, Miles writes, "We cannot enter the consciousness of a girl born into slavery who matures to give birth into slavery and can have no reasonable hope of escape. We cannot know Rose, but we can draw on the resources at our disposal ... to picture the woman she might have been and summon the shape of her daily life."[16]

Miles's work reminds us that uncovering the history of people held in captivity is always a daunting task, but never an inconsequential one. Meaning is often evasive and sometimes must be found where it seems most unlikely. In our study, the slave schedules of the 1850s and 1860s provide headcounts, but very little identifying information. An 1850 ledger page enumerating the "slave inhabitants" of Lower All Saints Parish, for example, provides only the age and sex of eighty-four enslaved men and women. The only person named is the white landowner, William A. Alston, who claimed these people as property. Records such as these provide sobering evidence of the many enslaved individuals who were considered chattel, unnamed in the population census, and forgotten. Because of such omissions, other primary sources have proven more fruitful for recovering the names of the enslaved, including wills, deeds, plantation inventories, contracts, and court, military, and church records. Letters, newspaper notices, and advertisements also provide valuable information. To locate these documents, we first needed to trace the history of Hobcaw's shifting borders from its 1663 land grant inception through bequests to heirs, private sales, and the multiple plantations that subdivided the peninsula into the Reconstruction era. Limiting the study to Hobcaw plantations also required learning the boundaries of proprietary counties in 1682, the Anglican parishes of 1767, and the districts and counties in 1785, many of which no longer exist.[17]

The former labels and boundary lines of districts, counties, and parishes help us distinguish the relevance of the records we encounter, but the geographical challenges are even more complex. Over the course of many years, Hobcaw Barony's sixteen thousand acres were divided into as many as fifteen plantations with twenty different names.

Alderly	Forlorn Hope
Annandale	Friendfield & "The Point"
Bellefield	Marietta (aka Pleasant Fields)
Calais (also known as [aka] Clegg's Point and Frasers Point)	Michau
	Oryzantia
Clifton	Rose Hill
Cogdell	Strawberry Hill (aka Belle Voir)
Crab Hall	Youngville

In addition, wealthier landowners held properties in several locations, some within the original Hobcaw Barony land grant and others outside it, which greatly complicates searches of landowner names. Suzanne Cameron Linder and Marta Leslie Thacker's *Historical Atlas of the Rice Plantations of Georgetown County and the Santee River* has proven immensely valuable.[18] Not only does this exhaustive work trace the ownership of rice plantations within the area; it also documents the shifting property lines of those plantations. The first thirteen chapters identify each known tract of land that resulted from the many subdivisions and sales of the original land grant. The most useful transactions span from John, Lord Carteret's sale in 1730 through Bernard Baruch's Hobcaw acquisitions between 1905 and 1907.

We combed the *Historical Atlas* and other sources for locations, landowners, dates, and events. Compiling over two hundred sixty rows of data in a spreadsheet, we developed a contextual timeline of the period (Table 4.1). Supported by maps and contextual research such as this, we could pursue the most important goal of our study: to recover the names of the thousands of enslaved people who toiled on this particular land.

Table 4.1. Sample Timeline Entries

Year	Event Description	Enslaver	Location
1807	Auctioneer William Payne announces in the *Charleston Daily Courier* an upcoming sale on February 17 of "77 Prime Country Born Negroes . . . being the property of Thomas Mitchell, Esq."	T. Mitchell, enabled by Wm. Payne	Forlorn Hope
1808	A law banning further importation of slaves takes effect, having been established as a statute on March 2, 1807.	—	—
1808	William Alston purchases the seashore tracts of Annandale and Youngville, renames the combined tract Crab Hall, and directs the building of "several slave houses."	Wm. Alston	Annandale Youngville Crab Hall

Note. — = information not applicable.

A single event description, such as the one describing William Alston's land purchases, would lead us to search the archives for William Alston at Annandale, Youngville, and Crab Hall plantations from 1808 forward. We could then seek his personal records, such as letters, wills, tax bills, and clothing allowances, all of which might provide information on the laborers who toiled on his properties. Identifying landowners, we discovered, is crucial for uncovering the names of enslaved people. In addition, the spreadsheet allows us to organize information by date, enslavers, and location. As shown in Table 4.1, organizing by date renders a sequence of events within an historical context. Then by isolating enslavers, we learned that at least sixty-nine individual landowners held captive thousands of people of African descent on Hobcaw soil from 1729 until 1865 when the Civil War ended.[19] Those enslavers' names are listed in Appendix A. Sorting the spreadsheet by sublevels—to include enslavers, dates, and locations—associates enslavers with plantations within estimated timeframes. For instance, twenty dated entries for William Alston reveal that from 1785 to 1865, he enslaved over six hundred seventy people. To date, we have found the names of sixty enslaved people who labored on his Hobcaw plantations. When we encounter a primary source that *does* name enslaved people, we record and tally those names in the spreadsheet also. For example, a timeline entry derived from a reward notice refers to two runaway adults, Fortune and Dinah, and an infant (Figure 4.2). Because only the enslaved parents are named in the reward notice, the "Count" column for the running total of recovered enslaved individuals' names increases by two (Table 4.2). Additional columns in the spreadsheet provide places for source information and notes, ensuring the collection of all relevant details for verification and suggesting further research, as needed. Drawing on these primary and secondary sources, our research team can then conceive a potential narrative for Fortune, Dinah, and their child.

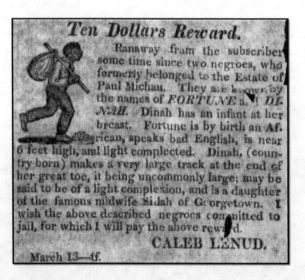

Figure 4.2. *Winyah Intelligencer,* March 10, 1819, page 5. Georgetown County Digital Library.

Table 4.2. Tallying the Recovered Names

Year	Event Description	Enslaved	Count	Enslaver	Location	Source	Researcher's Notes	Other Names
1819	Caleb Lenud posts a reward notice in a Georgetown newspaper, reporting Fortune, Dinah, and an unnamed infant as runaways and suggesting they could be hiding near Paul Michau's estate.	Fortune, Dinah	2	Paul Michau, Caleb Lenud	Michau Plantation	"Ten Dollars Reward," *Winyaw Intelligencer*, March 10, 1819, page 5.	This ad is reprinted every two weeks through August 18, which could suggest the runaways, Fortune and Dinah, had some level of success in avoiding apprehension.	Sidah, a "famous midwife" in Georgetown and mother of Dinah

Paul Michau had mortgaged his property on the southern end of Hobcaw Barony three times between 1795 and 1809, according to Linder and Thacker's *Atlas*. Michau died in 1812, leaving five children, one stepdaughter, and twenty-seven enslaved people "valued at 10,233.84."[20] The death of an enslaver often created intense anxiety for the enslaved, who were subject to sales and relocations that split their families and communities.[21] The complexities of Michau's unresolved debts and multiple heirs would have intensified these threats for the enslaved people on his property. After Michau's death, any number of people could have taken possession of Fortune and Dinah and sold or traded them away.

Subsequent searches on Caleb Lenud reveal that he had inherited his uncle Andrew Guerry's plantation in the Charleston District at the death of Guerry's wife.[22] Perhaps at some point, Lenud purchased Fortune and Dinah. Then, in late 1818 or early 1819, Fortune and Dinah escaped from captivity with their child. Suspecting that the runaways might return to the Georgetown area where Dinah's mother remained, Lenud placed the reward notice in the *Winyah Intelligencer* every two weeks, from March 13 until August 18, suggesting that the family might have had some success avoiding capture.[23]

Research on Laura Carr provides new insights about how Hobcaw's formerly enslaved can be discovered but also how evidence can be misleading. During the Baruch Era of Hobcaw Barony (1905–1964), Carr lived in Friendfield Village and was known as a midwife and medicine woman for her community.[24] Until her death, she occupied a small, two-room, former slave dwelling that was built before 1860 from "'recycled' material" and never had plumbing or electricity.[25] The staff and volunteer docents for the Belle W. Baruch Foundation have long known about a Laura Carr through oral histories that had been passed down from and about the residents of Friendfield Village. These stories included the names of several people who were born into slavery, including Bedford Carr (born ca. 1829), Tim McCants, (born ca. 1840), and Columbus Sands (born ca. 1861). In addition, Hobcaw's oral tradition indicated that Bedford Carr married a woman named Laura in 1891.[26] Our team encountered differing accounts of Laura Carr's lifespan, including her birth date, which would determine whether she, too, had been born into slavery. Our strategy for working with the uncertainty was to record each account and continue searching for additional clues that might verify others.

One piece of evidence generated significant excitement in February 2023. While cleaning away dirt, dust, and overgrowth in the Marietta Cemetery, Hobcaw Barony staff member Patricia Mishoe and a volunteer discovered

Laura Carr's gravesite.[27] They wiped off a metal marker posted by the Manigault Funeral Home, revealing that Laura Carr died at eighty years old on October 12, 1937, which means that she was born either 1856 or 1857, well before emancipation. The scrawled handwriting on the marker encouraged us to posit a fuller story—that Laura was a child of about six when President Lincoln issued the Emancipation Proclamation on January 1, 1863, and that by the end of the Civil War in 1865, she would have been eight or nine years old. Like the tattered sack at the center of Miles's narrative, this long-neglected grave marker seemed to provide new insights to a forgotten life.

At first, we trusted the grave marker, even though the mottled paper beneath the glass was likely added years after Laura Carr's death. We imagined that a relative might have requested the marker and provided the information to the Manigault Funeral Home. Months later, however, another handwritten document, the 1900 US Census, brought a corrective surprise.[28] In the record for the Waccamaw area of Georgetown County, Bedford Carr was listed as the head of a household that comprised six people, including Laura, his wife of nine years, age fifty-five, and four children: daughter Hanna, age twenty-seven; William, age twenty-five: Robert, age sixteen; and Nial, age ten. The census also recorded Laura Carr's birth date as March 1844, information that surely Bedford or Laura offered themselves. This self-reported date altered Laura's story once again, placing her at about age fifty in 1891 when she and Bedford married. The 1900 census also reveals that, in her lifetime, Laura Carr had eight children, five of whom were still living at the time. Perhaps the children identified in the 1900 household inventory were her own.

The 1910 census, instead of verifying the information from the previous decade, further complicated Laura Carr's story.[29] By this date, Carr was living alone as a widow. Despite the passage of a decade, her recorded age had decreased from fifty-five to fifty-two. Also, the total number of her children had decreased from eight to seven, leading us to wonder if one of the children whom the Carrs reported in 1900 had been stillborn or died in infancy. Ten years earlier, the loss of a young child might have been more fresh, warranting affirmation in a census count. A decade later, a woman alone could be excused for revising her losses. In either case, Laura's given age in each census places her birth before emancipation, whether in 1844 or 1856–1857.

The more information we find, the more questions we generate. By including even contradictory information in the timeline and adding cross-references in the Notes column, we have flagged the conflicting details for further study. As we search for additional evidence, Laura's story might alter again, resulting in revisions to recorded history and the stories we tell in our communities. More important, our information might fill in gaps for descendants who have incomplete family histories passed down through oral traditions, family Bibles, and other documents.

Rewards

This project from its inception has sought to discover as much information as possible about the people who were once enslaved on Hobcaw Barony. As the previous examples show, some information is retrievable but inconclusive. To find the names recorded below, we traced a path through a complicated landscape of time, geography, and culture to identify slave-owning families whose economic fortunes rose and fell through marriages, deaths, inheritance, legal disputes, bankruptcy, and civil war. Emancipation of the formerly enslaved and an undermined Reconstruction era resulted in further economic, social, and political dislocation. However, postemancipation records are both more plentiful and more detailed. Postbellum census records, for example, name formerly enslaved people with first names and surnames, list their occupations, and identify them as heads of household, spouses, and children. Freedmen's Bureau contracts list the names of people who chose to remain as paid workers on plantations. Additional civic records include birth dates, death dates, and marriages, many of which are now accessible in online genealogical databases, such as the South Carolina Historical Society Collections, or the South Carolina Department of Archives and History.[30] Using these resources, our team recorded data through the period of Reconstruction to collect the names of formerly enslaved people and compare those lists with earlier inventories.

Through this process, we have transcribed seven hundred thirty-one names of enslaved people held in bondage on Hobcaw Barony's former rice plantations. Appendix B lists the names of those individuals, many of whom were forgotten until now. During the next phase of the project, we hope to bring those names back where they belong—to their families and communities, to connect the past to the present. Today, the surnames of the enslaved and those who enslaved them are often still Georgetown names, the families are Georgetown families. We hope to connect with living descendants of the enslaved, share with them the histories we have found and hear their own oral histories to expand upon and enrich the work we have begun. In addition, we will compare enslaved names on a single plantation across several years to identify similarities and changes. By referring to our contextual timeline, we might then posit potential narratives for specific people, families, or communities. These insights would be most welcome in an environment where the paucity of historical detail has held firm for centuries. Using academic research and archival information in this way, we are partnering with the Baruch Foundation and area communities to raise awareness of the names and lives of the enslaved who lived on the southern end of the Waccamaw peninsula. If we work to ensure that their stories are told as part of the histories of Hobcaw Barony and Georgetown County, we can help the public hear the echo of voices from the past.

Conclusion

Like much of the American South, Hobcaw Barony is a landscape haunted by beauty and violence. Driving north toward the property from Georgetown on US 17, one is drawn in by the vast expanse of water, woods, and sunlight. The natural beauty arrests the senses when looking across Winyah Bay. Yet, nature alone does not define the view from the road. In the still-visible contours of the old rice fields, there is a scarred landscape that was once transformed into a wealth-generating machine through the forced toil of enslaved communities. Building and maintaining a rice plantation involved back-breaking work, with enslaved laborers moving tens of thousands of cubic yards of miry earth under the threat of the lash and amid the equally lethal dangers of wildlife, disease, and the unforgiving Carolina weather.[31] Slavery left scars on the land and its people.[32] The lines in the old rice fields should remind us that the brutality of the old South is not as long gone as we might hope. The pain it left behind has never completely subsided.

We do not presume that this project will heal all that needs to be healed, or make right that which was made wrong, but there is a responsibility to recognize the names and remember those communities whose history has been forgotten, neglected, or dismissed. As Pat Conroy wrote, geography can be a "wound," an "anchorage," or a "port of call."[33] At Hobcaw, we share the same land as thousands whose eyes opened and closed between the same waters and beneath the same skies that still define this place. We live and work in a place where freedom and dignity were "dreams deferred" for too long.[34] Yet, amid toil and terror, love was given, life was sustained, and people endured past the days of slavery. The survival of the enslaved and their descendants on Hobcaw is a history we must acknowledge. Although brought here as captives and forcibly held as property, these communities *made* the land called Hobcaw and Lowcountry, and many still call the area home.

Our work offers an intentional step to acknowledge these communities' proper place in what James Baldwin memorably termed "a more beautiful and more terrible history" of this property, state, and nation.[35] In doing so, we hope to reaffirm Baldwin's belief that this history belonged to people like his family and, by extension, to those descendants of the enslaved at Hobcaw Barony as well. The documents we discover and the stories we hear convey these difficult, resilient legacies. The lives and voices of those who came before us do indeed echo across the years. It is our duty to listen.

Appendix A: Names of Known Enslavers, Hobcaw Barony

Benjamin Allston Sr.

Benjamin Allston

Captain John Allston

Robert Francis Withers Allston

Thomas Allston

William A. Alston Jr.

Charles Cotesworth Pinckney Alston

Col. J. Alston

Colonel William Alston

John Ashe Alston

Joseph Alston

Mary Allston Young Alston

Thomas Pinckney Alston

William Algernon Alston

William Baker

Dr. Joseph Blyth

Frances Elizabeth Allston Blyth

J. Blythe Allston

Anna Alston

Charlotte Alston

Charles Alston Sr.

James Boyd

William June Buford

John Cheeseborough

Samuel Clegg

Samuel Clegg II

Samuel Clegg III

Elizabeth Clegg

Lydia Clegg III

Mehitabel Clegg

John Coachman

Charles Cogdell

John Cogdell

John Dawson

Benjamin D'Harriette

Samuel Dwight

Brice Fisher

Peter Foissin

Frances Fraser

Reverend Hugh Fraser

Benjamin Porter Fraser

Stephanus Ford

Rebecca Brewton Hayne

Mary Heriot

Mary Ouldfield Heriot

Robert Heriot

Roger Heriot

Benjamin Huger

Benjamin Huger, Jr

Joshua John Ward

Peter Johnson

D.W. Jordan

James Keith

Caleb Lenud

Nicholas Linwood
Edward Martin
John Martin
Samuel Masters
Paul Michau
John Izard Middleton, Jr.
Edward Mitchell
Thomas Mitchell
Mary Moore
Benjamin Porter
Elizabeth Clegg Porter
John Porter
Anzy Porter
William Bull Pringle

Mary Pringle
William Rhett
John Richards
John Roberts
F. Stuart
Elizabeth Towner
Lydia Towner
William H. Trapier
B. Huger Ward
Mayham Ward
Joshua J. Ward
Alexander Widdicom
Thomas Young

Appendix B: Names of Individuals Known to Have Been Enslaved at Hobcaw Barony

This list chronologically presents the recorded names of enslaved people on Hobcaw plantations beginning in 1739 through the early years of Reconstruction when Freedmen's Bureau records listed emancipated laborers. Further research is needed to determine whether any of the repeating names in the latter years refer to single individuals.

Cudjoe	Belly	Jerry	Snow
Judeth	Rose & child	June	Mingo
Liddy	Andrew	Polly-dove	Susy
Ceaser	Cate	Alia	Prince
Hope	Fillis	Tom	Mingo
Harculas	Old Fillis	Jenny	Kate
Mingo	Sampson	Bobb	Nancy
Samson	Carlos	Jack	Phobe
Loddy	Hector	Subina	Sampson
Blind Tom	Peter	Stattyra	Binkey
Hagar	Bell	Sue	Patty
Judy	Roxanna	Lenor	Jenny
Nanny	Emanual	Centry	Elsy
Hannah	Lilly	Mungo	Peter
Intram	Tryow	John	Amy

Silvia	Roger	Sam	Myrtilla
Betty	George	Toby	old Rose
Peter	Kate	Cuffee	Molly
Jack	Molly	Lilly's Philander	Tenah
Jenah	Daphne	Robert	Murria
Hester	Sue	John	Venus
Cretia	Toney	Scipio	Dido
Lewey	Bristol	Harry	Tenah
Phobe	Martilla	Will	Daphne
Hagar	Tommy	Old Harry	Mindah
Silvia	Abraham	Johnny	Rose
Polly	Cudjoe	Friday	Flora
Tommy	Fortune	Tommy	Martha
March	Dinah	Sawney	Phebe
Rose	Hercules	Solomon	Binkey
Lavinia	Bedford	Guy	Sally
Billy	York	Peter	Clarinda
Letty	Sam	Ben	Affee
Joe	Jimmy	Tom	Joan
Primus	Tom	Lye	Rachal
Sancho	Robbin	Francis	Levenia
Tyrah	Billy	Primus	Nelly
Diana	Chambers	Matthais	Elsey
See	Lilly	Old Scipio	Elizabeth
Maggy	Brap	William	Phillus
Frank	Primus	Ackemore	Peggy
Judith	George	Jack	Mary
Autron	Joe	Alfred	Levenia
Ben	Sam	Rachal	Old Sary
Agrippa	John	Clarinda	Old Fanny
Nanny	Mark	Lucy	Pendah
Sam	Moses	Mary	Silvya
Nanny	Prince	Luno	Lissy
Doll	Mary's Philander	Fanny	Rose
Philander	Joe	Dido	Will
Binkey	Israel	Grace	Peter
Venus	Sunderland	Maria	Alfred
Nelly	Abel	Elsey	Celia
Harry	Andrew	Elizabeth	Nelson

Harriet	Sary	Grace	Thomas
Saby	Fanny	Maria	Charles
Moses	Frederick	Robin	Pheno
Zelpher	Caroline	Prince	Hercules
Celia	William	Mark	Jack
Nancy	Louisa	John	Franny
Norrage	Betsey	Friday	Mary
Guilbert	Theophilus	Salley	Mendals
Nanny	Grace	Jenah	Joe
Clarifsa	Hardtimes	Frank	Rose
Eliza	Rebecca	Tom	Flora
Abby	Pierce	Guelbert	Martha
Charlotte	Thomas	Old Harry	Francis
Will	Phillis	Tom	Thomas
Selenia	Violet	Rachel	Julia
Prince	Washington	Massy	Affer
Silvya	Sarah	Clarissa	Peter
Lonnon	Gabriel	Moses	Bend
Amos	Betsy	Phoebe	Steph
Thomas	Old Rose	Binkey	Thomas
Hardtimes	Saml	Scipio	Olivia
Stephen	Jimmy	Sylvia	Tim
Hercules	Molly	Toby	Laura
Allick	Cuffee	Sundulund	Cuffee
Jack	Guy	Serenia	Will
York	Mary Ann	Nelly	Columbus
Adam	Sam	Sammy	Moses
Christmas	Lucy	Solomon	Jack
Charles	John	George	Cudjoe
Charlotte	Mary	Alfred	Windsor
Julia	June	Joe	William
Aimy	Franny	Alleck	Phillip
Nanny	Rachel	Andrew	Abey
Dianna	Dido	Ackemore	Daniel
Peggy	Elsey	Pendah	Prince
Cate	Brass	Old Scipio	May
Harriet	Primus	Amos	Peter
Esther	Billy	Charlotte	August
Bina	Sam	Adam	Dick

Thomas	Leeah	Dinah Izard	Lucy (a girl)
Columbus	Leinda	Hagar Green	John White
Amos	Reannuh	Joe Bengal	Phillis White
Lilly	Hertty	Henry (a boy)	Diana McCants
Sinclair	Tommy	Syke McCants	Brutas Car
July	Deliverance	Mary Ann	Sary Car
Jim	Thomas	McCants	Bedford Car
Celia	Boum	Frank Jenkins	Jno Car
Ned	Celia	Betsy Jenkins	Susan Car
Amy	Katrina	Dave Jabab	Edward Car
Zelieus	Moll	Molly Gregg	Eaphram Car
Molly	John Forsight	Price Bowen	Sip Days
Brutus	Frank Jackson	Molly Bowen	Bess Car
Fortune	Small Tommy	Robert Spikle	Toney Car
Abram	Beck	Blanch Spickle	Adam Jordan
Jack	Sam	William Draylin	Welbey Car
Grace	Gideon Simmons	Betsy Draylin	Meliar Gordan
Tina	Jenny Breck__	Hardtimes	Jno Shoobrick
Sary	Daniel Prince	Brockington	Rebecca
Assurance	Abel Lafree	Jeannette	Soobrick
Faith	Will Bunch	Brockington	Jane Gibs
Jenny	Gracie Cashing	Cato	Nickey Kershaw
John	Lindy Glasgow	Brockington	Sary Kershaw
Henrietta	John Haygood	Sally	Danl Bruice
Bedford	Jenny Carr	Brockington	Celear Bruice
Amelia	Frank Jackson	Cato (a boy)	Jim Brokedown
Lena	Ephraim Cuno	Jacob McCall	Jack Meril
Sep	Jim McCants	Sarah McCall	Lizzie Meril
George	Murriah	Nancy McCall	Moses Mirel
Molly	McCants	Robin Pinckney	Jimmey Ragg
Aggy	Lizzie McCants	Tenah Pinckney	Shurance
Psyche	Frederick Great	Murriah Fraser	Holmes
Teddy	Harriott Great	Mingo Bowen	Susan Holmes
Samuel	Ransom (a boy)	Nancy Bowen	Bram Blain
Heaster	Maria Scriven	Celia	Joe Lawyer
Tom	Venus Dixon	Brockington	Lazerous Becket
Nickey	Peter Johnson	Jacob (a boy)	Nelley Becket
Polly	Susannah	Carolina (a boy)	Jno Foreside
Bellu	Johnson	Rose Johnson	Elin Foreside

Isaac Shoobrick

Frank Bookey

Catherine
  Bookey

Antoney
  Richardson

Patience
  Richardson

Thos. Robertson

Louisa
  Robertson

Henryetta Blake

Jno. Pinckney

Louisa Pinckney

Faith Lawyer Jr.

Jno. White

Abram White

Daimon White

Hannah White

Joe White

Moley Pinkney

Wilcher Walker

Jiney Walker

Aggy Funeey

Bella Funeey

Charity Bunch

Thos. Alston

Hagar Grant

Rebecca Car

Caroline Car

Juba Kershaw

Tyra Rutlidge

Moley Blain

Hagar Stewarty

Nippy Blain

Tanzie Blain

Saml Alston

Nelessy Car

Glasco Lawyer

Mary Lawyer

Toney Small

Caty Drumer

Fortune
  Shoobrick

Marth Shoobrick

Hester Meril

B__ Coin

Solomon
  Rutlidge

Frank Jackson

Flora Jackson

Tryal Alston

Hetty Alston

Jack Bunch

Nanet Bunch

Moley Car

Abram Blain

Cesar Blain

Welington Blain

Venus Car

Nicy Blain

Danl Taylor

Hercules Fraser

Cassim Cambell

Cyrus Gadson

Jerry Vereen

Diana Vereen

Teed Hasell

Jobe Moultry

Bella Moultry

July Fraser

Levenia Fraser

Bob Murrell

Josey Moultry

Phoeby Moultry

Louisa Gadson

Jim Rutledge

Darcus Rutledge

Ely Butler

Abram Sumpter

Rachel Sumpter

Stephen Sherrill

Luna Sherrill

Deas

Nizah Pinckney

Joe Rutledge

Hanna Rutledge

Liddy Fraser

Dilly Right

Hariot Rutledge

Darinda Moultry

Sary Moultry

Molly Mas__

Amey Cambell

Emma Cambell

Agnes Moultry

Beuton Rutledge

Pompey Kinlock

Jonno Pyatt

Frank Alston

Hammon Fraser

Daniel Bruce

Celin Bruce

Solomon Keith

Severren Keith

Lazarus Bicket

Jim Brockinton

John Forsythe

Ellen Forsythe

John Car

Susan Car

John Pinckney

Louisen
  Pinckney

Edward Car

Rose Car

Tom Hamilton

Catherine
  Hamilton

Moses Small

Ephram Car

Willby Car

Henrietta Bake

Shurance
  Holmes

Patines Homes

Molly Blain

Tyra Rutledge

Lary Car

Catherine
  Bookey

Charity Bunch

Tony Car

Adam Sordan

Emilien Gadston

Minda Blain

Lozzy Marrell

Hestor Marrell

Ben Choln

Thomas Alston

Nelapy Alston

Molly Pinckney

Tom Robinson

Louisen
  Robinson

Lary Kenshaw

Glascow Sawyer

Mary Sawyer

Isaac Shubrick

Nancy Shubrick

Molly Car

Juba Kershaw

Lykie Brown

Aggy Tunny

Bella Tunny

Fortune Shubrick

Nippy Walker	Tim McCants	Amy Small	Joe Alston
Tanzen Blain	Netty Beck	Jack Cohen	August Ward
John Shubrick	Bess Carr	Phillis Cohen	Mazy Ward
Beckey Shubrick	Queen Sawyer	Charlo Gibson	Cuffy Funny
Anthony	Martha Shubrick	Alex McNight	Tilla Keeth
Richardson	Sophey Summers	Phillis McNight	Nanny Parker
Patience	Marcus Tunny	Caesar Becket	George Giffs
Richardson	Jimmy Car	Sue Becket	Moses Jenkins
Solomon	Dianna Siprey	Cain Fraser	Molly Becket
Rutledge	Frank Jackson	Tom Fraser	Morris
Thomas Keith	Jack Bunch	Mary Ann Fraser	Columbus Sands
Cinda Mention	Nanny Bunch	Oliver Fraser	Sylvia Dease
Netty Taylor	George Gibbs	Hagar Fraser	Frank Spring
Laura Carr	Johnny Rivers	Will Fraser	Caly Small
Robert Shankel	Andrew Rivers	Caesar Shubrick	Moses Pinckney
Sam Gibbs	Harmon Becket	Minda Shubrick	Wesley White
Fayette Sawyer	Bella Becket	Lucy Lawyer	Venus Car
Eliza Keith	Robert Small	Affy Lawyer	

Richard A. Almeida is John Monroe Marshall Holliday professor of political science at Francis Marion University, where he has been on the faculty since 2007. His research and teaching interests include elections, interest groups, and political thought. He lives in Conway, SC, with his wife and daughter.

Patti Burns is director of the Marion County SC Library System. In her previous position as the head of adult services at the Georgetown County Library, Patti was able to assist many African-American patrons with their genealogy and document several African-American cemeteries. Patti is currently working to recover local African-American genealogy resources and document African-American cemeteries in Marion County.

Madison Cates is assistant professor of history at Coastal Carolina University and the co-director of the Belle W. Baruch Institute for South Carolina Studies. His research examines the environmental history of the American South and has appeared in publications such as *Southern Cultures* and *The Journal of Southern History*.

Greg Garvan is an avid public historian who has served as a volunteer at Hobcaw Barony, Middleton Place, the International African American Museum, The Slave Dwelling Project, and the McLeod Plantation Historic Site.

Megan Hammeke received her undergraduate degree in history from Coastal Carolina University in 2023 and is currently completing a master's degree in library and information science. She has always loved history and research, and her experience with Hobcaw Barony has inspired a wider love of cultural heritage and personal histories.

Lynn Hanson is professor emerita from Francis Marion University, where she taught in the English department and served as a founding co-director for the Belle Baruch Institute for South Carolina Studies.

Adam Houle is the author of *Stray*, a finalist for the Colorado Books Awards. His work has appeared in *AGNI*, *Shenandoah*, *Post Road*, and elsewhere. He is an assistant professor of English at Francis Marion University and co-editor of *Twelve Mile Review*.

Steven C. Sims-Brewton is Head of Access Services librarian/associate professor in the James A. Rogers Library of Francis Marion University.

NOTES

1. King Charles II established the Charter of Carolina on March 24, 1663, to reward his supporters during his family's restoration to the crown. The original Hobcaw Barony land grant was assigned to Sir Charles Carteret, a knight and baronet. The bequest later passed to his great-great-grandson, John Carteret, in 1718. See Charles H Lesser, "Lords Proprietors of Carolina," *South Carolina Encyclopedia* (https://www.scencyclopedia.org/sce/entries/lords-proprietors-of-Carolina). See also the transcribed text of the charter in Yale Law School Avalon Collection of documents in law, history, and diplomacy (https://avalon.law.yale.edu/17th_century/nc01.asp).

2. "Last Will and Testament of Charles Cogdell, 1776," South Carolina County, District and Probate Courts, 1670–1980, database with images, *Ancestry*, https://www.ancestry.com.

3. Walter Edgar, *South Carolina: A History* (Columbia: University of South Carolina Press, 1996), 286.

4. "Last Will and Testament of Belle W Baruch," March 23, 1964, 9.

5. The Belle W Baruch Foundation officially approved a mission revision to include "conservation of natural *and cultural* resources" [italics added] on May 9, 2011. A subsequent mission revision in 2016 further emphasizes the importance of history and culture. For the most recent mission statement, see https:///www.hobcawbarony.org.

6. Published studies include Cameron Moon, "Timber-Framed Dwellings of the Enslaved and Freedmen in the South Carolina Lowcountry: Continuities and Innovations in Building Practices and Housing Standards," *Buildings & Landscapes: Journal of the Vernacular Architecture Forum* 28, no 1 (2021): 9–131; Lynn Hanson, "The Wealth of Information in Belle Baruch's Checkbooks."

Interdisciplinary Humanities 36, no 2 (2019): 21–53; Heathley A Johnson, "Archaeology on the Widdicom Tract at Hobcaw Barony," *Legacy* 23, no 2 (2019): 24–27; Christina Brooks, "Enclosing Their Immortal Souls: A Survey of Two African American Cemeteries in Georgetown, South Carolina." *Southeastern Archaeology* 30, no 1 (2011): 176–186; Mary Miller, *Baroness of Hobcaw: The Life of Belle W Baruch* (Columbia: University of South Carolina Press, 2006); Lee G Brockington, *Plantation Between the Waters: A Brief History of Hobcaw Barony* (Charleston, SC: The History Press, 2006) Additional research reports are accessible through the Belle W Baruch Foundation, such as James Liphus Ward, "Back to the Land, Back to its People: A Strategic Response to Researching the Cultural Landscape at Hobcaw Barony" (Unpublished manuscript, 2015, Hobcaw Barony, https://hobcawbarony.pastperfectonline.com/archive/51B83865-C879-4459-9150-112329083656); Carolyn Dillian, "Holocene Sea Level Rise and Shell Midden Development and Destruction" (Unpublished manuscript, 2019, Hobcaw Barony); Allison Steadman, "An Inventory and Archive of Garments Removed from Belle Baruch's Basement" (Unpublished manuscript, 2019, Hobcaw Barony); Elizabeth Howie and Melissa Hydock, "Art Historical Research on Works of Art in Hobcaw House" (Unpublished manuscript, 2019, typescript); and Thomas McConnell, "Bernard Baruch Library: An Annotated Bibliography" (Unpublished manuscript, 2008, https://hobcawbarony.pastperfectonline.com/archive/EDEEF599-CAB0-4C28-9429-366406311966). See also James L Michie, "Search for San Miguel de Gualdape," Research Manuscript Series 1, Waccamaw Center for Historical and Cultural Studies (Conway, SC: Coastal Carolina University, 1991) SCETV's interactive website, BetweenThe Waters.org, provides a virtual tour of Hobcaw Barony and showcases additional studies, interviews, and programs on the property. See also SCETV's associated blog, *Making History Together: A Collaborative Blog for SCETV's "Between the Waters"* at https://makinghistorybtw.wordpress.com.

7. Miller, *Baroness of Hobcaw*, 169.

8. SCETV's interactive website, BetweenTheWaters.org, allows visitors to explore conditions of enslaved Africans and their African-American descendants Although some details refer specifically to the enslaved people on Hobcaw's former plantations, the information drawn from contributing scholars describes the generalized conditions of rice cultivation in South Carolina.

9. Mary Battle, "Africans in Carolina," Lowcountry Digital History Initiative (Charleston, SC: College of Charleston). See also the South Carolina Maritime Museum exhibit, "The Atlantic Slave Trade," curated by Justin McIntyre, https://www.scmaritimemuseum.org. Although there exists some debate on the "Black rice thesis," the works of Dan Littlefield and Judith Carney provide support for these claims. See Dan Littlefield, *Rice and Slaves: Ethnicity and the Slave Trade in Colonial South Carolina* (Champaign: University of Illinois Press, 1991), and Judith A Carney, *Black Rice: The African Origins of Rice Cultivation in America* (Cambridge, MA: Harvard University Press, 2001). For an accessible discussion of the Black rice thesis in relation to early American culinary culture, see Hendricks, "The Multicultural Nature of Eighteenth-Century Cooking in British America: The Southern Rice Pie," in *Carolina Currents: Studies in South Carolina*

Culture, vol 1, "New Directions," edited by Christopher D Johnson (Columbia: University of South Carolina Press, 2024), 28–42.

10. See Charles Joyner, *Down by the Riverside: A South Carolina Slave Community* [25th anniversary edition] (Champaign: University of Illinois Press, 2009), 221.

11. Joyner, *Down by the Riverside*, 221.

12. "1850 Census: The Seventh Census of the United States," United States Census Bureau, https://www.census.gov/library/publications/1853/dec/1850a.html. Compare with "United States Census (Slave Schedule), 1850," database with images, *FamilySearch*, https://www.familysearch.org.

13. Frederick Douglass's *Narrative of the Life of Frederick Douglass, an American Slave* (New York: Bedford, 1845), was published in 1845 and became one of the most influential abolitionist texts. Harriet Jacobs's *Incidents in the Life of a Slave Girl, Written by Herself* (Cambridge, MA: Belknap Press, 2009) was published in 1861 after Jacobs escaped to New York. For a guide to these and other slave narratives, see Audrey Fisch, editor, *The Cambridge Companion to The African American Slave Narrative* (Cambridge, MA: Cambridge University Press, 2007).

14. Miles, *All That She Carried: The Journey of Ashley's Sack, a Black Family Keepsake* (New York: Random House, 2021), 18.

15. Miles, *All That She Carried*, 77.

16. Miles, *All That She Carried*, 77–78.

17. See the "Maps Tracing the Formation of Counties," South Carolina Department of Archives & History https://www.archivesindex.sc.gov/guide/County Records.

18. Suzanne Linder and Marta Thacker, *Historical Atlas of the Rice Plantations of Georgetown County and the Santee River* (Columbia: South Carolina Department of Archives and History, 2001), 3–73. See also Julian Stevenson Bolick, *Waccamaw Plantations* (Clinton, SC: Jacobs Press, 1946), 1–2.

19. One of the earliest known enslavers on Hobcaw Barony was Samuel Masters, who purchased two hundred acres of Cogdell Plantation in 1729 from Lewis John to raise cattle and run tar kilns for ships. Within three years, he mortgaged his Cogdell land and home, along with all of his tar kilns and associated equipment, his livestock, and two unnamed enslaved people. The records pertaining to Samuel Masters provide evidence of enslaved labor on Hobcaw properties before landowners cultivated rice. See Linder and Thacker, *Historical Atlas*, 13.

20. Linder and Thacker, *Historical Atlas*, 8.

21. See Miles, *All That She Carried*, 92.

22. As established in Andrew Caleb Guerry's will, August 3, 1796, Guerry's wife was granted a life estate on his Charleston area plantation until her death. At that time, the property transferred to Caleb Lenud, who was Guerry's nephew. The exact year is currently unknown. Guerry's will did not include his wife's name, and the 1790 US Census did not even count women. See "South Carolina, U.S., Wills and Probate Records, 1670–1980," database with images, *Ancestry*, https://www.ancestry.com.

23. See the series of *Winyah Intelligencer* newspapers in the Georgetown County Digital Library's Historical Newspaper Collections, beginning with the March 10, 1819, issue; http://www.gcdigital.org/digital/collection/p163901coll8.

24. Bernard Baruch began purchasing South Carolina estates in 1905. He agreed to sell five thousand acres to his eldest daughter, Belle, in 1935; by 1956, she owned all her father's Hobcaw holdings. Her death in 1964 precipitated the transfer of her property to the Belle W Baruch Foundation to protect and manage in perpetuity. See Miller, *Baroness of Hobcaw*. Friendfield Village is a former slave-dwelling community on Hobcaw property where several buildings still stand, including a church and a doctor's office. Many of the Baruch family's African-American employees continued to live in Friendfield Village until the 1950s, despite the absence of electricity and plumbing.

25. National Register of Historic Places Registration Form, submitted for Hobcaw Barony, September 19, 1994, 18.

26. Former staff member Lee Brockington, "African Americans at Hobcaw," file folder, currently held at Hobcaw Barony.

27. Richard Lancaster, the volunteer who assisted staff member Patricia Mishoe.

28. "US Census Records," database with images, *Ancestry*, https://www.ancestry library.com.

29. *Ancestry*'s transcription of the handwritten 1910 census was another obstacle. The transcriber misread the first letter as a "B" rather than an "L," recording her name as Baura Carr, rather than Laura Carr. See the "1910 United States Federal Census," database with images, *Ancestry*, https://www.ancestrylibrary.com.

30. See the South Carolina Historical Society and the South Carolina Department of Archives and History, https://www.schistory.org/archives; and https://www.scdah.sc.gov.

31. According to historian Mart A Stewart, enslaved laborers preparing an eighty-acre rice plantation worked "with shovels in ankle-deep mud and water [and] had to move well over thirty-nine thousand cubic yards of fine-grained river swamp muck to construct an eighty-acre plantation, in addition to clearing the land and leveling the ground in the fields." See Mart A Stewart, "Rice, Water, and Power: Landscapes of Domination and Resistance in the Lowcountry, 1790–1880," *Environmental History Review* 15, no 3 (1991): 47–64, especially 50.

32. This idea is most clearly explored in David Silkenat, *Scars on the Land: An Environmental History of Slavery* (Oxford, England: Oxford University Press, 2022); Erin Stewart Mauldin, *Unredeemed Land: An Environmental History of the Civil War and Emancipation in the Cotton South* (Oxford, England: Oxford University Press, 2018); and Stewart, "Rice, Water, and Power."

33. Pat Conroy, *Prince of Tides* (New York: Bantam Books, 1986), 1.

34. Langston Hughes, "Harlem," 1951 *Poetry Foundation*, https://www.poetryfoun dation.org/poems/46548/harlem.

35. James Baldwin, "A Talk to Teachers," *The Saturday Review*, December 21, 1963.

WORKS CITED

"1910 United States Federal Census." *Ancestry*. https://www.ancestrylibrary.com.

Baldwin, James. "A Talk to Teachers." *The Saturday Review*, December 21, 1963.

Ball, Charles. *Fifty Years in Chains: Or, the Life of an American Slave*. Chapel Hill: University of North Carolina Press, 2012.

Baruch, Belle. Last Will and Testament. 23 March 1964.

Battle, Mary. "Africans in Carolina." Lowcountry Digital History Initiative. Charleston, SC: College of Charleston. https://ldhi.library.cofc.edu.

"Between The Waters: Exploring Hobcaw Barony." SCETV. http://www.Between theWaters.org/.

Blight, David W. *Race and Reunion: The Civil War in American Memory*. Cambridge, MA: Belknap Press, 2001.

Bolick, Julian Stevenson. *Waccamaw Plantations*. Clinton, SC: Jacobs Press, 1946.

Brockington, Lee G. "African Americans at Hobcaw." Unpublished manuscript.

Brockington, Lee G. *Plantation Between the Waters: A Brief History of Hobcaw Barony*. Charleston, SC: The History Press, 2006.

Brooks, Christina. "Enclosing Their Immortal Souls: A Survey of Two African American Cemeteries in Georgetown, South Carolina." *Southeastern Archaeology* 30, no. 1 (2011): 176–186.

Brundage, W. Fitzhugh. *The Southern Past: A Clash of Race and Memory*. Cambridge, MA: Harvard University Press, 2005.

Carney, Judith A. *Black Rice: The African Origins of Rice Cultivation in America*. Cambridge, MA: Harvard University Press, 2001.

Cogdell, Charles. "Last Will and Testament. 1776. South Carolina County, District and Probate Courts, 1670–1980." Database with images. Ancestry. https://www .ancestry.com.

Conroy, Pat. *The Prince of Tides*. New York: Bantam Books, 1986.

Cox, Karen. *Dixie's Daughters: The United Daughters of the Confederacy and the Preservation of Confederate Culture*. Gainesville: University Press of Florida, 2003.

Dillian, Carolyn. "Holocene Sea Level Rise and Shell Midden Development and Destruction." Unpublished manuscript, 2019. Hobcaw Barony.

Douglass, Frederick. *Narrative of the Life of Frederick Douglass, an American Slave, Written by Himself*. New York: Bedford, 1845.

Douglass, Frederick. "Speech delivered in Madison Square, New York, Decoration Day." 1878. Washington, DC: Library of Congress, Manuscript Division.

Edgar, Walter. *South Carolina: A History*. Columbia: University of South Carolina Press, 1996.

Fisch, Audrey, ed. *The Cambridge Companion to The African American Slave Narrative*. Cambridge, MA: Cambridge University Press, 2007.

Foster, Gaines M. *Ghosts of the Confederacy: Defeat, the Lost Cause, and the Emergence of the New South, 1865 to 1913*. Oxford, England: Oxford University Press, 1987.

Guerry, Andrew Caleb. "Last Will and Testament." August 3, 1796. Database with images. *Ancestry*, https://www.ancestry.com.

Hanson, Lynn. "The Wealth of Information in Belle Baruch's Checkbooks." *Interdisciplinary Humanities* 36, no. 2 (2019): 21–53.

Hendricks, Christopher E. "The Multicultural Nature of Eighteenth-Century Cooking in British America: The Southern Rice Pie." In *Carolina Currents: Studies in South Carolina Culture*, vol. 1, "New Directions," edited by Christopher D. Johnson, 28–42. Columbia: University of South Carolina Press, 2024.

Howie, Elizabeth, and Melissa Hydock. "Art Historical Research on Works of Art in Hobcaw House." Unpublished manuscript, 2019, typescript.

Hughes, Langston. "Harlem." 1951. *Poetry Foundation.* https://www.poetryfoundation.org/poems/46548/harlem.

Jacobs, Harriet. *Incidents in the Life of a Slave Girl, Written by Herself.* 1861. Reprint. Cambridge, MA: Belknap Press, 2009.

Johnson, Heathley A. "Archaeology on the Widdicom Tract at Hobcaw Barony." *Legacy* 23, no. 2 (2019): 24–27.

Joyner, Charles. *Down by the Riverside: A South Carolina Slave Community.* [25th anniversary edition]. Champaign: University of Illinois Press, 2009.

Lesser, Charles H. "Lords Proprietors of Carolina." *South Carolina Encyclopedia.* https://www.scencyclopedia.org/sce/entries/lords-proprietors-of-Carolina.

Linder, Suzanne, and Marta Thacker. *Historical Atlas of the Rice Plantations of Georgetown County and the Santee River.* Columbia: South Carolina Department of Archives and History, 2001.

Littlefield, Daniel C. *Rice and Slaves: Ethnicity and the Slave Trade in Colonial South Carolina.* Champaign: University of Illinois Press, 1991.

"Maps Tracing the Formation of Counties." Columbia: South Carolina Department of Archives & History. https://www.archivesindex.sc.gov/guide/CountyRecords.

Mauldin, Erin Stewart. *Unredeemed Land: An Environmental History of the Civil War and Emancipation in the Cotton South.* Oxford, England: Oxford University Press, 2018.

McConnell, Thomas. "Bernard Baruch Library: An Annotated Bibliography" Unpublished manuscript, 2008 https://hobcawbarony.pastperfectonline.com/archive/EDEEF599-CAB0-4C28-9429-366406311966.

Michie, James L. "Search for San Miguel de Gualdape." 1991. Research Manuscript Series 1. Waccamaw Center for Historical and Cultural Studies. Conway, SC: Coastal Carolina University.

McIntyre, Justin. "Atlantic Slave Trade." Georgetown: South Carolina Maritime Museum. https://scmaritimemuseum.org.

Miles, Tiya. *All That She Carried: The Journey of Ashley's Sack, a Black Family Keepsake.* New York: Random House, 2021.

Miller, Mary. *Baroness of Hobcaw: The Life of Belle W. Baruch.* Columbia: University of South Carolina Press, 2006.

"Minutes: Belle W. Baruch Foundation Trustees Board Meeting." May 9, 2011. Hobcaw Barony. https://hobcawbarony.pastperfectonline.com/archive/21C78BF3-815A-44F3-947A-275646634220.

Moon, Cameron. "Timber-Framed Dwellings of the Enslaved and Freedmen in the South Carolina Lowcountry: Continuities and Innovations in Building Practices and Housing Standards." *Buildings & Landscapes: Journal of the Vernacular Architecture Forum* 28, no. 1 (2021): 9–131.

National Register of Historic Places Registration Form, submitted for Hobcaw Barony, September 19, 1994.

Navin, John. *The Grim Years: Settling South Carolina, 1670–1720.* Columbia: University of South Carolina Press, 2019.

Silkenat, David. *Scars on the Land: An Environmental History of Slavery.* Oxford, England: Oxford University Press, 2022.

Steadman, Allison. "An Inventory and Archive of Garments Removed from Belle Baruch's Basement." Unpublished manuscript, 2019. Hobcaw Barony.

Stewart, Mart A. "Rice, Water, and Power: Landscapes of Domination and Resistance in the Lowcountry, 1790–1880." *Environmental History Review* 15, no. 3 (1991): 47–64.

Swanson, Drew. *Remaking Wormsloe Plantation: The Environmental History of a Lowcountry Landscape*. Athens: University of Georgia Press, 2012.

"Ten Dollars Reward." *Winyah Intelligencer.* March 10, 1819, 5.

"United States Federal Census." Database with images. *FamilySearch*. http://familysearch.org.

Ward, James Liphus. "Back to the Land, Back to its People: A Strategic Response to Researching the Cultural Landscape at Hobcaw Barony." Unpublished manuscript, 2015. Hobcaw Barony. https://hobcawbarony.pastperfectonline.com/archive/51B83865-C879-4459-9150-112329083656.

Sight, Symmetry, and the Plantation Ballad

Caroline Howard Gilman and the Nineteenth-Century Construction of South Carolina

Michael S. Martin

Charleston, South Carolina, as one of the largest cities in the nascent United States, a major port for slave trading, and a southern destination spot for American and world travelers, surely loomed large in the nineteenth-century cultural imagination. In William Faden's 1780 map, Charleston is surrounded by wide-open spaces both north and south of the harbor. The southern border showcases James and Johns Islands and is surrounded by wavy, dark lines indicative of marshlands.[1] This early, postrevolution image emphasizes the harbor, too, with quadrant points indicating westward movement into the meandering harbor. Perhaps in adherence to Jeffersonian notions of sequestered natural spaces, the city is surrounded by large tracts of undisturbed land, suitable for lowland farming.

An 1844 map of the city by Charleston engraver William Keenan reveals another Jeffersonian design, this one centered on rectangle and quadrangle city divisions based on the even demarcation of space.[2] The design aesthetic reveals order, with roughly even sections of space across horizontal and vertical lines associated with prominent Charleston roadways and neighborhoods, including Cannons Borough in the central part of the map, adjacent to the Ashley River, which forms the southern border with the nearly peninsular city. The same impulse to partition, recreate, and memorialize Charleston and, on a larger level, the state of South Carolina, exists within early southern writings, too, particularly within travelogues, nonfiction writings, and sketches. Although Charleston itself was in flux as a major, expanding southern port city, its projection both in maps in literary texts, such as those by Caroline Howard Gilman, suggest a cultivated, symmetrical, and ordered environment. Gilman uses various aesthetic elements to affect this stasis, including Romantic recreations of the coastline and historic downtown, as well as naturalist depictions that provide early insight into southern lowlands ecology. In doing so, she also normalizes South Carolina's rigid social hierarchies and becomes an unexpected defender of enslavement.

Gilman is the rare, antebellum female sketch and regional writer who was based south of the Mason-Dixon line. Originally from Massachusetts, she became fully invested in southern culture and identified as a Charlestonian after moving to South Carolina in 1819 with her husband, a Unitarian minister. Recent scholarship on her has not been abundant, although her racial beliefs have been a topic of interest in some journal articles.[3] Others have framed Gilman's writing as part of the larger, national impulse in the nineteenth century for travel into the Appalachian highlands.[4] According to Jan Bakker, "her literary fame was [from] the nationwide dissemination of her popular young people's magazines printed in Charleston from 1832 to 1839."[5] She maintained some connections with New England, though, as we see in her repeated quotations from the early Boston children's author, Anna Maria Wells. Gilman worked not only in children's literature but also in domestic fiction, with two published novels, *Recollections of a Northern Housekeeper* (1834) *and Recollections of a Southern Matron* (1835), on semi-autobiographical family life in New England and then Charleston, respectively. She is a somewhat forgotten and rarely anthologized, but nonetheless important, figure in antebellum, southern letters. Her most enduring work may be her travelogue, *The Poetry of Travelling in the United States* (1838), a series of sketches, collective writings, and epistles that showcases her synthesis of British poetic conventions, including metrical forms, thematically framed within a "discoverable" New World landscape and local southern idiom. The book contains picturesque travel stories from her group ventures into southern and northern highlands and points of interest, includes poetry and letters from other authors, and mixes prose depictions of towns and picturesque landscapes and buildings, most notably, St. Michael's Cathedral in Charleston, with Romantic poetic accompaniments of such places.

Gilman acknowledges New England letters and emphasizes northern travel within her works, including a section of *The Poetry of Travelling in the United States* titled "Notes on a Northern Excursion," which takes the narrator to Niagara Falls, Trenton Falls (New York), and elsewhere. Yet she clearly envisions herself as an editor and contributor to southern letters and its nascent literature, and Charleston is always present in her imagination. Even the postscript to "Notes on a Northern Excursion" begins and ends with a shifting vision of Charleston. The city is either coming into focus or receding out of her line of vision, as she composes from the perspective of standing on a boat deck. Within *The Poetry of Travelling in the United States*, Gilman also serves as editor for a series of War of 1812–era letters composed by the "young, beautiful widow" and Charlestonian Eliza Wilkinson.[6] Moreover, she repeatedly references William Gilmore Simms, perhaps the most preeminent southern fiction writer in the first half of the nineteenth century, with hagiography bordering on adulation. Her assimilation into southern culture is completed by her sketch and poetic recollections of both the Revolutionary War and the War of 1812, which she offers from a distinctly southern, Charlestonian perspective. As with the Wilkinson letters, she views herself as a sort of translator of southern customs for antebellum, cosmopolitan reading audiences, regardless of their regional affiliation.

Moreover, much like the Faden and Keenan maps of the antebellum city, Gilman centers her axis of vision upon Charleston—its church spires, rivers, and social fabric. Although Charleston was a dynamic, growing city, full of new immigrants and deeply involved in the brutal business of the enslavement, for Gilman, it becomes a place of peace and stasis, a sort of welcoming oasis. At the end of "Notes of a Northern Excursion," as Gilman recalls her return passage from Norfolk via boat, she espies from "a distance, St. Michael's spire," an object that takes on a domestic affiliation for her, as it generates "tender thoughts of home."[7] She extends the domestic association through verse: "When, returning to our land,/This summer exile nears his home."[8] More important, the vision of the spire, which becomes representative of the city as whole, inspires a sort of conceptual ordering for Gilman:

> *Symmetric* spire! Our city's boast,
> In scientific grandeur piled!
> The guardian beacon of our coast,
> The seaman's hoe when waves are wild.[9]

In this portion of the narrative, the stability of the spire counters Gilman's constant movement as she travels through northern and southern climes, a dynamic she emphasizes in the poem's opening lines:

> Over the winds and waves, far out
> From the shadows of the shore,
> I see the mariner's beacon
> Its silvery splendor pour.[10]

Charleston, recreated by moonlight and from the moving perspective of a boat deck as the solitary traveler looks "Over the winds and waves," becomes a welcome place of stability. The static object, lying in "silverly splendor" on Charleston's shoreline, establishes both the spatial order of land meeting ocean and that of the personal—an extension of domestic, familiar space.

The dramatic return to Charleston then transitions to "Notes of a Southern Section," with a prose opening and subsequent poetic interludes. Gilman's discussions of her time in Charleston combine to form the most prolonged, single-stay recounting of *The Poetry of Travelling the United States*. The relative stasis that follows her return voyage is somewhat jarring compared with the preceding "quick-cut" travel accounts and cultural studies of life and customs in Northern climes, whether of Burlington, Vermont, or of Salem, Massachusetts. At this point, while centering her axis of vision in and around Charleston, she extends her vision outward to domestic, plantation spaces as if they were branch tendrils. The stasis of location continues until Gilman introduces other southern travel narratives and poems, including one from the New England writer Anna Maria Wells, who recounts a coach trip from "Charleston to Columbia."[11] At this point, the travelogue once again becomes a series of mini-sketches, most notably of the Appalachian Mountains and their springs, and caves.

Gilman and Southern Cultural Symmetry

Gilman's axis of vision, Charleston, centers her world, which is extended in a gentrified, conditioned way throughout her nonfiction and fiction. From a modern perspective, Gilman comes across as a racial apologist. Part of the stasis that she celebrates in Charleston and the surrounding area is from enslaved people remaining obedient and not disrupting the existing systems of racial servitude. In Gilman's world, enslaved people or "servants"— a comfortable euphemism of racial hierarchies commonly used in the first half of the nineteenth century—know their place. For example, in *Recollections of a Southern Matron*, Jacque, the "young master's" slave, is temporarily given rein over the plantation on the shores of the Ashley River outside of Charleston.[12] Notably, Jacque uses his moment of authority to maintain the southern racial social order. In this way, he is the opposite of Grandison in Charles Chesnutt's titular North Carolina story and will never "ascend the hall stairs" when white visitors enter the family plantation home.[13] Even Gilman's poetry romanticizes and thus supports the racial social order. For example, she laments the death of white children in a heavily sentimental tone but ignores the suffering of enslaved children.[14] The "order" here is suggestive of an invisible and visible social world, separated by race and class, that shapes antebellum Charleston and the South in general. Gilman is content as long as this social order is maintained and is part of her "symmetrical" vision of Charleston overall.

Gilman's sense of "order" extends from southern social and labor roles into other areas, including the natural world and its spatial demarcations. A cartographic illustration may be helpful here. The center of Keenan's 1844 Charleston map features clear spatial divisions between genteel, manicured riverside neighborhoods adjacent to a small pond ("Mill Pond"). North of this pond is a public square—perfectly shaped and partitioned—nearly adjacent to the southern border of the Cooper River and, tellingly, marshland, indicated by dark, squiggly lines. The low-country marshes and ecosystem are divided from, and separated by, ideological projections of cultural and urban planning. Gilman articulates a similarly ordered vision for waterways, predominant landscapes, and architectural markers, such as St. Michael's Cathedral. These perspectives are taken both from miniature and panoramic perspectives, varying between daytime and by moonlight. She alternates, for instance, between poetry and prose in recreating a nighttime scene in Charleston, this time at Grace Church: "[T]here is a supernatural brightness in the stars, gemming their far and wide canopy; and the waters, tinged by moonbeams, seem like deathly upturned faces."[15] At times, Gilman almost simultaneously, through aesthetic and affective conventions, positions the stasis of Charleston and her axis of vision with some degree of changeability, adding dramatic conflict in the process.

At the same time that Gilman uses her imaginative depictions of people and places to defend the practice of slavery, she also works to define Charleston—and, by extension, South Carolina and its neighboring states—as part of a vital, patriotic, and united nation. She does so largely by looking backward through the lenses of history and cultural memory. Much of the extended Charleston section of "Notes of a Southern Excursion" centers on history, particularly through heroic stories from the War of 1812. In the poem "Mary Anna Gibbes," Gilman introduces a female heroine who saves "Colonel Fenwick," while another poem, "Hurrah for Sullivan's Isle," serves as a patriotic ode to that battle similar to Alfred Tennyson's "Charge of the Light Brigade."[16] Later, Gilman references a gift vase that features a patriotic ode ("Hail, our country's natal morn,/Hail, our spreading kindred-born!" is the first couplet) on one side, with an accompanying, patriotic inscription dedicated for the "4th of July" on the other.[17] Collectively, these reminiscences of the past elide the fact that, in the 1830s, Charleston was in the middle of a moral and cultural battle that would quickly lead the nation into the

Civil War. Recounting a time when Charlestonians helped defeat an external threat, Gilman diverts attention away from the internal forces that were dividing the nation and would soon erupt into open battle. Just as her celebratory depictions of enslaved people, such as Jacque, mask the horrors of chattel slavery, so too does her historical vision hide the gruesome realities that surround her.

Charleston is the center of Gilman's imagined South, but it is not her only point of focus. She extends her exploration of geographic and cultural stasis outward to the southern plantation, which becomes, unsurprisingly, a place of domestic harmony, not brutal oppression. Michael O'Brien, writing on intellectual life in antebellum southern culture, contends that Gilman, "writing very much as a mother," uses the plantation trope as a didactic, learning device.[18] In making his argument, O'Brien references Gilman's seven children and her background in children's periodicals. He also cites *Recollections of a Southern Matron*, where Gilman's narrator imagines a plantation working as a school.[19] The lessons of that school, one discovers, reinforced the rigid social structures Gilman consistently defends. At the beginning of *Recollections of a Southern Matron*, for example, she offers a vivid description of wholesome childhood memories that effectively erase the exploitation of enslaved African Americans. Speaking through an imagined character, Gilman states:

> I write in my paternal mansion. The Ashley, with a graceful sweep, glitters like a lake before me, reflecting the sky and the bending foliage. Occasionally a flat, with its sluggish motion, or a boat, with its urging sail, passes along, and the woods echo to the song or the horn of the negro, waking up life in the solitude. The avenue of noble oaks, under which I sported in childhood, still spread their strong arms, and rustle in the passing breeze. My children are frolicking on the lawn where my first footsteps were watched by tender parents, and one of those parents rests beneath yonder circling cedars. Change! Sameness! What a perpetual chime those words ring on the ear of memory![20]

The quasi-fictitious narrator composes this family drama as if the central vision begins at the "paternal mansion" and extends outward. Social order is referenced with "the negro" who lives on the outskirts of the antebellum mansion, whereas natural order is suggested by the oak alley, providing aesthetic effect and practical shade, in front of the plantation home. These spatial partitions separate the "paternal mansion" from the surrounding marshlands and undeveloped plots of land. The idyllic scene also reinforces and normalizes the rigid gender and racial hierarchies of southern culture. We notice, for example, that the "negro" becomes a part of the natural world, his song announcing daybreak and "waking up" the world around him. The reader experiences him through his song and his horn, not his forced labor, suggesting that he, like Jacque, joyfully participates in the social order that deprives him of liberty. Social order and aesthetic symmetry seem to be intertwined in Gilman's gaze. Similarly, the female narrator focuses her attention, again willingly and without question, on the domestic concerns of child raising. For her, the boats along the Ashley River serve as aesthetic decorations rather than instruments of trade. The historian Steven M. Stowe contends that separate spheres existed by sex in the antebellum South: "Culture appeared as Nature; thus the social arrangements based on the belief in separate spheres—the division of labor, intense same-sex friendships, political activity for men, domestic authority for women—seemed not only orderly and rich but also unlikely to be altered."[21] Gilman showcases "domestic authority" through identification with the paternal mansion as an avatar for the genteel South, the space where parlor entertainment and other bourgeoisie "social arrangements," as portrayed in her fiction and nonfiction, occur and are celebrated. Stowe's point here, though, emphasizes the separate spheres for the sexes and, later, visible social orders, "hierarchical" in their nature, that counter invisible ones.[22] The patrilineal plantation estate, a site that serves as the starting point for Gilman's angle of vision, extending outward, portrays such an invisible social order and visible natural order.

Elsewhere in "Notes on a Southern Excursion," Gilman composes a ballad, "The Plantation on Ashley River."[23] The piece alludes to a genre of antebellum southern writing that I would term the "plantation tradition" in ballad poetry. In its uncritical celebration of social stratification, plantation ballad poetry hearkens to depictions of a reconstructed South in both postbellum writings and the midcentury works of Joel Chandler Harris, John Pendleton Kennedy, and others.[24] The well-read Gilman, part of both northern and southern literati, seems aware of these southern traditions or is at least hearkening toward them, albeit not fully in the way that southern historical reconstructionists significantly and anachronistically posit antebellum southern memory. Gilman's ideology here, centered on the War of 1812, suggests that postbellum notions of a romanticized pre–Civil War Southern past had earlier precursors. Gilman's ballad begins with a welcoming quatrain that contrasts urban hurriedness with rural tranquility:

Farewell, awhile, the city's hum,
Where busy footsteps fall,
And welcome to my weary eye
The Planter's friendly Hall.[25]

The subsequent stanzas include rich, emblazoned lists, similar to those in Walt Whitman's poetry, of peoples and forms of labor throughout the greater Charleston area. Her poetic eye scans the city and perceives "the dairy on the stream," "the poulterer" watching over his "charge," "the nurse" practicing her "skill," and the "Negro labourer" outside his "humble hut."[26] Juxtaposing the social and ecological, Gilman's gaze normalizes as part of the natural order the division of labor and even the economic exploitation of the Black laborer, who lives in a "humble hut" rather than a proper house. In some ways, her treatment of nature and society connects her to earlier writers, such as William Bartram, J. Hector St. John de Crèvecoeur, and Thomas Jefferson. Pamela Regis argues that these "eighteenth-century thinker[s]" understood "science" as one, large conglomerate, not separate epistemologies for differing phenomena studies."[27] Like Gilman, they found that the social reflected the natural and that natural order, in turn, justified the social order. A twenty-first-century perspective would surely separate the two realms: Only the most strident racist would defend racial injustice as a "natural" phenomenon. Gilman, however, gleefully conflates them. In both her study of Charlestonian labor and her systematizing of southern ecologies, the reader finds that one and the same idea is in play.

Natural Tableaus, the Charleston Landscape, and Orderly Nature

Although Gilman envisions herself as a cataloguer of nature, eighteenth-century notions of natural history only go so far for contextualizing Gilman's early nineteenth-century nonfiction sketches, poetry, and fiction writings. "Order" could also be considered in terms of aesthetics and design principles, and the categories of thinking that inform literary portrayals of naturescapes, countrysides, and the celestial bodies. Order is invariably conceptual in its schema, as with the extended domestic world that Gilman envisions spreading from Charleston outward or the blend of social relations, both visibly and invisibly hierarchical in makeup, that her poetic eye scans and catalogues. Both her prose and poetic renderings of Charleston and, more broadly speaking, southern locales, naturalistic or otherwise, are done within the genre of travel writing. Markus Heidde argues that, despite the "supposedly descriptive quality of travel writing and its documentary style," the genre is marked by "imaginary elements [that] . . . involve the invention of other cultures, societies, peoples, communities, and landscapes."[28] These "imaginary elements" for Gilman include an intermingling of the documentary style of the travel genre within Romantic aesthetic conventions. Literary portrayals of the natural world in antebellum thinking, whether on northern or southern locales, were often marked with the same tension that Heidde identifies between ideological poles: "the dichotomy of civilization and wilderness merged into American pre-national mythology."[29] Gilman sought such a division conceptually, though the slippage between genteel Charleston culture and the natural persists in her writings.

In her antebellum travel writings, Gilman emphasizes entertaining scenes and quick visits within her city. Like other southern travel writers, except perhaps William Bartram, she does not fastidiously catalog the local ecology. Moreover, Gilman wrote during the interlude of Enlightenment rationalism and Romanticism; her portrayal of the natural world synonymously reveals orderly conventions reminiscent of Jefferson's grid design in mapmaking *and* the solitary figure immersed in a general, imaginative naturescape usually associated with the Romantic ego. In general, Romantic poetry rarely documents particular ecologies. William Wordsworth's "Ode: Intimations of Immortality from Recollections of Early Childhood," for example, teaches us little about the flora and fauna of the English Lake District.[30] The same could be said of William Cullen Bryant's poetry and the Boston countryside. In each case, the natural world provided inspiration and metaphor, not a subject to be studied for its own sake. Nature poetry was not really about nature *qua* the natural world. Southern antebellum poets, as Joesph M. Flora demonstrates, seemed even less interested in the natural world than their New England counterparts.[31] For these writers, nature became a commodity, something to be developed through labor and capital or consumed for sporting pleasure. Strangely, in her poetry, though, Gilman *does* document the natural world of coastal South Carolina without much affectation or allegorizing. If northern poets, such as Philip Freneau, discovered beauty in nature, southern poets found opportunity.

Unlike her southern peers, Gilman focuses her nature poetry on the aesthetics shaped by British Romanticism. In this way, her poetry is thematically similar to that of her northern contemporaries, as we see in "A Southern Scene," "The Crow-Minder," and the aforementioned "Ashley River," all of which appeared within "Notes of a Southern Excursion."[32] Here, the reader finds Romantic tropes, such as the solitary figure in nature

("The Crow-Minder") and Wordsworthian childhood recollections occasioned by a specific locale ("A Southern Scene"). Even in urban poems, such as "She sleeps," which apostrophizes Charleston, Gilman offers a nocturnal catalogue envisioning everything from a "fond mother" sleeping "o'er her infant child" to an "old man" sleeping "through dreamless hours," all of which evoke the powerful sentimental feelings of Romantic poetry.[33]

Still, Gilman's poetic southern tableaus have a distinctly naturalist tendency that is not often found in Romantic poetry. For example, in the Ashley River plantation poem, after the initial garden lane opening scene, Gilman provides a brief compendia of southern flora and fauna, beginning with the "Cedar's gloom" and shifting into other tree species: the "rich Magnolia," the "Hickory bough," the "Holly, with its polish'd leaves," and the "broad oak's shade."[34] Similarly, "The Crow-Minder of the South," which is ostensibly about a Romantic, solitary figure watching over the fields, also reads like a veritable natural history of low-country, Southern ecology. Once again, a natural compendium of plants and animals is listed, from nearly half a dozen bird species (the "Mocking bird," the "Oriole," the "Goldfinch, Waxbird," the Turtle Dove, the "Blue Jay," and the Woodpecker," among others).[35] Other animal species, from the "Lizard" to the "Butterfly" to the "Frog," are included in sustained re-creations of landscape types, including "forest trees" and "damp brakes," perhaps of the Laurel variety.[36] This naturalist bent belies the Romantic ethos that frames the poem. Nature is not nondescript but instead catalogued with relative fastidiousness. On the level of aesthetic principle, Gilman consciously orders her poetry around Romantic conventions, only for a classificatory system more befitting a naturalist to emerge.

Gilman's primary focus, however, remains on her characters and how they respond to the natural world. In "The Crow-Minder of the South," Gilman utilizes a Romantic ordering device, one where the solitary figure in nature "feels a present Deity" within the natural surroundings, in this case, among the South Carolina fields.[37] Although she is ostensibly cataloguing a solitary figure in nature, Gilman simultaneously reinscribes social hierarchy. The farm laborer does not toil to earn his pay but rather remains "idly busy."[38] Reducing the hard work of agriculture to something closer to a hobby, Gilman suggests that worker is as happy in his occupation as she is in hers. The social structures that force him to work and allow her to write become normalized. Each reflects natural design, and each serves individuals equally well. In more subtle ways, Gilman also reinforces racial hierarchies that, she suggests, are not only natural but also benevolent. The poem's protagonist, referred to pejoratively as the "boy," passes by and may even "share" some "plain food" with the "dark laborer" with whom he briefly socializes.[39] With this pastoral description, Gilman effectively erases the violence of enslavement, as the two figures become companions rather than adversaries. She also ascribes generosity to the white laborer who, in sharing his food, becomes a provider rather than an oppressor.

Natural "order," in Gilman's writing is tinged both with Romantic aesthetics and Enlightenment philosophy, both imaginatively recreated within southern ecological and social systems. Gilman recreates her northern identity into a distinctly southern one throughout *The Poetry of Travelling the United States*. She was clearly conversant in antebellum southern letters and its literary preoccupations, and she wanted to participate in a conversation initiated by other writers. More important, Gilman's desire for literary and conceptual order, with Charleston serving as the nexus for an extended, domestic worldview, is linked to larger sociopolitical upheaval

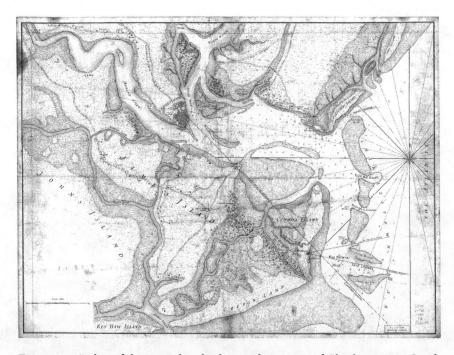

Figure 5.1. A plan of the town, bar, harbor, and environs of Charlestown in South Carolina: with all the channels, soundings, sailing-marks &c. from the surveys made in the colony, by William Faden, ca. 1780. Library of Congress, Geography and Map Division.

Figure 5.2. Plan of the city and neck of Charleston, SC, engraved by William Keenan, 1844. David Rumsey Map Collection, David Rumsey Map Center, Stanford Libraries.

in the antebellum South. In addition to the intractable issue of slavery, the nineteenth-century South was, as historian Peter W. Bardaglio argues, going through "profound social change" linked to "the rise of the cotton kingdom" and "the first stirrings of industrialization and urbanization."[40] Bardaglio argues that such cultural upheaval led to "new channels of legal control over family norms and behaviors," so much so that they "severely disrupted the traditional structure of power in the households and larger society of the South."[41] Gilman envisioned herself as more than a cataloguer of the South. She was immersed in Charleston culture and the southern economy through her husband and surely was aware of such nascent cultural upheaval. Her desire to discover (in actuality, create) social and natural order, or the surety of particular aesthetic designs, is assuredly a reaction to such economic and cultural changes. She tries to ground herself within such a shifting world by making recourse to historical dimensions that define and illustrate the South. Her imagined southern plantation, with its picturesque oak alleys, orderly gardens, and content slaves might be a natural reaction to such external "stirrings."

Michael S. Martin is associate professor of English at Nicholls State University. Martin specializes in nineteenth-century American literature. He has recently published *Appalachian Pastoral: Mountain Excursions, Aesthetic Visions, and the Antebellum Travel Narrative* (Clemson University Press). His essays have appeared in *A Journal of Melville Criticism, The Nathaniel Hawthorne Review, Postmodern Culture,* and *Studies in American Indian Literature.*

NOTES

1. See Figure 5.1, William Faden, A plan of the town, bar, harbor, and environs of Charleston in South Carolina.
2. See Figure 5.2, William Keenan, Plan of the City and Neck of Charleston, SC.
3. See, for example, Jan Bakker, "Another Dilemma of an Intellectual in the Old South: Caroline Gilman, the Peculiar Institution, and Greater Rights for Women in the Rose Magazines," *The Southern Literary Journal* 17, no. 1 (1984): 12–25; and Calvin Schermerhorn, "Arguing Slavery's Narrative: Southern Regionalists, Ex-Slave Autobiographers, and the Contested Literary Representations of the Peculiar Institution, 1824–1849," *Journal of American Studies* 46, no. 4 (2012): 1009–33.
4. See my chapter "'The beautiful of the awe and sublime': Appalachia's New Testing Ground for Burke's Conceit" in Michael S. Martin, *Appalachian Pastoral: Mountain Excursions, Aesthetic Visions, and the Antebellum Travel Narrative* (Clemson, SC: Clemson University Press, 2022), 105–30.
5. Bakker, "Another Dilemma," 12.
6. Caroline Howard Gilman, "Preface," in *Poetry of Travelling in the United States* (New York: Scatcherd and Adams, 1838; reprint, London: Forgotten Books, 2018), v.
7. Gilman, "Notes of a Northern Excursion," in *Poetry of Travelling,* 206.

8. Gilman, "Notes of a Northern Excursion,"207, lines 37–40.

9. Gilman, "Notes of a Northern Excursion," 206, lines 13–16; emphasis added.

10. Gilman, "Notes of a Northern Excursion," 206, lines 1–4.

11. Gilman, "Notes of a Northern Excursion," 327.

12. Caroline Howard Gilman, *Recollections of a Southern Matron* (New York: Harber, 1838; transcribed 1998, Archive.org; https://docsouth.unc.edu/fpn/gilman/gilman.html), 11, 9.

13. Gilman, *Recollections*, 11. Charles W. Chesnutt's satirical short story "The Passing of Grandison" was published in *The Wife of His Youth and Other Stories of the Color-Line* (New York: Houghton, Mifflin, 1899), 168–202. For a helpful discussion of the story and its depictions of race, see Delmar, "Mask."

14. See, for example, lines such as "I kissed his pale and suffering brow" in Gilman, "The Overseer's Children," in *Poetry of Travelling*, 231.

15. Gilman, *Poetry of Travelling*, 248.

16. Tennyson's famous 1854 poem recounts an encounter of British light cavalry and Russian military forces in the Crimean War. See Alfred, Lord Tennyson, *Poems*, edited by Hallam Lord Tennyson, 2nd ed., Vol. 2, 225–226 (London: Macmillan Publishing, 1908), 369.

17. Gilman, *Poetry of Travelling*, 216–17.

18. Michael O'Brien, *Conjectures of Order: Intellectual Life and the American South, 1810–1860* (Chapel Hill: University of North Carolina Press, 2004), 766.

19. O'Brien, *Conjectures of Order*, 766. See especially Chapter VI, "Parental Teaching," of *Recollections of a Southern Matron*: "One would suppose that the retirement of a plantation was the most appropriate spot for a mother and her children to give and receive instruction," 47.

20. Gilman, *Recollections*, 10, 11.

21. Stephen C. Stowe, "City, Country and the Feminine Voice." In *Intellectual Life in Antebellum Charleston*, edited by Michael O'Brien, et al. (Knoxville: University of Tennessee Press, 1998) 296.

22. Stowe, "City, Country," 296–97.

23. Gilman, *Poetry of Travelling*, 222.

24. See, for example, Joel Chandler Harris's infamous Tar Baby plotline in his *Uncle Remus* stories (1881). For a secondary source study of this Southern literature, see Nicholas Cords and Patrick Gerster, *Myth and Southern History*, Vol. 5: *The New South* (Champaign: University of Illinois Press, 1989).

25. Gilman, *Poetry of Travelling*, 223, lines 1–4.

26. Gilman, *Poetry of Travelling*, 225–26, lines 42, 50, 58, 54.

27. Pamela Regis, *Describing Early America: Bartram, Jefferson, Crèvecoeur and The Rhetoric of Natural History* (DeKalb: Northern Illinois University Press, 1992), xi.

28. Marcus Heide, *Framing the Nation, Claiming the Hemisphere: Transnational Imagination in Early American Travel Writing (1770–1830)*, Vol. 4: Stockholm English Series (Stockholm, Sweden: Stockholm University Press, 2022), 36, emphasis added.

29. Heide, *Framing the Nation*, 37.

30. Wordsworth, "Intimations of Immortality from Recollections of Early Childhood," Poetry Foundation, https://www.poetryfoundation.org/poems/45536/.

31. See Joseph F. Flora, "Nature," in *The Companion to Southern Literature*, edited by Joseph F. Flora et al., 530–35 (Baton Rouge: Louisiana State Press, 2002), 530–35.

32. Gilman, *Poetry of Travelling*, 217–219, 232.

33. Gilman, "She Sleeps," in *Poetry of Travelling*, 248, lines 3, 20.

34. Gilman, "The Plantation on the Ashley River," in *Poetry of Travelling*, 225, lines 16, 18, 26, 30.

35. Gilman, "The Crow Minder of the South," in *Poetry of Travelling*, 218, lines 7, 19, 24, 30, and 31. Gilman includes vivid descriptions of birds elsewhere as well. In multiple instances, throughout "Notes of a Southern Excursion," she recalls the sound of the "merry mock-bird" echoing through the "winding lane," or perhaps oak alley, that surrounds her Ashley River plantation. See Gilman, "Southern Scene," in *Poetry of Travelling*, 233, line 38. In "The Crow-Minder," the poet recounts that "The Mocking bird" serves as a "partner of [the laborer's] walk," leaving a brief "orchestral tone" in Romantic cadences at "the midnight hour" See Gilman, "The Crow-Minder," in *Poetry of Travelling*, 218, lines 7, 11, and 12. These references not only capture the richness of her ecosystem but also connect her to other Southern writers. Flora notes, "In place of the English nightingale, Southern poets specialized in descriptions of the mockingbird." See Gilman, "Nature" in *Poetry of Travelling*, 532.

36. Gilman, *Poetry of Travelling*, 218, lines 29, 39.

37. Gilman, *Poetry of Travelling*, 66.

38. Gilman, *Poetry of Travelling*, 55.

39. Gilman, *Poetry of Travelling*, 58, 67.

40. Peter Bardaglio, *Reconstructing the Household: Families, Sex, and the Law in the Nineteenth-Century South* (Chapel Hill: University of North Carolina Press, 1998), xv.

41. Bardaglio, *Reconstructing the Household*, xv.

WORKS CITED

Bakker, Jan. "Another Dilemma of an Intellectual in the Old South: Caroline Gilman, the Peculiar Institution, and Greater Rights for Women in the Rose Magazines." *The Southern Literary Journal* 17, no. 1 (1984): 12–25.

Bardaglio, Peter. *Reconstructing the Household: Families, Sex, and the Law in the Nineteenth-Century South*. Chapel Hill: University of North Carolina Press, 1998.

Chesnutt, Charles W. "The Passing of Grandison." In *The Wife of His Youth and Other Stories of the Color-Line*, 168–202. New York: Houghton, Mifflin, 1899.

Cords, Nicholas, and Patrick Gerster. *Myth and Southern History*. Vol. 5: *The New South*. Champaign: University of Illinois Press, 1989.

Delmar, Jay P. "The Mask as Theme and Structure: Charles W. Chesnutt's 'The Sheriff's Children' and 'The Passing of Grandison.'" *American Literature* 51, no. 3 (1979): 364–75.

Flora, Joseph F. "Nature." In *The Companion to Southern Literature,* edited by Joseph F. Flora, et al., 530–35. Baton Rouge: Louisiana State Press, 2002.

Gilman, Caroline Howard. *The Poetry of Travelling in the United States.* New York: Scatcherd and Adams, 1838. Reprint. London: Forgotten Books, 2018.

Gilman, Caroline Howard. *Recollections of a Southern Matron.* New York: Harber, 1838. Transcribed 1998. Archive.org. https://docsouth.unc.edu/fpn/gilman/gilman.html.

Heide, Marcus. *Framing the Nation, Claiming the Hemisphere: Transnational Imagination in Early American Travel Writing (1770–1830).* Vol. 4: Stockholm English Series. Stockholm, Sweden: Stockholm University Press, 2022.

Martin, Michael S. *Appalachian Pastoral: Mountain Excursions, Aesthetic Visions, and the Antebellum Travel Narrative.* Clemson, SC: Clemson University Press, 2022.

O'Brien, Michael. *Conjectures of Order: Intellectual Life and the American South, 1810–1860.* Chapel Hill: University of North Carolina Press, 2004.

Regis, Pamela. *Describing Early America: Bartram, Jefferson, Crèvecoeur and The Rhetoric of Natural History.* DeKalb: Northern Illinois University Press, 1992.

Schermerhorn, Calvin. "Arguing Slavery's Narrative: Southern Regionalists, Ex-Slave Autobiographers, and the Contested Literary Representations of the Peculiar Institution, 1824–1849." *Journal of American Studies* 46, no. 4 (2012): 1009–33.

Stowe, Steven C. "City, Country and the Feminine Voice." In *Intellectual Life in Antebellum Charleston,* edited by Michael O'Brien, et al., 295–324. Knoxville: University of Tennessee Press, 1998.

Tennyson, Alfred, Lord. "The Charge of the Light Brigade." In *Alfred Lord Tennyson, Poems,* edited by Hallam, Lord Tennyson, 2nd ed., Vol. 2, 225–226. London: Macmillan Publishing, 1908.

Wordsworth, William. "Intimations of Immortality from Recollections of Early Childhood," Poetry Foundation. https://www.poetryfoundation.org/poems/45536/.

Putting John Calhoun to Rest

The Northern Imagination and Experience of a Charleston Slave Mart

Michael Emett

"If it had not been for Mr. Beecher, there would have been no *Oceanus* voyage," claimed Stephen M. Griswold, a Brooklyn jeweler and congregant of the Plymouth Church.[1] Writing about the expedition of northerners aboard the steamer *Oceanus* in April 1865 to attend the return of the American flag to Fort Sumter, Griswold admitted that it was the appointment of Reverend Henry Ward Beecher as the event's keynote speaker that led him and at least one hundred eighty people to head to Charleston.[2] The *Oceanus* travelers constituted only a fraction of the approximately three thousand people who filled the ruined fort to celebrate the flag re-raising.[3] Their experiences, however, illuminate the northerners' experience in the "cradle of secession" immediately after the Civil War. Visiting Charleston made the imagined institution of slavery tangible, even visceral. Using the "History of Experience" approach developed by Robert Boddice and Mark M. Smith, in this essay, I seek to recreate the sensory experiences of the *Oceanus* passengers as they traveled through war-ravaged Charleston and visited the grave of John C. Calhoun, which some of the travelers defaced.

The History of Experiences approach allows us to weave together the senses and emotions with other facets of historical investigation, including material culture, gender, intellectual and political issues, animal history, and foodstuff. This approach treats historical actors in their own terms and contexts, refraining from presentism epistemologies that impose modern values and sensibilities on past events. Boddice and Smith, scholars of emotions and the senses, respectively, remind us that historical actors are "biocultural historical artifacts" situated in lived experiences, which we should reconstruct as contextually as possible. Analyzing the emotions and senses as these actors understood them becomes the foundation for fleshing out what particular experiences meant to the people who were present.[4]

When the passengers of the *Oceanus* arrived in Charleston, they experienced a city undergoing a remarkable transformation as the enslaved Black people became free and the wealthy white citizens became impoverished.

Slavery was officially gone, but its vestiges remained. For many of these travelers, who were essentially tourists, these remnants of slavery, along with the sensory experiences of the city itself, were defined by their earlier experiences with printed texts and Henry Ward Beecher's "freedom auctions," dramatic recreations of slave auctions, which were performed in northern churches and city buildings to advance the abolitionist cause. The fictional and the authentic merged in immediate and emotional ways for the northerners, assuring them that John Calhoun's ghost, which had haunted the North long after his death, was now safely buried in St. Phillip's cemetery.

As soon as word reached Washington, DC, that General William T. Sherman's forces had captured Charleston in February 1865, President Abraham Lincoln and Secretary of War Edwin Stanton began preparing a celebratory ceremony.[5] They designed the event to focus on reraising the same American flag that was lowered from Fort Sumter during the evacuation of April 14, 1861, purposefully choosing to hold the ceremony on the four-year anniversary of the beginning of the Civil War.[6] In New York City, semiretired Brevet Major General Robert Anderson, who endured more than thirty-four hours of severe bombardment at Fort Sumter in 1861, was ordered to reraise that flag he had since secured in a mailbag and bank vault.[7]

Stanton and Lincoln invited northern governors, legislators, Supreme Court justices, military leaders, and prominent individuals, including General Ulysses S. Grant and Vice President Andrew Johnson. Many northern civilians also garnered tickets and passes to attend.[8] With Lincoln's selection of Brooklyn-based Reverend Henry Ward Beecher of the congregationalist Plymouth Church, many more northerners desired to go, especially his congregants. Persuading Stanton for more passes, these congregants formed a committee and secured the *Oceanus* steamship and over one hundred eighty passes. Hundreds of other congregants wished to attend the ceremony but were unable to do so because of limited space.[9] The committee planned stops in Virginia and North Carolina on their return trip to Brooklyn.[10] The committee also hired a band to provide entertainment. Baptist music composer William Bradbury used his time onboard to test his new song, "Victory at Last!," which he performed during the flag reraising ceremony.[11]

The passengers of the *Oceanus* included ministers, businessmen, local politicians, churchgoers, and a few military veterans and active-duty officers. Many belonged to the Plymouth Church and were staunch antebellum abolitionists.[12] Beecher, an internationally recognized abolitionist minister known for his dramatic, charismatic oratory, had made Plymouth Church the central hub of New York's Underground Railroad.[13] Beecher had endeared himself to Lincoln, first by inviting him to speak in Brooklyn, which played a pivotal role in his 1860 presidential victory, and later for defending the war effort while in England in 1863.[14] The American minister to England, Henry Adams, reported to Lincoln that Beecher's efforts in important industrial cities, including Liverpool, Manchester, and Edinburgh, had "done more for our cause in England and Scotland than all that has been before said or written." Lincoln agreed, writing, "If the war was ever fought to a successful issue, there would be but one man—Beecher—to raise the flag at Fort Sumter, for without Beecher in England there might be no flag to raise."

Adams and Lincoln recognized the role Beecher played in keeping England out of the Civil War. Indeed, tensions between England and the Union had been high since the *Trent* affair of 1861 when the US Navy boarded a British vessel carrying Confederate statesmen to England. Insulted, Parliament prepared for a vote to respond, even to the point of declaring war on the United States. If not for Prince Albert's timely cool head prevailing, shortly before his death, England might have intervened at that time. The underlying tension between the two nations, however, remained and became especially high in 1863 when the Union imposed a naval blockade on the South, creating a "cotton famine" that threatened British industrial cities and pushed thousands of workers into unemployment and poverty. According to Applegate, Beecher had originally not wanted to speak on anything political while in England, but threats from detractors, the urging of his British supporters, and the Union victories at Gettysburg and Vicksburg prompted him to undertake a series of lectures, which doubtlessly encouraged England to stay out of the war.[15]

The *Oceanus* and its passengers left for Charleston on April 10.[16] Their most profound experiences with the institution of enslavement, however, took place after the April 14 flag ceremony. What they had heard, read, and imagined for years from Beecher and others was now material. They encountered freed slaves on the streets and in gatherings, entered an abandoned slave market, and stood before the resting place of the Father of Secession, John C. Calhoun.

On April 15, Beecher, *Oceanus* passengers, and many others gathered at Zion's Presbyterian Church, which stands near the original location of The Citadel, for the "Freedmen Meeting."[17] Before the war, the white church allowed owners to bring enslaved people to worship and provided a communal space for the city's freed and enslaved Black populations. With the war over and emancipation ensured, the church became a site of celebration. An estimated three thousand freedmen gathered at the church, spilling over into the nearby grounds of The Citadel, to listen to several speakers, including William Lloyd Garrison, George Thompson, Martin Delaney, General Rufus Saxton, Senator Henry Wilson of Massachusetts, and Pennsylvania Representative Judge William Kelley.[18] About halfway through this celebration, another one formed spontaneously in Citadel Square, drawing away much of the crowd and some of the speakers.[19] According to Beecher's account and those of the *Oceanus* passengers, several such meetings took place. Beecher, for example, preached a sermon at the same church the next day.[20] With these gatherings, Charleston proper had become an extension of the celebration at Fort Sumter the day before.[21]

During the initial meeting on April 15, *Oceanus* passenger J. L. Leonard recorded a touching scene with an older gentleman and his family. Seeing "an old negro" about "seventy years of age," Leonard noticed how the old man "was much too absorbed in the spectacle."[22] As Mr. Leonard tried conversing with him, he noticed his "wooden leg," and noted, "I went up and inquired how he lost his leg" only to see tears rolling down the man's face and hearing him exclaim, "'My God! My God! what a sight'" and "'Peace! Peace!'" A loud noise, however, interrupted the old man's excitement: "[H]earing the report of a fire-arm," he "startled up in alarm, asking 'What's that?' his thoughts going back to former days."[23] Mr. Leonard, unable to get the man to escape the present moment, was aware that the report of the firearm caused the older man's mind's ear to recall the violence of southern slavescapes. He recognized the significance of the report because similar sounds were used at abolition gatherings to inform northern audiences of southern sounds that instilled fear in the enslaved.[24]

The old man then "turned his attention again to his children, and was so completely overcome that it was some time before he could reply" to Leonard's question. Nevertheless, it was the scene of "intense interest manifested by this poor old man" that made a "strong impression" upon Leonard, who found it "an illustration of the peculiar emotional nature of that race, of which I had often heard, but which I had never before seen."[25] Leonard's words reveal that his perceptions were shaped by what he had previously heard or read about Blacks' "emotional nature." It demonstrates a northern reformist disconnect, innocent or not, toward those they labored to free. Charleston may have offered Leonard his first in-the-flesh experience with a formerly enslaved person. His presuppositions, however, caused him to recognize the profound meaning of the past. The old man, aware of his wooden leg, seemed to recall his slave past only through the sound of the gunshot.[26] Still, the present experience of being with family, all now free, awaiting to hear the words of those who helped free them, overpowered the pain of the past and what it took from him. Noticing the man's "intense interest" for his now-free family, Leonard recognized the future was overwhelming both the past and present. The opportunities now realized generated hope and happiness for the old man.[27]

On another day, the *Oceanus* passengers found themselves along Chalmers and State streets, possibly retracing the path of Union war correspondents James Redpath, Charles Coffin, and Kane O'Donnell in February. The group passed several stores, some having reopened with meager supplies, and a few firms. Members of the group claimed that some of those firms owed them money. One was said to "owe us money in sums from one thousand to eleven thousand dollars," while another firm located on Broad Street owed a member of the group "over a thousand dollars!"[28] These comments demonstrate the financial connections between North and South, especially for New Yorkers. It was, however, "the slave-mart that attracted the most attention, especially, "the veritable slave pens in which families were kept, at the auction block, separated forever."[29] For the visitors standing in the defunct, unnamed mart, the building's emptiness and silence testified that "the day of traffic in human flesh is past–the dreadful marts are closed, and the wail of their agonized victims will never be heard in the streets of Charleston."[30] Entering the mart's jail, the travelers noticed the "dark dungeons and instruments of torture" used to perpetuate the "obsolete institution [of slavery] destined to become so throughout every State of the free Republic."[31]

As we will see, these northerners imagined the slave marts, jails, and auction sites through the experiential machinations of abolitionism. These intersensorial tactics included visual and tactile means found through literature, photography, the oral and aural experiences from lecture halls and speaking circuits given by freed slaves and fugitives, and Beecher's own dramatic freedom auctions, which were performed from 1848 to 1860 to raise money to emancipate enslaved persons. Collectively, these abolitionist tools provided the multisensory lenses through which many onboard the *Oceanus* experienced the sights and sounds of Charleston.

Print culture, unsurprisingly, offered northern abolitionists an early and powerful exposure to the South's long history of enslavement. Abolitionist travelogues of southern journeys, publications from expatriate southerners, and narratives of and by fugitive slaves informed the North that the South was an alien culture. In his history of slave narratives, Michaël Roy argues that, in some ways, these documents were more powerful than the spoken words of the formerly enslaved. The aurality of an authentic voice, he notes, was not enough to "convert" the North into the ideology of abolition.[32] Printed words, which involve at least three senses, provided a means for readers to "feel" words internally and thus encouraged a commitment to moral and political reform.[33] Although the sights and sounds of the formerly enslaved and slavery's attendant artifacts served as powerful representations of the slave South, the ability to see and (re)hear their words and persons while touching covers and pages made what was temporary all the more permanent.[34]

Many of the travelers seemed to recognize the authority of printed words. One *Oceanus* passenger, Dr. J. Allen, found in the Charleston library a monograph, "The *Philosophy* of Kidnapping," which he kept as a souvenir.[35] This work "contains many curious passages of curious interest, as a commentary upon the humanity of the 'Slave business.'"[36] Another passenger obtained several papers "whose dates was [sic] lost," containing enactments and regulations regarding the treatment of enslaved people. "£740, for the wilful [sic] murder of a slave—£350 for the unintentional murder of the slave in the ordinary process of whipping—£70 fine *for putting out the eye, cutting off the ears, pulling out the tongue, and otherwise maiming a slave.*"[37] William Spicer found a bill of sale for "a slave who was described as 'a negro fellow named Simon,'" included a chilling but, thankfully, denied promise: "The seller's name was Mordecai, and the buyer of 'the sole use of Simon forever,' was a Mr. Lazarus."[38] These print artifacts fit squarely with abolitionists' employment of diverse objects, presenting the South as foreign, brutal, and antithetical to American republicanism and liberty. As Roy indicates, they also serve as durable, visceral objects that can both create and sustain the ideology of abolitionism.

Roy also posits that photographs and sketches added greater authenticity to the slave narrative as developed by abolitionists.[39] After 1839, when the culture of photographic mementos blossomed, daguerreotypes quickly became infused into abolition tactics. As with print, owning images made a visualized South more permanent. His point has been recently reinforced by Jessie Morgan-Owens, who examines the use of photography by abolitionists, especially the image of seven-year-old Mary Mildred Williams. Morgan-Owens demonstrates that southerners used photography to show off prized slaves in ways that concealed cruelty and sexualization and made their institution appear humane and dignified. Northerners understood their tactics and developed their own slave images replete with chains, scars, and bodies commodified as objects. The case study of Mary Mildred Williams demonstrates this point. The image of the biracial child circulated throughout the

North and horrified the mind's eye at the barbary put upon children and helped transform sympathy into action.[40] As Mark M. Smith notes, such pictorial practices appealed to the "capitalist, humanitarian modernity," enflaming the North's righteous indignation toward slavery.[41]

The published and spoken words of runaway slaves, including Frederick Douglass's, also authenticated the southern soundscapes and imagined landscapes. Douglass's antebellum accounts of hearing the "dreadful sounds" of slavery anticipated the northerners' experiences in Charleston.[42] In slave pens and markets, Douglass writes, a "quick snap, like the discharge of a rifle; the fetters clank, and the chains rattle simultaneously, your ears are saluted with screams . . ." and "the crack you heard, was the sound of the slave-whip; the scream you heard was from the woman you saw with the babe."[43] For the northern visitors, these sounds reverberated within the walls of markets and plantation landscapes, where they were both ghastly and unnerving. The recreated and published sounds impressed themselves on northerners' minds, forming the imagined reality of the South.[44]

It was through their ears and eyes that northerners became accustomed to the sounds of the South and learned to detest them. Smith thoroughly analyzes how the North learned to hear and see what made the South un-American to their sensibilities. During meetings, abolitionist speakers not only displayed various shackles and chains but also shook them, echoing the clanking of bondage. During a gathering in Boston, for example, an abolitionist speaker held up chains, "its clankings touched a cord, and the City Hall was thunderous with emotion."[45] In print and speech, northerners created a multisensory impression of the South and the institution of slavery. However, the South and slavery were not merely a region of brutal cacophony—they were simultaneously silent and noisy, and chains assisted in this portrayal. The silence of over four million enslaved people "echoed loudly" in northern ears, pressing reformers to maintain a "moral and republican obligation" to combat slavery.[46]

Inside this slave mart, one *Oceanus* passenger "secured a pair of manacles, which had been in use in one of the slave-pens."[47] For him, those devices might very well have held meaning created by abolitionist texts and performance. Manacles and other enslaving implements, including muzzles and collars, helped stoke indignation, dread, and sympathy from northerners when displayed by abolitionists. Typically made of wrought iron, these heavy manacles, placed on various body parts such as necks and ankles, bound multiple enslaved people together to prevent escape. On the body, these devices were rough and burdensome, leaving bruises, scars, and sometimes infections. Although these iron devices were shocking in themselves, lecture circuit speakers used sensorial and sometimes exaggerated methods to further generate within the northern imagination the horrors of slavery.[48]

The chains placed on radical abolitionist John Brown after his failed raid at Harper's Ferry made rounds throughout the North, becoming a dual symbol of slavery's potential future effects on all of humankind and of slavery's demise if abolitionists acted. Some time after the appearance of Brown's chains in Boston, Henry Ward Beecher wielded them in a heated 1859 sermon, denouncing the South for its institution and the North for its complicity and calling Brown a God-fearing humanitarian martyr for radical abolitionism.[49] Beecher, "in the frenzy of eloquence," grabbed the "clanking irons and threw them violently onto the stage" and stamped down on them repeatedly. Reports of the moment claimed this action "awakened a sentiment in his vast audience."[50] The sight of slavery's bindings being crushed by the abolition's heel became a profound trifecta of the sight, sound, and touch for northern indignation. The presence of shackles that bound a white man possibly presented seductive speculation that many in the crowd viewed the power that shackled John Brown as their future enslavement if the South

Figure 6.1. "A Dramatic Scene, Throwing the Slave Chains," from *Life and Work of Henry Ward Beecher*, by Thomas Wallace Knox. Hartford Publishing Company, 1887, p. 160.

ultimately prevailed. These powerful sensory experiences encouraged abolitionists to silence the markets, plantations, and the instruments of bondage before the war and later to heal the wounds each caused upon human flesh and the nation.[51]

Although artifacts from Charleston's slave marts invoked provocative experiences of abolitionist culture and imagination, this was not the first time several of *Oceanus*'s passengers found themselves in such a building. Beecher's freedom auctions had allowed these travelers to imaginatively enter slave markets and auction blocks. Beecher created these dramatic events from his experiences watching actual slave auctions in northern Kentucky. Congregants participated in these auctions, bidding to secure the freedom of actors representing enslaved people. According to Applegate, for the northern audience, "it was as if they were witnessing a live slave auction, and they were the saviors."[52]

Encouraging his flock to imagine an absent enslaved person, Beecher first called for his congregation to see themselves and their neighbors as enslaved. He asked, "Could logic frame an argument strong enough to satisfy you that you ought not to try to escape? Should it not burn in your veins?"[53] With these words, Beecher aurally transformed spiritual language into physical sensation. For his Christian audience, his reference to fiery sensation held both negative and positive associations. On the one hand, his words invoked hell's flames and eternal condemnation. On the other hand, they summoned the sensation of spiritual cleansing and the affirmation of God's blessing through the spiritual freedom from sin. By imagining themselves as enslaved people, antebellum white congregants now had the fiery feel of those who sought physical freedom; through references to fire, freedom became both spiritual and physical. Beecher next led his congregation to visually imagine an enslaved person having the appearance of a daughter, mother, wife, or sister.[54] This exercise brought the issue of slavery closer to human perception, as one would hear the sounds and the physical descriptions of a loved one seen not only as property but also as flesh to satisfy the enslavers' sexual desires and as people placed in perpetual bondage.[55] Beecher's aural use of sexually charged language, typically shouted to condemn sins such as lust and adultery inside church buildings, would have shocked the audience's nineteenth-century sensibilities by loudly expressing subject matter usually shunned by polite classes.[56] Having brought the issue forth in full force, Beecher ushered in more fantastic emotions and feelings, as his audience now sensorially envisioned enslaving men sexually assaulting loved ones.

THE "FREEDOM RING." Mr. BEECHER PLEADING FOR MONEY TO SET A SLAVE CHILD FREE.

Figure 6.2. The "Freedom Ring": Mr. Beecher Pleading for Money to Set a Slave Child Free," from *Life and Work of Henry Ward Beecher*, by Thomas Wallace Knox. Hartford Publishing Company, 1887, p. 301.

When a formerly enslaved person was present, Beecher heightened his efforts to use sensory experience to bring slavery uncomfortably close to home. In one instance, Beecher pressed his congregation to look into the eyes of an enslaved woman to see if she could "read 'Liberty' in your eyes."[57] With this instruction, Beecher essentially turned the tables on his congregation, making them feel the gaze of the enslaved person, an experience that reversed the expected power structures. In the antebellum era, the experience of being looked upon, of being captured in someone's gaze, generated the sensation of being controlled as one imagined the pressing touch of another's eyes upon them.[58] By being gazed upon by an enslaved person, the white congregation perceived the sensations of control. For these northern Christians, the evils of slavery were now more than words heard or read and images seen; they were vividly felt, even transformative, sensations. Just as white eyes had gazed on enslaved people to stimulate specific behaviors, especially those of obedience, the gaze of the enslaved now pushed the white congregants to act.[59]

Beecher himself took on a visual and oral–aural role in these performances by replicating the vernacular language, accents, and loud voices of the auctioneers he had witnessed in Kentucky.[60] He seems to have been a capable actor. Beecher's son would later write that his father made the freedom auctions so lifelike that he "would have made a capital auctioneer."[61] More important, his play acting caused a "perfect frenzy" among the audience as his performance became all too real. Beecher created a scene of "sobbing, hysterical women, with shining-eyes," and "trembling-handed men."[62]

The aural, visual, and tactile experiences that Beecher generated made real the printed accounts his congregations would have read. Primary sources from the time of the freedom auctions include the memoirs of runaway slaves and those who were kidnapped into slavery, such as Frederick Douglass and Solomon Northup. These writers provided scenes where auctioneers presented "properly trained" slaves before a crowd.[63] The invasive physical inspections performed on the enslaved were akin to a "jockey [examining] a horse," as men and women were stripped, poked, and prodded. Potential buyers often performed private, erotic examinations on women, driving prices higher.[64] White witness accounts reveal how traders washed, scented, and "oiled" enslaved men and women to improve their appearance and highlight muscle tone, female curvature, and health.[65] Anne C. Bailey's recent research supports these accounts. She documents how buyers, often with unwashed hands, would physically touch and grope female slaves, especially their hips, to feel their breeding potential. They also checked mouths for disease and tooth decay.[66]

As he became more experienced with his freedom auctions, Beecher went further with haptics. To strengthen his congregation's abolitionist convictions, he would shout, "Christ stretched forth his hand and the sick were

Figure 6.3. Charleston slave auction, 1861. The flag was one of the early flags of the Confederate Government and not the American flag. New York Public Library.

restored to health; will you stretch forth your hands and give that without which is of little worth? Let the plate be passed and we shall see."[67] In reaction, the people hurriedly grabbed cash, banknotes, and jewels. Through the tactile actions of reaching out, grabbing valuables, and putting them into a collection plate, the people physically redeemed the slaves.[68] Christ, as the New Testament describes, placed his hands on the head or over their eyes, at times using earthy objects such as clay to restore the afflicted from physical and spiritual ailments. The Plymouth Church congregants used their hands and money, like clay, to redeem people, giving political health to those physically ill from slavery and freeing them from the sins of their oppressors. Emancipation was now more than something said and heard in church, secular meetings, or Congress. It was more than what was read in print. It was now something physically enacted through the senses.

Beecher was especially skilled at creating these kinds of powerful experiences. When a congregant threw in her gold ring to help purchase a young girl's freedom, Beecher placed the ring on the girl's finger, proclaiming, "With this ring, I wed you to freedom," and telling her to "remember that this is your freedom ring."[69] With this small golden ring, he bound the girl to her eternal "bride-groom": freedom. Christianity often portrays binding as a sign of a covenant with God, a promise that enables eternal liberty at the end of earthly life. Scholars of touch often view this sort of binding as a mechanism of control that uses both pain and pleasure to ensure spiritual freedom.[70] Beecher, however, asserted that there was no pain in this binding, only the gentle sensation of freedom. He later commissioned a painting depicting this young girl gazing upon this small binding symbol in a relaxed, thus free, posture and expression. The ring's golden color and smooth surface contrast the roughness of the large, black shackles. The ring feels comforting and tender, and its color and texture promise peace and safety.[71]

Not everyone approved of Beecher's auctions. Newspapers, especially those with antiabolitionist leanings, accused him of insincerity and claimed he used the freedom auctions to foment war between the states. Modern scholarship has also critiqued Beecher, arguing that the auctions created a theatrics of northern white supremacy. For these scholars, Beecher and his congregation offered just another version of slave markets because they appropriated Black bodies for profit. There was no actual freedom for those auctioned in the Plymouth Church, only a new form of white oppression. Others have noted that Beecher reinforced racist associations of skin color and human value, pointing out that most of the actors portraying enslaved people in the church were biracial and looked more white than Black.

Figure 6.4. *That Freedom Ring*, by Eastman Johnson, ca. 1860. Beecher commissioned local artist Eastman Johnson to paint Pinky with her ring soon after her freedom was purchased. Brooklyn Newspapers and Microfilm Collection, BCMS.0028, Brooklyn Public Library Center for Brooklyn History.

Applegate responds to these critiques by stating that Beecher used people with white features to appeal to the sensibilities of his congregation. To persuade even his fellow abolitionists to feel genuine kinship with the enslaved, Beecher first had to make them familiar. Only then could his congregants recognize Black people as fellow citizens.[72]

These critiques notwithstanding, Beecher's freedom auctions were moving and effective. They caused audiences not only to donate money but also to cry and clap. These actions, as well as the physical space of the Plymouth Church, enhanced the congregants' experiential religious perceptions and the meanings they drew from them. Churches are, of course, designed as places for spiritual salvation through physical gatherings. The freedom auctions extended this role and made Plymouth Church a place for a new kind of experienced redemption.[73] Enthusiastic clapping and the church's vibrant acoustics created thunderous booms, seemingly from heaven. In the Bible, thunder carries multiple meanings. It signals destruction; reveals God's wrath; announces a cleansing rain; and, along with angelic trumpets, proclaims the coming of Christ. During the freedom auctions, the clapping-thunders also created multiple associations. It indicated God's wrath for the sin of slavery, pushing the nation to free itself from divine displeasure. It also suggested God's pleasure as the congregations freed another person from bondage and cleansed the nation in preparation of Christ's reign.[74]

Crying, too, has multifaceted meanings within Christianity. It can signify sincerity, grief, celebration, angst, and the catharsis of spiritual redemption. Churchgoers at Beecher's freedom auctions cried out in grief and indignation when they saw an enslaved person, especially when Beecher invited them to see their female loved ones in an enslaved woman. They also cried in shame at the very existence of slavery. During a successful auction, their tears transformed into tears of celebration, happiness, and cleansing. Newspapers tellingly described the tears and the clapping as "rapturous."[75] The theologically charged language invokes the culmination of God's wrath upon earth to destroy sin and the redemption of believers rewarded with a sinfree world.[76]

Several historians have recently connected sensory experience, especially smell and sight, to the slave trade. In his haunting investigation of slave markets, Walter Johnson notes how auctioneers rubbed "sweet oil" over enslaved faces as they prepared them for sale. Scent, cleanliness, and appearance, Johnson argues, played critical roles in the purchasing decisions of enslavers who saw the clean, healthy, proper looking, and smelling enslaved individuals as fitting representations of their plantations.[77] Andrew Kettler sees the control of an enslaved person's odor as a way of asserting white paternal rights over the enslaved body by disguising signs of disease and falsely presenting a clean, bright body ready for labor.[78] Slave traders and auctioneers played to their customers biases and expectations. In her examination into the largest slave auction in American history, held in the Georgia Sea Islands in 1859, Anne C. Bailey records how the auctioneer had to "repeatedly reassure the boisterous buyers that there was no attempt at subterfuge," regarding concerns raised over the possibility of a sick enslaved presented as healthy.[79] These modern studies—as well as Mark M. Smith's investigation of the southern soundscape of bells, shackles, noise ordinances and whistling, and Erin Dwyer's timely book on slavery and fear—all shed light on how Beecher's performances influenced the imaginations of Plymouth Church's congregants and defined the Charleston that the *Oceanus* passengers discovered in 1865.[80]

Even six years after the last freedom auction, Beecher's imagined slave mart ingrained an experiential bias in the postbellum visitors to Charleston. Only now, the pens were empty of enslaved bodies, the instruments of torture and control lay useless, even dead, and the imagined echoes of suffering had faded away. As with Charleston, so went the South and the nation. The manacles taken north clanked hollowly before becoming encased in museum displays to teach future generations that abolitionists and the Union army had defeated slavery. In the empty slave mart, the passengers of the *Oceanus* found their abolitionist work validated. Reading the *Oceanus* account, one discovers that their imaginative antebellum experiences of slavery's selling place determined their perceptions inside a real one. It was as if they had already entered such spaces, fighting against their inhuman purposes. They could now carry home evidence of their years-long struggle.

For some visitors, John Calhoun's vandalized tomb became the primary symbol of slavery's legacy. Quoting from a fellow passenger, Reverend Theodore Cuyler offered a summation of visiting the grave site. Beecher, William Lloyd Garrison, British abolitionist George H. Thompson, and others gathered around the grave in St. Philip's cemetery, which Cuyler describes as "a plain brick oblong tomb, covered with a marble slab, and bearing the single word 'CALHOUN.'"[81] Garrison remarked that the name, synonymous with slavery, "is decayed worse than his moldering body; the one may have a resurrection, the other never!" Noticing that several Union shells had burst around the tomb, Garrison added, "Did none of the bones in the sepulcher *rattle*" on hearing the shells explode "at the grave's mouth?"[82] Garrison envisioned the demise of Calhoun's body, once standing loud and bold, now shaking in its grave because of northern armaments.[83] Beecher declared the marble slab as "the record of the rebellion," bearing the "great crop of war" from "the dragon-toothed doctrines that were sown by the hands of that dangerous man." He recalled how Calhoun's words held significant "effect upon the minds of young men."[84]

Some northerners, however, did more than philosophize over the tomb's meanings. They wished to take the marble slab. When doing so proved impractical, they desecrated the grave marker by chipping away fragments that they kept as mementos. K. Stephen Prince argues that these actions provide an apt metaphor for the South's demise, a point he supports by citing northern journalist Sidney Andrews: "'Down in the churchyard . . . is a grave which every stranger is curious to see'"; this grave "'of the father of the Rebellion,'" Andrews notes, "had seen better days.'" A site guarded during the war and considered a "holy spot" now, like the city, lay in ruins. "Scavengers had even broken off pieces of the great statesman's grave for keepsakes."[85] For Prince, the grave "damaged and desecrated . . . once a revered monument to the intellectual champion of slavery and state's rights—lay in ruin."[86]

Grave of John C. Calhoun, in front of St. Philip's church, Charleston, S. C.

Figure 6.5. John C. Calhoun's grave, ca. 1865, seemingly taken not long before its desecration. Courtesy of the Library of Congress.

The destruction of Calhoun's grave did not please Theodore Tilton and Henry Ward Beecher. Tilton found it disturbing. Instead of damaging the stone further, he chose to pluck "some clover growing near the ruins of Institute Hall."[87] Beecher offered his opinion on why people wanted a piece of the grave site. Standing before Calhoun's "monument, brooding over his dust," he called the marble a "record of rebellion," pointing to the South's vain hope of preserving the Confederacy and Calhoun by chiseling his name into stone, resulting in "a ruined, shattered city, demoralized and destroyed." Now the tomb resembled the city as "vandal hands were beginning to chip off the marble to bring back as memorials."[88] These actions puzzled Beecher: "What on earth should a man want a memorial of Calhoun for? And if one wanted it, what must be the measure of that want that would lead him to desecrate a grave, and break down gravestones, that he might have something to put on his mantle-piece, or on his cabinet shelf?" Beecher answered his own question: it was so these northern vandals could say, "'I stole that from the grave of Calhoun.'"[89] Beecher felt that the desecration fulfilled a petty, prideful, and consumerist need to show off an unnecessary souvenir. The end of slavery and the destruction of Charleston should have been enough.[90]

It may also be that the northern hands that chipped these pieces away saw in this action the experiential memory of reclaiming their power from Calhoun, tangibly proving that they no longer had to fear him. The northerners reconstructed the lost sense of order destroyed by—ironically—breaking down Calhoun's grave, placing the power it represented tangibly under their control, and making the feared past a harmless display that announced the presence of a freer postbellum stability and order.

A performance of mirthful music blossomed before the eyes and ears of Garrison, Tilton, Beecher, and Thompson, ending these discussions at Calhoun's grave. As Carl Schulz notes, the sight and sound of Black children singing "'John Brown's Body' within earshot" of the remains "perfectly encapsulated" Calhoun's South as "dead and gone."[91] The marble fragments, representative of slavery's intellectual champion, became artifacts that could be handled, shared, and preserved in a private home or museum. Like the manacles, the fragments provided physical, tactile evidence that slavery sat dead and silent before them. Those who took them could see and feel the demise of slavery, just as Beecher and his companions could hear and see it in the children's song. Slavery and Calhoun had been encased in polished white marble, the gravesite symbolizing the imagined grandeur of the South's institution even after its creator's death. Now chipped away and defenseless, transformed into rough, shapeless pieces, it mocked the man, his institution, and the South, allowing Calhoun's opponents to officially pronounce slavery as "dead and gone," as its most fervent advocate. Calhoun's ghost no longer loomed over them.[92]

Michael Emett is a full-time lecturer at the University of Alabama in Huntsville. He is the author of several book reviews and has presented internationally on topics ranging from special treasury agents in Port Royal, South Carolina, to Robert Anderson and catharsis over Fort Sumter. Focusing on the history of the United States up to 1877, he specializes in the History of Experiences. He also volunteers at Fort Sumter National Park.

NOTES

I thank the two anonymous reviewers for their hard work in getting this article in ship shape and for their questions and suggestions. I also thank Drs. Mark M. Smith and Patricia Sullivan at the University of South Carolina for helping me unpack the scene at Calhoun's tomb further when this idea was presented before a body of scholars and graduate students. Their push allowed for greater depth of analysis of why the northerners desired "a piece" of Calhoun.

1. Stephen M. Griswold, *Sixty Years with Plymouth Church* (New York: Fleming H. Revell Co., 1907), 152.

2. Griswold, *Sixty Years*, 152. See also Debby Applegate, *The Most Famous Man in America: The Biography of Henry Ward Beecher* (New York: Doubleday Press, 2006), 94–95, 101, 109–118, 146–148, 169–70, 188, 195–96, 210–11.

3. Justus C. French and Edward Cary, *The Trip of the Steamer Oceanus to Fort Sumter and Charleston, S.C.: Comprising the Incidents of the Excursion, the Appearance, at That Time, of the City, and the Entire Programme of Exercises at the Re-Raising of the Flag over the Ruins of Fort Sumter, April 14, 1865* (Brooklyn, NY: The Union Steam Printing House, 1865); and Frank Decker and Lois Rosebrooks, *Brooklyn's Plymouth Church in the Civil War Era: A Ministry of Freedom* (Charleston, SC: The History Press, 2013), 23–30, 42–44.

4. Robert Boddice and Mark M. Smith, *Emotion, Sense, Experience* (Cambridge, UK: Cambridge University Press, 2020), 18–26. See also Robert Boddice, "What Is the History of Experience?" HEX: CoE in the History of Experiences, April 18, 2019. https://www.tuni.fi/alustalehti/2019/04/18/.

5. See Daniel S. Lamont, George B. Davis, Leslie J. Perry, and Joseph W. Kirkley, *The War of the Rebellion: A Compilation of the Official Records of the Union and Confederate Armies: Part II.*, series 1, vol. 47, part 2, (Washington, DC: US Government Printing Office, 1895), 979, and series 1, vol. 47, part 3, 17–18, 34–35, 41, 51–52, 59, 99, 109, 116–117 128, 161; and David Alan Johnson, *The Last Weeks of Abraham Lincoln: A Day-By-Day Account of His Personal, Political, and Military Challenges* (New York: Prometheus Books, 2018), 119–20.

6. Johnson, *Last Weeks*, 119–120; see also French and Cary, *Trip of the Steamer*, 5.

7. Newspaper accounts of these events appeared in *The Buffalo Commercial* (New York), February 24, 1865; *Pomeroy Weekly Telegraph* (Ohio), March 2, 1865; *Burlington Times* (Vermont), February 25, 1865; and *The New York Times*, February 22, 1865. For examples of southern papers reprinting the resolution, see *Montgomery Daily Mail* (Alabama), March 5, 1865; and *Edgefield Advertiser* (South Carolina), March 8, 1865.

8. "Fort Sumter," *New York Herald*, April 9, 1865, 8, https://www.loc.gov/resource/sn83030313/1865-04-09/ed-1/?sp=8.

9. Griswold, *Sixty Years*, 143–144, French and Cary, *Trip of the Steamer*, 5–8; *New York Daily Herald*, "Fort Sumer Celebration," April 8, 1865, and *Brooklyn Union*, "For Fort Sumter," April 10, 1865.

10. William A. Spicer, *The Flag Replaced in Sumter: A Personal Narrative* (Providence, RI: Providence Press Co., 1885), 16, 18. See also French and Cary, *Trip of the Steamer*, 14–19.

11. See Griswold, *Sixty Years*, 143–144; Spicer, *Flag Replaced*, 16, 18; and French and Cary, *Trip of the Steamer*, 14–19, 163–165. It remains unclear whether Bradbury originally wrote "Victory at Last!" for the ceremony or for national distribution. Reports in the *New York Times* and *Brooklyn Union* show that "Victory at Last!" provided an extra boon to the celebrants' euphoria. See also "Fort Sumter," *New York Times*, April 18, 1865, 8, https://www.nytimes.com/1865/04/18/archives/fort-sumter-restoration-of-the-stars-and-stripes-solemn-and.html; *Brooklyn Union*, April 20, 1865; and French and Cary, *Trip of the Steamer*, 15–16, 47.

12. See Griswold, *Sixty Years*, 81–84, 87, 101, 152; Applegate, *The Most Famous Man*, 94–95, 101, 109–18, 146–48, 169–70, 188, 195–96, 210–11, 281–85, 309–15, 321–26, 344–50; and Decker and Rosebrooks, *Plymouth Church*, 23–30, 42–44, 74–82, 95–97, 109.

13. Decker and Rosebrooks, *Plymouth Church*, 23–30, 42–44, 74–82, 95–97, 109.

14. Jason Phillips, *Looming Civil War: How Nineteenth-Century Americans Imagined the Future* (Oxford, UK: Oxford University Press, 2018), 30–31, 80–84, 87–88, 116; Lionel Crocker, "Henry Ward Beecher at Fort Sumter, April 14, 1865." *The Southern Speech Journal* 27, no. 4 (1962): 273–83; Harold Holzer, *Lincoln at Cooper Union: The Speech That Made Abraham Lincoln President* (New York: Simon & Schuster, 2004), 10–11, 23–24, 59, 66, 73–74.

15. See French and Cary, *Trip of the Steamer*, 26–27, 145–51, 167–68; Spicer, *Flag Replaced*, 34, 70, and C. R. Horres Jr., "Charleston's Civil War 'Monster Guns,' the Blakely Rifles," *South Carolina Historical Magazine* 97, no. 2 (1996): 115–38.

16. *Brooklyn Union*, April 10, 1865; Spicer, *Flag Replaced*, 12–13.

17. French and Cary, *Trip of the Steamer*, 88, 95–96; Spicer, *Flag Replaced*, 60–62; and Blain Roberts and Ethan J. Kyrtle, *Denmark Vesey's Garden: Slavery and Memory in the Cradle of the Confederacy* (New York: The New Press, 2019), 51–52.

18. *Oceanus* passengers Theodore Tilton and Reverend Dr. J. Leavitt were also in attendance, as was Beecher. See French and Cary, *Trip of the Steamer*, 88, 95–96.

19. Records of the speeches appear in French and Cary, *Trip of the Steamer*, 97–118. Roberts and Kyrtle provide a useful summary of their content in *Denmark Vesey's Garden*, 51–52.

20. See Henry Ward Beecher and T. J. Ellinwood, "Narrative by Henry Ward Beecher of His Trip to Charleston, S.C., as Orator of the Day at the Restoration of the Flag over Fort Sumter, April 12, 1865." (Delivered in Plymouth Church, April 23, 1865; Reported and published by T. J. Ellinwood. 1892), 35–37.

21. See French and Cary, *Trip of the Steamer*, 88, 95–96; Spicer, *Flag Replaced*, 60–62; Roberts and Kyrtle, *Denmark Vesey's Garden*, 51–52; and Beecher and Ellinwood, "Narrative," 35–37.

22. French and Cary, *Trip of the Steamer*, 96–97.

23. French and Cary, *Trip of the Steamer*, 96–97.

24. French and Cary, *Trip of the Steamer*, 96–97. We can never know if the sound was an actual gunshot. Any similar sound, however, may have triggered someone who was formerly enslaved. Frederick Douglass compares the "quick snap" of the whip to the "discharge of the rifle," both sounds commonly heard in the enslaved Southern landscape. See Mark M. Smith, *Listening to Nineteenth-Century America* (Chapel Hill: University of North Carolina Press, 2001), 175, 303 n51; and Erin Austin Dwyer, *Mastering Emotions: Feelings, Power, and Slavery in the United States* (Philadelphia: University of Pennsylvania Press, 2021), 49, 57, 138, 141, 145–47.

25. French and Cary, *Trip of the Steamer*, 97.

26. It is possible, of course, that the "old man" suffered from posttraumatic stress, caused by the fear-filled atmosphere in which he lived. As suggested by Frederick Douglass's experiences, masters and overseers used loud noises to instill fear. See Dwyer, *Mastering Emotions*; French and Cary, *Trip of the Steamer*, 97.

27. French and Cary, *Trip of the Steamer*, 97.

28. French and Cary, *Trip of the Steamer*, 95.

29. French and Cary, *Trip of the Steamer*, 94–95.

30. French and Cary, *Trip of the Steamer*, 94–95.

31. French and Cary, *Trip of the Steamer*, 95.

32. Michaël Roy, *Fugitive Texts: Slave Narratives in Antebellum Print Culture*, translated by Susan Pickford (Madison: University of Wisconsin Press and ENS Editions 2007, 2022), 5.

33. Roy, *Fugitive Texts*, 63–64.

34. Roy, *Fugitive Texts*, 82.

35. Emphasis in the original. It is unclear as to whether the stress on "Philosophy" is made by French and Cary or if that is how the frontispiece portrayed the title. See French and Cary, *Trip of the Steamer*, 169–170.

36. French and Cary, *Trip of the Steamer*, 170.

37. French and Cary, *Trip of the Steamer*, 170, emphasis in original.

38. Spicer, *Flag Replaced*, 59.

39. Roy, *Fugitive Texts*, 69–72.

40. Jessie Morgan-Owens, *Girl in Black and White: The Story of Mary Mildred Williams and the Abolition Movement* (New York: W. W. Norton and Co., 2019). See also Matthew Fox-Amato, *Exposing Slavery: Photography, Human Bondage, and the Birth of Modern Visual Politics in America* (Oxford, UK: Oxford University Press, 2019).

41. Mark M. Smith, "Getting in Touch with Slavery and Freedom," *The Journal of American History* 95, no. 2 (2008): 382.

42. Smith, *Listening*, 175.

43. Quoted in Smith, *Listening*, 172–77, 182–83.

44. Smith, *Listening*, 172–77.

45. Smith, *Listening*, 144–45.

46. Smith, *Listening*, 160–65.

47. French and Cary, *Trip of the Steamer*, 170.

48. For a contemporary account of these practices, see Weld, *Slavery As It Is*; see also Smith, "Getting in Touch," 390. For some southerners, images of shackled people may have had a very different effect. Walter Johnson finds that, in some cases, the images of female slaves in chains heightened sexual fetishes for some slave masters and traders. See Walter Johnson, *Dark River of Dreams: Slavery and Empire in the Cotton Kingdom* (Cambridge, MA: Harvard University Press, 2013), 383–84.

49. Decker and Rosebrooks, *Plymouth Church*, 91–92.

50. Applegate, *Most Famous Man*, 310–12.

51. Applegate, *Most Famous Man*, 310–12.

52. Applegate, *Most Famous Man*, 226–29, 285–85, 316–17, 322.

53. William Constantine Beecher, Rev. Samuel Scoville, and Henry Ward Beecher, *A Biography of Rev. Henry Ward Beecher* (New York: Charles L. Webster & Co., 1888), 293; and Applegate, *Most Famous Man*, 226–27.

54. Applegate, *Most Famous Man*, 226–229; Decker and Rosebrooks, *Plymouth Church*, 11–22.

55. Wayne Shaw, "The Plymouth Pulpit: Henry Ward Beecher's Slave Auction Block," *American Transcendental Quarterly* 14, no. 4 (2000): 335–43.

56. For a useful introduction to nineteenth-century constructions of sexuality, see Jan Marsh, "Sex & Sexuality in the 19th Century," Victoria and Albert Museum, 2010 (http://www.vam.ac.uk/content/articles/s/sex-and-sexuality-19th-century/).

57. Applegate, *Most Famous Man*, 284, 316–17; Decker and Rosebrooks, *Plymouth Church*, 81, 95.

58. See Martin Jay, *Downcast Eyes: The Denigration of Vision in Twenty-Century French Thought* (Berkeley: University of California Press, 1994), 410–13.

59. Jay, *Downcast Eyes*, 287–88, 294–95, 410–13.

60. See Applegate, *Most Famous Man*, 109–10, 116, 118, 226–29, 284, 316–17; and Decker and Rosebrooks, *Plymouth Church*, 11–22, 81–95.

61. Beecher, Scoville, and Beecher, *Biography*, 292–93; and Paxton Hibben, *Henry Ward Beecher: An American Portrait* (New York: George H. Doran Company, 1927), 111–13.

62. Applegate, *Most Famous Man*, 226–29, 284, 316–17; see also Shaw "Plymouth Pulpit," and James Stupp, "Slavery and the Theatre of History: Ritual Performance on the Auction Block," *Theatre Journal* 63, no. 1 (2011): 63–71.

63. Frederick Douglass, *My Bondage and My Freedom* (New York: Miller & Miller, 1855).

64. Solomon Northup, *Twelve Years A Slave* (New York: Derby & Miller, 1852).

65. See, for example, William Wilberforce, "Account of a Slave Auction," in *A Letter on the Abolition of the Slave Trade, Addressed to the Freeholders and Other Inhabitants of Yorkshire*, London, 1807; "Slave Auction, 1869"; John Zaborney, "The Domestic Slave Trade in Virginia," *Encyclopedia Virginia*, 2020 (https://www.encyclopediavirginia.org/Slave_Sales); Lucius C. Matlack, *Narrative of the Life and Adventures of Henry Bibb, an American Slave, Written by Himself* (New York: Author, 1849; https://hdl.loc.gov/loc.rbc/General.05639), 103–04; and Henry Watson, *Narrative of the Life of Henry Watson, a Fugitive Slave* (Boston, MA: Bela Marsh, 1850), 7–9.

66. Anne C. Bailey, *The Weeping Time: Memory and the Largest Slave Auction in American History* (Cambridge, UK: Cambridge University Press, 2017), 5, 11, 18.

67. Applegate, *Most Famous Man*, 228–29, 284–85, 316.

68. Applegate, *Most Famous Man*, 284–85, 316.

69. Applegate, *Most Famous Man*, 316–17; and Decker and Rosebrooks, *Plymouth Church*, 92–95.

70. On binding, touch, and religion, see David Chidester, "The American Touch: Tactile Imagery in American Religion and Politics," in *The Book of Touch*, edited by Constance Classen (New York: Routledge Press, 2005), 51–53. For more on ancient, medieval, and Reformation religious interpretations of binding, see Darrell Thorpe, "Handclasps and Arm Gestures in Historical Christian Art," LDS Temple Endowment (http://ldstempleendowment.blogspot.com/2009/08/laws-of-god.html).

71. Applegate, *Most Famous Man*, 316–17; and Decker and Rosebrooks, *Plymouth Church*, 92–95.

72. For treatment of period criticism, see Applegate, *Most Famous Man*, 228–29, 284–85, 316. For an example of modern critiques, see Stupp, "Slavery," 61–84. Although most of those slaves on stage were of whiter complexion, the first two to be "auctioned" were daughters of a freed slave father and enslaved mother, the latter and the girls were held in New Orleans at the time of the auction. The Plymouth Church met the father and had a photograph of the girls, later meeting the girls in person. Their dark skin color was not a topic of controversy for these church goers, as evidenced in extant records.

73. See Applegate, *Most Famous Man*, 226–29, 284.

74. Applegate, *Most Famous Man*, 226–29, 284; Decker and Rosebrooks, *Plymouth Church*, 21, 95.

75. Applegate, *Most Famous Man*, 226–29.

76. For the culture and history of crying and its role in religion, see Tom Lutz, *Crying: The Natural & Cultural History of Tears* (New York: W.W. Norton and Co., 1999).

77. Walter Johnson, *Soul by Soul: Life Inside the Antebellum Slave Market* (Cambridge, MA: Harvard University Press, 1999), 117–34; see also Johnson, *Dark River*, 11, 16, 41, 48, 159–61, 171, 183–84, 200–204, 250.

78. Andrew Kettler, "Odor and Power in the Americas: Olfactory Consciousness from Columbus to Emancipation," PhD dissertation, University of South Carolina, 2017 (https://scholarcommons.sc.edu/etd/4139/), 235–36.

79. Bailey, *Weeping Time*, 15.

80. Smith, *Listening*; and Dwyer, *Mastering Emotion*. See also Bailey, *Weeping Time*, 5, 11, 18, 68; Peter Kolchin, *American Slavery, 1619–1877* (New York: Hill & Wang, 2003), 21–22; Shaw "Plymouth Pulpit"; Stupp, "Slavery," 63–73; Damian Alan Pargas, *Slavery and Forced Migration in the Antebellum South* (Cambridge: Cambridge University Press, 2014), 106–11; and Mark M. Smith, *How Race Is Made: Slavery, Segregation, and the Senses* (Chapel Hill: University of North Carolina Press, 2008).

81. Theodore Cuyler, as quoted in French and Cary, *Trip of the Steamer*, 119. The *Oceanus* account claims that these are remarks were taken from a Cuyler article printed in the *Evangelist* newspaper upon his return to Brooklyn, New York. To date, this edition of the *Evangelist* has yet to be located.

82. Emphasis in the original.

83. However, residents disinterred Calhoun's remains in another location before the Union occupation in February of the same year. So, although the bones did not physically "hear" Garrison, they would have vibrated at Union shelling. Still, the incendiary image is manageable symbolically.

84. French and Cary, *Trip of the Steamer*, 119.

85. K. Stephen Prince, "Making Sense of Ruins in the Postwar South," in *The World the Civil War Made*, edited by Gregory P. Downs and Kate Masur (Chapel Hill: University of North Carolina Press, 2015), 106–31. After the war, Calhoun's body was restored to St. Philip's, and a new grave marker, an obelisk, replaced the destroyed marble slab.

86. Prince, "Making Sense," 106–31. See also Roberts and Kyrtle, *Denmark Vesey's Garden*, 51.

87. Roberts and Kyrtle, *Denmark Vesey's Garden*, 48.
88. Beecher and Ellinwood, "Narrative," 31–32.
89. Beecher and Ellinwood, "Narrative," 33–34.
90. An incident with a young boy before entering the cemetery at St. Philip's church might have also influenced Beecher's opinion toward the desecration of Calhoun's grave. "One of the most interesting visits I paid was to St. Philip's church and the graveyard that lies opposite to it. As I drew near this graveyard there sat upon the wall a little one-armed boy, saying, 'Please sir, I lost my arm by a shell.' No one could withhold a charity on such an application. It was not an uncommon thing to hear it said, 'The shell that took off the top of that column came down and struck a boy and killed him.' So this point and that are marked by various experiences such as these." See, Beecher and Ellinwood, "Narrative," 31. Although Megan Kate Nelson focuses on wounded soldiers with missing limbs, the presence of such injuries for civilians is informative. See Megan Kate Nelson, "Empty Sleeves and Government Legs," in *Ruin Nation: Destruction and the American Civil War* (Athens: University of Georgia Press, 2012), 160–227.
91. As quoted in Price, "Making Sense," 120.
92. Price, "Making Sense," 120.

WORKS CITED

Applegate, Debby. *The Most Famous Man in America: The Biography of Henry Ward Beecher*. New York: Doubleday Press, 2006.

Bailey, Anne C. *The Weeping Time: Memory and the Largest Slave Auction in American History*. Cambridge, UK: Cambridge University Press, 2017.

Beecher, Henry Ward, and T. J. Ellinwood. "Narrative by Henry Ward Beecher of His Trip to Charleston, S.C., as Orator of the Day at the Restoration of the Flag over Fort Sumter, April 12, 1865." Delivered in Plymouth Church, April 23, 1865. Reported and published by T. J. Ellinwood. 1892.

Beecher, William Constantine, Rev. Samuel Scoville, and Henry Ward Beecher. *A Biography of Rev. Henry Ward Beecher*. New York: Charles L. Webster & Co., 1888.

Boddice, Robert. "What Is the History of Experience?" HEX: CoE in the History of Experiences, April 18, 2019. https://www.tuni.fi/alustalehti/2019/04/18/what-is-the-history-of-experience/.

Boddice, Robert, and Mark M. Smith. *Emotion, Sense, Experience*. Cambridge, UK: Cambridge University Press, 2020.

Chidester, David. "The American Touch: Tactile Imagery in American Religion and Politics." In *The Book of Touch*, edited by Constance Classen, 49–69. New York: Routledge Press, 2005.

Crocker, Lionel. "Henry Ward Beecher at Fort Sumter, April 14, 1865." *The Southern Speech Journal* 27, no. 4 (1962): 273–283.

Decker, Frank, and Lois Rosebrooks. *Brooklyn's Plymouth Church in the Civil War Era: A Ministry of Freedom*. Charleston, SC: The History Press, 2013.

Douglass, Frederick. *My Bondage and My Freedom*. New York: Miller & Miller, 1855.

Dwyer, Erin Austin. *Mastering Emotions: Feelings, Power, and Slavery in the United States*. Philadelphia: University of Pennsylvania Press, 2021.

Fox-Amato, Matthew. *Exposing Slavery: Photography, Human Bondage, and the Birth of Modern Visual Politics in America*. Oxford, UK: Oxford University Press, 2019.

French, Justus C., and Edward Cary. *The Trip of the Steamer Oceanus to Fort Sumter and Charleston, S.C.: Comprising the Incidents of the Excursion, the Appearance, at That Time, of the City, and the Entire Programme of Exercises at the Re-Raising of the Flag over the Ruins of Fort Sumter, April 14, 1865*. Brooklyn, NY: The Union Steam Printing House, 1865. https://www.loc.gov/item/02010572/.

Gaddis, Elijah. *Gruesome Looking Objects: A New History of Lynching and Everyday Things*. Cambridge, UK: Cambridge University Press, 2022.

Griswold, Stephen M. *Sixty Years with Plymouth Church*. New York: Fleming H. Revell Co., 1907.

Hibben, Paxton. *Henry Ward Beecher: An American Portrait*. New York: George H. Doran Company, 1927. (Reprint Whitefish, MT: Kissinger Publishing, 2003.)

Holzer, Harold. *Lincoln at Cooper Union: The Speech That Made Abraham Lincoln President*. New York: Simon & Schuster, 2004.

Horres, C. R. Jr. "Charleston's Civil War 'Monster Guns,' the Blakely Rifles." *South Carolina Historical Magazine* 97, no. 2 (1996): 115–138.

Jay, Martin. *Downcast Eyes: The Denigration of Vision in Twenty-Century French Thought*. Berkeley: University of California Press, 1994.

Johnson, David Alan. *The Last Weeks of Abraham Lincoln: A Day-By-Day Account of His Personal, Political, and Military Challenges*. New York: Prometheus Books, 2018.

Johnson, Walter. *Dark River of Dreams: Slavery and Empire in the Cotton Kingdom*. Cambridge, MA: Harvard University Press, 2013.

Johnson, Walter. *Soul by Soul: Life Inside the Antebellum Slave Market*. Cambridge, MA: Harvard University Press, 1999.

Kettler, Andrew. "Odor and Power in the Americas: Olfactory Consciousness from Columbus to Emancipation." PhD diss., University of South Carolina, 2017. https://scholarcommons.sc.edu/etd/4139/.

Kettler, Andrew. *Smell of Slavery: Olfactory Racism in the Atlantic World*. Cambridge, UK: Cambridge University Press, 2020.

Kolchin, Peter. *American Slavery, 1619–1877*. New York: Hill & Wang, 2003.

Lamont, Daniel S., George B. Davis, Leslie J. Perry, and Joseph W. Kirkley. *The War of the Rebellion: A Compilation of the Official Records of the Union and Confederate Armies: Part II*. Series 1, Vol. 47. Washington, DC: US Government Printing Office, 1895. https://texashistory.unt.edu/ark:/67531/metapth142234/.

Lamont, Daniel S. *The War of the Rebellion: A Compilation of the Official Records of the Union and Confederate Armies: Part III*. Series 1, Vol. 47. Washington, DC: US Government Printing Office, 1895. https://texashistory.unt.edu/ark:/67531/metapth154639.

Lutz, Tom. *Crying: The Natural & Cultural History of Tears*. New York: W.W. Norton and Co., 1999.

Marsh, Jan. "Sex & Sexuality in the 19th Century." Victoria and Albert Museum, 2010. http://www.vam.ac.uk/content/articles/s/sex-and-sexuality-19th-century/.

Matlack, Lucius C. *Narrative of the Life and Adventures of Henry Bibb, an American Slave, Written by Himself.* New York: Author, 1849. https://hdl.loc.gov/loc.rbc/General.05639.

Morgan-Owens, Jessie. *Girl in Black and White: The Story of Mary Mildred Williams and the Abolition Movement.* New York: W. W. Norton and Co., 2019.

Nelson, Megan Kate. "Empty Sleeves and Government Legs." In *Ruin Nation: Destruction and the American Civil War,* 160–227 (Athens: University of Georgia Press, 2012).

Northup, Soloman. *Twelve Years a Slave.* New York: Derby & Miller, 1852.

Pargas, Damian Alan. *Slavery and Forced Migration in the Antebellum South.* Cambridge: Cambridge University Press, 2014.

Parry, Tyler D., and Charlton W. Yingling. "Slave Hounds and Abolition in the Americas." *Past & Present* 246, no. 1 (2020): 69–108.

Phillips, Jason. *Looming Civil War: How Nineteenth-Century Americans Imagined the Future.* Oxford, UK: Oxford University Press, 2018.

Prince, K. Stephen. "Making Sense of Ruins in the Postwar South." In *The World the Civil War Made,* edited by Gregory P. Downs and Kate Masur, 106–31. Chapel Hill: University of North Carolina Press, 2015.

Roberts, Blain, and Ethan J. Kyrtle. *Denmark Vesey's Garden: Slavery and Memory in the Cradle of the Confederacy.* New York: The New Press, 2019.

Roy, Michaël. *Fugitive Texts: Slave Narratives in Antebellum Print Culture.* Translated by Susan Pickford. Madison: University of Wisconsin Press and ENS Editions 2007, 2022.

Shannon, Richard. *Gladstone, Vol. 1: 1809–1865.* London: Methuen Publishing, 1982.

Shaw, Wayne. "The Plymouth Pulpit: Henry Ward Beecher's Slave Auction Block." *American Transcendental Quarterly* 14, no. 4 (2000): 335–43.

"Slave Auction, 1859." EyeWitness to History, 2005. http://www.eyewitnessto history.com/slaveauction.htm.

Smith, Mark M. "Getting in Touch with Slavery and Freedom." *The Journal of American History* 95, no. 2 (2008): 381–91. https://www.jstor.org/stable/25095624.

Smith, Mark M. *How Race Is Made: Slavery, Segregation, and the Senses.* Chapel Hill: University of North Carolina Press, 2008.

Smith, Mark M. *Listening to Nineteenth-Century America.* Chapel Hill: University of North Carolina Press, 2001.

Spicer, William A. *The Flag Replaced in Sumter: A Personal Narrative.* Providence, RI: Providence Press Co., 1885. https://www.gutenberg.org/files/23846/23846-h/23846-h.htm.

Stupp, James. "Slavery and the Theatre of History: Ritual Performance on the Auction Block." *Theatre Journal* 63, no. 1 (2011): 63–71.

Thorpe, Darrell. "Handclasps and Arm Gestures in Historical Christian Art." LDS Temple Endowment. http://ldstempleendowment.blogspot.com/2009/08/laws-of-god.html.

Watson, Henry. *Narrative of Henry Watson, a Fugitive Slave.* Boston, MA: Bela Marsh, 1850.

Weld, Theodore Dwight. *American Slavery as It Is: Testimony of a Thousand Witnesses.* New York: American Anti-Slavery Office, 1839.

Wilberforce, William. "Account of a Slave Auction" taken from William Wilberforce, *A Letter on the Abolition of the Slave Trade,* Addressed to the Freeholders and Other Inhabitants of Yorkshire. London, 1807.

Wilson, A. N. *Prince Albert: The Man Who Saved the Monarchy.* New York: Harper-Collins, 2019.

Zaborney, John. "The Domestic Slave Trade in Virginia." *Encyclopedia Virginia,* 2020. https://www.encyclopediavirginia.org/Slave_Sales.

The Lamar Bus Riots

School Choice and Violent Desegregation in South Carolina

Lakin Hanna and Erica Johnson

Public school desegregation in the American South was violent. After the monumental *Brown v. Board of Education* Supreme Court decision in 1954, desegregation on a national scale took almost two decades, and parts of the South have yet to achieve full integration.[1] In South Carolina, many white parents sought to bypass desegregation measures with school choice because they were still deeply concerned about having Black and white children attend the same classrooms. When officials tried to force desegregation, some white southerners resisted violently. One such episode in South Carolina took place on March 3, 1970. White community members overturned three school buses in front of Lamar High School, making national news. Several African-American students suffered injuries, but authorities only held a small handful of the white organizers responsible for their violent actions. The Lamar bus riots negatively affected the Black community's perceptions of public schools, the justice system, and white people.

Historiography

The 1970 riots in Lamar, SC, mimicked other forms of white resistance that occurred throughout the South during public school desegregation. One of the most well-known instances took place in Little Rock, Arkansas. Nine Black high school students enrolled in the formerly all-white Central High School in 1957. White people verbally threatened and threw rocks at the Black students and their parents as they tried to enter the school. The state's governor, Oral Faubus, even blocked the school entrance, preventing the nine students from attending school that day.[2] Desegregation efforts at Americus High School in Georgia led to a similar outcome. As the Black students arrived at the all-white school, white students and parents attacked their shared vehicle with rocks, racial slurs, and threats. These students were able to make it inside of the school but still faced violence even after the school day had started.[3] White South Carolinians were watching these events unravel in larger locales, seeing that the rioters faced few, if any, consequences. Even though Lamar was a much smaller town than Little Rock or Americus, the 1970 bus riots had a significant impact on discussions of desegregation throughout the country.[4]

Although the Lamar bus riots attracted nationwide attention in the 1970s, scholars have not given the incident sufficient attention. Most historical studies only discuss the events in Lamar within larger studies of desegregation and the civil rights movement with an emphasis on the political and legal contexts. For example, Philip G. Grose included the incident in his analysis of South Carolina Governor Robert McNair's overall civil rights politics.[5] Similarly, Timothy J. Minchin used the riots to hook readers into his study of the National Association for the Advancement of Colored People's (NAACP) fight for civil rights in the South.[6] Although these and other studies include the riots in Lamar, there has not been a fully developed discussion of the events.[7] However, addressing what happened in Lamar is important in understanding the educational and racial politics of South Carolina and the United States in the 1950s, 1960s, and 1970s, as well as the legacies of those politics in the twenty-first century.

As the fiftieth anniversary of the Lamar bus riots approached, public interest in memorializing the events gained momentum. In the spring of 2019, South Carolina State Senator Gerald Malloy presented a resolution and recognized three survivors on the floor: Ronald Bacote, Clarence Brunson, and Reverend David Lunn.[8] The next year, the University of South Carolina's Center for Civil Rights and Research hosted the three survivors to share their stories.[9] These three men became the voices of the riots, but they were only three of the six on their bus, and there were three buses that day carrying about thirty young people. The students' experiences varied and influenced their lives in differing ways. The renewed public attention encourages scholars to revisit the events with additional perspectives and to resituate the story in different historical contexts. Although it happened more than fifty years ago, the event's effects still linger, and segregation still exists in many school districts across South Carolina.

Methodology

In the years leading up to the riots, white academics, ministers, and politicians delivered sermons, made speeches, and circulated pamphlets reinforcing white supremacy and condemning desegregation. These influential individuals provided encouragement and validation for white southern parents who feared public school integration. Local and national newspapers and magazines reported on Lamar in the wake of the events and around the fiftieth anniversary, including the *Florence Morning News*, *The New York Times*, *Time*, and *Jet*. However, these sources represent the perspectives of adults. Our research combines magazines, newspapers, pamphlets, and court records with recently recorded oral testimonies of survivors of the Lamar bus riots, as well as by students who experienced desegregation in nearby communities. We interviewed Clarence Brunson and Robert Hammonds Jr., two of the Black teenage bus drivers on March 3, 1970. We also incorporated public testimonies and oral histories of other teens who experienced segregation and desegregation in the area, including Dr. Alvin Heatley, David Lunn, and Dr. Carol McClain. Combining printed sources with oral accounts provides a fresh perspective on the riots as well as on the educational politics and race relations in the 1960s and 1970s in South Carolina.

Debates Over Desegregation

For much of the twentieth century, segregation permeated southern society, but people began to call for change in the 1950s, 1960s, and 1970s. The 1896 Supreme Court case *Plessy v. Ferguson* allowed segregation based on the "separate but equal" ruling. Public facilities had "colored" sections and items for all nonwhite individuals to use. For instance, Heatley shared that his earliest memory of racial discrimination was drinking from a "whites-only" water fountain at Sears in nearby Florence, SC.[10] Furthermore, Hammonds described purchasing a hot dog in Lamar: Black customers had "to go to the back window" for service.[11] As the civil rights movement made headway in desegregating public facilities and schools, white South Carolinians pushed back. Lunn, an African-American student who was on one of the buses on March 3, described tensions in Lamar during this time as "a Coke bottle shaken up . . . you don't want to take the top off!"[12] South Carolina's young people who were growing up in the Jim Crow era, such as Brunson, Hammonds, and Lunn, were ready for change, but ending segregation was not going to be easy or peaceful.

By the early 1950s, civil rights activists, legislators, and a growing number of Americans realized that the schools designated for Black students were separate but substantially unequal and saw desegregation or integration as necessary and desirable.[13] White southern parents, however, did not want to send their children to Black schools, because they knew that those schools were unequal. In 1950, *Briggs v. Elliot* was the first case to address segregated schools in South Carolina. Black residents of Clarendon County sued the local school district, chaired by Roderick Elliot. In a pretrial hearing, the school district admitted to some inequities in its Black schools. South Carolina Governor James Byrnes asked the legislature to create a school equalization program. The program was intended to provide equal facilities, transportation, and teachers' salaries in Black schools funded by a three-cent sales tax. Because of the governor's directive, the court ruled in favor of Elliot and the school district.[14] Although Americans increasingly sought desegregation, South Carolinians used equalization to keep Black and white students separate, at least for several more years.

The equalization program, even if properly administered, never solved racial disparities, nor could it meet the standards of federal mandates. The 1954 *Brown* decision ruled that even if the facilities and supplies were equal, segregation still deprived Black students of "equal educational opportunities."[15] The equalization program could not be a substitute for desegregation or integration. Still, the state moved forward with Governor McNair's plan. The Darlington County School District established Spaulding Elementary and Spaulding High School as equalization schools in 1953. Black students in Lamar attended these supposedly equal but still segregated schools. In an oral history, Hammonds shared that it was quite clear how Spaulding High School was very unequal. He spoke about hand-me-down equipment and outdated textbooks that were sometimes ripping at the seams. He was excited to integrate at Lamar High School, because Black students would finally have access to better facilities and materials.[16]

Despite federal court rulings ordering desegregation, many white southerners attended churches where their ministers used scripture to justify segregation. In some cases, those ministers published their racist sermons for distribution throughout the South. For instance, Presbyterian Reverend G. T. Gillespie gave an address in Mississippi in favor of segregation, and in 1954, the Synod of Mississippi printed it as a pamphlet that is now part of the papers of the Wallace family of Florence, SC. In the address, Gillespie used both Old and New Testament passages to argue that God intended the separation of races. Although acknowledging that "the Bible contains no clear mandate for or against segregation as between the white and 'negro' races," he believed that he could infer God's true intentions through his interpretations.[17] Many southern families clung to Reverend Gillespie's claims because Christianity was, and still is, a cornerstone of southern culture, especially in rural communities, such as Lamar.[18] Despite the *Brown* ruling, white southerners had leaders who defended segregation and legitimized their racial biases.

Many white politicians also defended white supremacy and openly defied segregation in speeches and interviews. In 1956, approximately one fifth of the US Congress signed a document resisting desegregation and agreeing to take all necessary actions to maintain segregation. Former South Carolina Senator Strom Thurmond and former Georgia Governor Richard B. Russell Jr. authored the document they officially titled *The Declaration of Constitutional Principles*, which is commonly known as *The Southern Manifesto*. *The Declaration* argued that the US Supreme Court had overstepped its judicial power in the decision to end public school segregation and that southern states should "use all lawful means to bring about a reversal of this decision, which is contrary to the Constitution and to prevent the use of force in its implementation."[19]

Once integration became a federal law and trickled down into small towns throughout the South, white families that could not afford expensive private academies rallied behind "freedom of school choice" and "neighborhood school" initiatives, which allowed Black parents to select their children's schools but provided no assistance with transportation. In most cases, these parents had no choice but to select the school closest to their homes. This gesture toward integration, in fact, perpetuated segregation.[20] White parents found these plans beneficial in making sure their children attended all-white schools, while the district claimed to abide federal and state legislation concerning public school integration. These plans effectively maintained white supremacy by putting a heavier strain on Black families. In an article for *Jet*, Warren Brown asserted, "The favorite desegregation dodges of whites were the 'freedom of choice' and the 'neighborhood school' concepts."[21]

Florence, SC, offered school choice to families, allowing Black students to attend previously all-white schools. Dr. Carol Maurice McClain shared her experiences with school choice in an oral history. Her parents discussed the choices McClain had for junior high school. She could have attended all-Black Williams Junior High School, but she chose to attend Poynor Junior High School, mainly because it offered honors classes not available at Williams. For her, it was about the quality of the curriculum and course offerings in the desegregated school. She shared how she hated Poynor because the teachers did not provide the same quality of instruction to the Black students as they did to the white students. However, she attended Poynor for all three years of junior high.[22] Although school choice was an option for Black families, it did not guarantee an equal education, even for students able to attend previously all-white schools.

White educators and parents of white students in desegregated southern classrooms found justification for their views toward Black students in segregationist pamphlets and magazines. William S. Milburn was a veteran educator from Kentucky who presented at the 1966 Citizens' Councils of America Annual Leadership Conference.[23] The organization's magazine, *The Citizen*, later published his presentation, which asserted that "the capacity of the white students to learn is markedly greater than that of the Negroes."[24] Milburn also expressed concern about the "temperament" of Black students in comparison with that of white students. He claimed that "the Negro student's emotions seem to be more intense, to operate over a wider range and with less self-restraint than those of the white students."[25] Emeritus Professor of Psychology Henry E. Garrett also published a pamphlet making similar claims. He argued that, because the average IQ of a white child was twenty points higher than that of a Black child, desegregated classrooms required a reduction in standards, meaning that white children would "work below their capacity with resultant inferior education."[26] The publication of such misinformation by educated leaders who supported racist ideologies led whites almost to hysteria once the federal government forced school districts to desegregate.

Although *Brown v. Board of Education* was a monumental Supreme Court case, the "all deliberate speed" clause stifled its efforts of public school desegregation because southern states used the broad statement to stall public-school desegregation. Legislators started to realize that these school districts used this vague description, possibly done to appease southern Democrats, as a justification for keeping schools mostly segregated with only a few Black students. In 1965, Charles C. Green challenged freedom of choice plans in the US District Court for the Eastern District of Virginia. The US Supreme Court settled the case in 1968. With a unanimous verdict, the Supreme Court rejected freedom of choice plans and required districts to develop realistic plans for desegregation. More than fourteen years after the *Brown* decision, the "the Court now required school boards to eliminate affirmatively all vestiges of segregation."[27] In other words, school choice was no longer an option by 1968. Both Black and white families had their reservations about desegregation but did not necessarily know what to do after the court rulings.

Two years after *Green v. New Kent County*, families in Lamar faced desegregation. In early 1970, the federal courts ordered the Darlington County School District to create a plan of action for desegregation that state and federal officials would have to approve. Rezoning the Lamar area seemed like the best option for desegregation, so the Darlington County School Board redrew the lines to determine where students would attend public schools based on their address. There was perceived socioeconomic bias to the new zoning. One white parent claimed, "Not a single doctor, lawyer, school-board member or anybody prominent got put in the nigger schools."[28] Anger over desegregation now became focused on both class and race in South Carolina.

Some African-American students also resisted integration. For example, Brunson, a senior at Spaulding High School in 1970, shared that many of his classmates did not want to attend and graduate from a school in which they had no pride. Moreover, the students had already purchased graduation caps and gowns, class rings, and varsity athletic jackets, and most students would not have been able to afford to repurchase these items for Lamar High School. Brunson's mother provided for him and his three siblings, earning only thirteen dollars a week.[29] Like many parents, she struggled to provide for her children and had little money for duplicative purchases.

Beyond the financial hardships on families, many Black teachers lost their jobs during public school desegregation through consolidation. Florence County, the neighbor to Darlington, ended up with a largely unbalanced ratio of Black to white teachers once desegregation began in their schools.[30] In losing teachers who looked like them, "Black parents feared that the children would be forced to adopt White culture and lose their own rich culture and identity."[31] Moreover, some white teachers discriminated against their new Black students.[32] McClain explained how she attended clinics where Black adults prepared them for desegregated classrooms. The adults told the Black children to sit in the front of the classroom so the white teacher could not miss them, but the teachers "would leave the front of the room" and "stand beside" the desks of Black students so they did not have to look at them.[33]

Not surprisingly, African-American families felt that the new desegregation decision still left African-American students underserved, but they recognized that advocacy for true equality could jeopardize their livelihoods and homes. Many of these families sharecropped on land owned by white families. Some white employers gave Black parents the ultimatum to do as white community members told them or face the consequences. Despite these obstacles, "Black children in Lamar boycotted their schools almost one hundred percent because their parents didn't think the plan brought enough integration."[34] These students faced strong resistance. Leading up to the events on March 3, white families met to protest desegregation. The "Freedom of Choice" organization in Darlington County developed plans to resist desegregation. One newspaper article claimed, "More than 800 persons met at St. John's High School" and "voted to oppose court ordered integration of Darlington County public schools."[35] St. John's was a "white" high school for the city of Darlington and made a favorable location for white families to discuss these matters while inherently excluding the Black community and their perspectives on the federal order of immediate integration. At another rally at Lamar High School, Congressman Albert Watson "congratulated the group for carrying out their protest in a calm manner," and "said that because of the interest and non-violent manner of the protest," Americans were listening to southern "problems."[36]

Many white families in Lamar were upset over desegregation because they believed the government had "forced" it upon them. This perception was so pervasive in Darlington County that even white students espoused it. According to the *Florence Morning News*, white students from Lamar wrote a letter to President Richard Nixon in response to the desegregation order. They claimed that Lamar would have sixty-five percent Black enrollment, making white students the minority. Echoing white educators like Milburn and Garrett, the students argued that "we will suffer both academically and psychologically."[37] With emotions running high, the nonviolent approach praised by Albert Watson would not last long.

Lamar Bus Riots

Desegregated classes in Darlington County officially began on February 18. Many white families boycotted the school and petitioned to shut it down.[38] Even when these attempts began to lose steam, white parents were unwilling to watch their way of life disrupted in the name of progress. They now turned to violence. On the morning of March 3, 1970, a large crowd of white citizens formed along the roadside where public school buses would transport Black students from Spaulding High School to Lamar High School. Many of these citizens armed themselves with chains and ax handles, but there were city and state police present at multiple points along the bus route to stop the crowd from breaking into a riot.[39] Darlington County viewed these precautions as necessary because other incidents of violence had taken place during desegregation, including the attacks on the Little Rock Nine in Arkansas.

That morning, South Carolina Highway Patrol officers were not supposed to route the buses carrying the African-American students to Lamar High

School, but they did so anyway. As the buses approached the school, the white citizens entered the road and began throwing rocks and glass objects into the buses, harming almost every Black student aboard. "I screamed: 'Oh Lord, help us. . . . I was so afraid that I was going to be killed," Sally Mae Wilds recounted to Darlington County NAACP President Arthur Stanley.[40] Students were able to evacuate the buses moments before the mob over-turned them. Police released pepper spray and gas to disperse the crowd; however, many students commented that the state troopers and county law enforcement officers seemed unconcerned with their safety. For instance, Lunn told Stanley that "one of the patrolmen seemed to think it was funny to see some 'nigger' child assaulted."[41] After the students were safely inside of the school, Dr. Sidney Griffith came to treat their wounds.[42] School officials told the African-American students who had been attacked that they were going to be sent home for the day. Many of the students decided to have their parents pick them up or have police officers escort back to their residences.

As news reached Columbia, state officials were horrified. Governor McNair classified the attack as "an act which defies all human reasoning and understanding."[43] On March 3, McNair ordered the school to remain closed for an undisclosed amount of time and worked with South Carolina Attorney General John N. Mitchell to deploy approximately one hundred National Guard troops stationed in Hartsville to Lamar to deter additional violence. On a federal level, Vice President Spiro T. Agnew stated, "violence was aimed unbelievably . . . at children who are innocent participants in the court-ordered desegregation of a Southern school district" and prom-ised that those responsible for the attacks would be "brought to the bar of justice."[44]

By March 6, 1970, local law enforcement officers had initially taken twenty-seven white rioters into custody on varying charges. After less than a day, a magistrate judge of Darlington County, the Honorable Sam Chapman, released all the men on a mere two-thousand-dollar bond. After the judge's decision, one white male spectator remarked, "I don't think there'll be any more trouble, not on the surface leastways. Remember the raccoon goes hunting at night."[45] Multiple other white citizens present in the courtroom that day made similar comments. The use of threatening language to scare African Americans out of exercising their rights was not a new phenomenon of the 1960s. In the late 1800s, the Ku Klux Klan used intimidation tactics to prevent African Americans from pursuing legal actions against others in the community. Richard Schaefer noted, "The Klan became fairly success-ful in undermining the actions of the Radical Republicans in Congress by intimidating the freed slaves to keep them from voting."[46] These methods of terrorism continued throughout the twentieth century not only through lynchings, arson, and other acts of violence, but also through Confederate memorials, which were designed to oppress and silence African Americans.[47]

The white citizens' remarks in the courtroom showed their willingness to intimidate Black people. It also demonstrated their confidence that whites would face few consequences for doing so. In fact, only three of the twenty-seven people arrested were charged, and they received light sentences, ranging from twelve to twenty-four months and fines of differing amounts. The men served only six months, and after they paid their fines, they were released on probation. These actions highlight how southern circuit courts showed leniency toward white convicts, in this case, finding ways to lessen the consequences for those who incited violence against the Black community.

The NAACP appealed the light punishments given to those who incited a riot, destroyed state-owned transportation, and injured multiple minors. By 1972, the NAACP had secured a hearing before the South Carolina Supreme Court in hopes that justice would be served to the Black community in Lamar and that the three main organizers who had been charged, Jeryl Best, Delmar Kirven, and James Dewey Marsh, would serve substantial sentences for their crimes.[48] Notably, Best owned Mr. B's Seafood House in Lydia, SC, about ten miles North of Lamar. His own daughter attended school in neighboring Lee County, so his leadership in Darlington County was somewhat surprising and suggests that some of the rioters were not seeking to protect their own children but simply wanted to prevent integration in any South Carolina school.[49] In seeking to overturn the ruling, the NAACP hoped to deter similar crimes as school boards adhered to federal legislation concerning integration. The lawyers for the NAACP questioned whether Wade S. Weatherford Jr., the initial presiding judge, had the power to reduce the defendants' sentences. The South Carolina Supreme Court overruled the lower court's decision and required the defendants to serve the remainder of their sentences. This ruling was a great victory for the NAACP and the Black community within South Carolina.[50]

Even after the courts carried out justice, many white southerners still believed that the attackers were heroes for standing up for what they believed was right. According to an essay in *The Afro-American*, one local resident, George Dority, "regretted not being with the two hundred whites who attacked the buses and highway patrolmen with bricks, chains and clubs."[51] Others were not supportive of the violence but backed the sentiments of the protestors. One *New York Times* article summarized this notion quite clearly as: "Condemn the act but condone the motives."[52] As evidenced by the interviews and oral histories, many white residents seemed to have been fine with living around Black people, having Black employees, and maybe even sharing public spaces with the Black community, but they opposed school desegregation because it might allow for the dismantling of the racial ideologies and hierarchy that many of their ancestors fought to maintain in the Civil War.

One of the hardest realizations for the Black community was that people they *knew* were members of the mob—people they had worked under, sharecropped with, and knew as acquaintances. Lunn shared, "The FBI showed us pictures. These people were our next-door neighbors. . . . We knew all of them."[53] These white southerners were not out-of-state agitators storming into Lamar and harming African-American children. They were fellow local citizens. Hammonds recounted a similar feeling. He shared a childhood story of white neighbors playing basketball with him and his brothers. On the day of the riot, Hammonds remembered looking out the windows of the bus he was driving and seeing those same white boys taking part in terrorizing African-American students. Brunson also shared a similar reaction. He often asked himself, "How was I good enough to play with you and work with you but could not go to school with you?"[54] The idea of living among people willing to use violence to stop desegregation was not only terrifying for African Americans but also confusing and dehumanizing.

The Black community, especially its youths, was resilient despite the physical and psychological harm suffered that day. Both Brunson and Hammonds spoke of the peaceful coexistence of white and Black students within the schools after Lamar's desegregation.[55] When the school finally reopened in March, one student told a newspaper that she was unhappy about desegregation, but her education took priority: "Somehow we have a feeling that if adults speak less, the students and teachers would find the situation manageable—even perhaps profitable. It's worth an honest try."[56] Progress may have been slow and hampered by violence, but eventually it came. A newspaper article written five years after the riots discussed how unified this desegregated school had become. The Southern Association of Schools and Colleges accredited all the public schools in the Lamar area, with an "emphasis on quality education," and that body declared, "The transition . . . in Lamar has gone far better than almost anyone dared believe it could."[57] Reflecting on the events, Lunn advocated for reconciliation: "We cannot forget, but we must be able to forgive."[58] His statement reflects how many African Americans living in Lamar have been able to reckon with those who harmed them and their families.

Although this event occurred only for a few hours, it shaped local and national debates on public school desegregation, especially the issue of busing. In fact, President Nixon included antibusing as a part of his presidential reelection campaign platform in 1972. In a speech, he claimed he wanted to put a stop to the "anger, fear and turmoil in local communities, and worst of all, agonized concern among hundreds of thousands of parents for the education and safety of their children who have been forced by court to be bused miles away from their neighborhood schools." He proposed legislation to provide funds to improve schools in poorer neighborhoods instead—reminiscent of South Carolina's equalization school program. Although he admitted, "There's no escaping the fact that some people do oppose busing because of racial prejudice," he added "but to go on from this to conclude that antibusing is simply a code word for prejudice is a vicious libel on millions of concerned parents who oppose busing—not because they are against desegregation, but because they are for better education for their children."[59] *Jet* magazine published a lengthy response. The author explained that some Black Americans opposed busing because it was a "bankrupt, suicidal method of desegregating schools, based on the false notion that Black children are unable to learn unless they are in the same setting with white children."[60] The article featured multiple pictures from the Lamar bus riots. Although court-ordered busing continued until 1999, many American schools remain segregated and the fight to keep them that way continues.[61]

Legacies of Choice

One legacy of the Lamar bus riots is the question of whether parents should be able to choose their children's public school. Leading up to the events of March 3, 1970, many white families leaned into the idea of choice to avoid exposing their children to an integrated student body. Although there has been some progress in public school integration across the United States, the freedom of choice movement has been revived within the past few years, especially in the South. This time, the movement includes racial as well as social issues, such as critical race theory; issues pertaining to lesbian, gay, bisexual, transgender, queer/questioning, intersex, and asexual/aromantic/agender plus other individuals; social–emotional learning; and basic sex education. American political polarization has begun to play out in schools as religious and political leaders are feeding parents misinformation yet again.[62] *Vouchers, school choice,* and *education savings accounts* have all become buzzwords for politicians within the past few years. Vouchers allow parents to use the money allotted for their student within a public school to offset the cost of private school tuition. Education savings accounts are public funds placed in special accounts for parents to access and use for private educational costs, such as tuition, textbooks, and other types of programs.[63] Many proponents argue that these programs allow parents to spend the money they pay into the school system as they see fit, whereas opponents argue that the programs deprive low-income schools of the funding needed to serve large populations of at-risk students.

Moreover, public schools remain highly segregated, largely on the basis of race and socioeconomic status, because of the way the United States funds public schools. In South Carolina, as in other states, property taxes fund a significant portion of public school budgets. The value of the homes within the district determines how much funding a district receives.[64] Under this system, lower income neighborhoods will always have poorer funded schools, and even today, many of those impoverished neighborhoods have majority-Black populations. In large part, this "racial residential segregation" stems from the redlining practices of the 1930s, 1940s, and 1950s.[65] Redlining deemed those living in certain areas low-income and high-risk loan applicants, which often prevented African-American families from obtaining mortgages and other loans. During the 1950s and 1960s, middle-class white families moved to suburban neighborhoods with high property values and well-funded schools, "a process facilitated by federal government housing and transportation investments."[66] However, redlining laws kept Black families out of suburban housing developments, and the property values of the houses in African-American neighborhoods remained low. Therefore, schools in predominantly Black neighborhoods had and continue to have less funding. Current policy makers argue that Black families can use school choice to overcome the impacts of racial residential segregation on their children's educations.[67] However, these arguments ignore the challenges, especially those related to transportation, that Black families face in placing their children in districts where they do not live. Scholars sometimes refer to these burdens as the "parent tax." Along with paying this "tax," there are also discrepancies in the information concerning school choice given to white families and families of color.[68]

Magnet schools are another form of school choice that emerged in the 1970s, but most studies on them have focused on urban areas, not rural areas such as Lamar.[69] Magnet schools are public institutions with specialized programs and curricula intended to create "an alternative to mandatory reassignment and forced busing." Districts should manage enrollments "to ensure a racially balanced student population."[70] In 2007, the Supreme Court ruled that magnet schools could not use race as an admission criterion, but they could use neighborhood demographics and socioeconomic status.[71] The lasting legacies of redlining ensure some level of diversity. There are currently seven magnet programs or magnet schools within Darlington County.[72] However, they are in the county's two larger towns. Families from a smaller town such as Lamar would still have to find transportation, which is especially burdensome for low-income families.

Conclusion

Desegregating schools in the South is still underway, and evasion policies such as school choice, as well as outright violence, have marred public school integration efforts. This study shifts away from a focus on the political and legal history of the Lamar bus riots to emphasize the educational context and legacies. Incorporating oral testimony from African Americans who experienced desegregation as young people in Darlington and Florence Counties helps to decenter the perspectives of predominantly white adults. Although Lamar was unique because of its small size, the riots grew out of the same racial tensions present across the South. The Lamar bus riots were senseless acts of violence that harmed innocent children. They were carried out by individuals who wanted to maintain white supremacy in southern public schools. Ministers, educators, and politicians misinformed parents and community members about the benefits of integration. As a result, misguided individuals went so far as to defend those who broke the law. The Lamar bus riots provide not only a lens to study developments concerning race relations within South Carolina's educational system but also an important lesson regarding the work still needed to achieve integration.

Lakin Hanna is from Lancaster, South Carolina. She is a recent graduate from Francis Marion University with a degree in secondary history education. She plans to teach history in the Lancaster County School District.

Erica Johnson is an associate professor of history and faculty coordinator for Universities Studying Slavery at Francis Marion University. She has published two books and numerous articles on various elements of the African diaspora and the legacies of slavery in the Americas.

NOTES

1. Although scholars and the public alike often use the terms *desegregation* and *integration* interchangeably, they are not synonymous. Warren Brown explained the difference in 1972. He noted that desegregation involves adding just one Black student to a white school. Integration would only occur if peoples of different races accept one another. Integration is about more than numbers of students. He identified a third category: racial balance. This would mean that a school maintained "a fixed number of students of one race in proportion to the number of students of another race attending a school." See Warren Brown, "Busing: Bigots Battle to Keep Blacks Separate and Unequal," *Jet*, 42, no. 8 (May 18, 1972): 24. https://books.google.com/books?id=trEDAAAAMBAJ.

2. See David L. Chappell, "Diversity within a Racial Group: White People in Little Rock, 1957–1959." *The Arkansas Historical Review*, 66, no. 2 (2007): 181–93.

3. See Jim Auchmutey, *The Class of '65: A Student, a Divided Town, and the Long Road to Forgiveness* (New York: PublicAffairs, 2015).

4. Little Rock had a population of nearly one hundred thousand people. Americus had a population of about thirteen thousand people. In contrast, Lamar had only twelve hundred residents. National news outlets were quick to point out Lamar's small population when reporting on the bus riots. See, for example, "South Carolina: Rebellion at Lamar." *Time*, March 16, 1970. https://content.time.com/time/subscriber/article/0,33009,909055,00.html; William F. McIlwain, "On the Overturning of the Two School Buses in Lamar, S. C." *Esquire*, January 1971, 98; and "A Bad Day in Lamar." *Newsweek*, March 16, 1970, 26."

5. Philip G. Grose, *South Carolina on the Brink: Robert McNair and the Politics of Civil Rights* (Columbia: University of South Carolina Press, 2006), 278–81.

6. Timothy J. Minchin, "Making Best Use of the New Laws: The NAACP and the Fight for Civil Rights in the South, 1965–1975," *The Journal of Southern History* 74, no. 3 (2008): 669–70.

7. See also Billy B. Hathorn, "The Changing Politics of Race: Congressman Albert William Watson and the South Carolina Republican Party, 1965–1975," *South Carolina Historical Magazine* 89, no. 4 (1988): 232; and Winfred B. Moore and Orville Vernon Burton, eds., *Toward the Meeting of the Waters: Currents in the Civil Rights Movement of South Carolina during the Twentieth Century* (Columbia: University of South Carolina Press, 2008), 16–17.

8. South Carolina Senate, "Senate Resolution to Recognize an Incredible Group of South Carolina Citizens from Darlington County for Their Role in the Fight for Desegregation and for Their Outstanding Resiliency in the Face of Trauma," 123rd Session, April 24, 2019, S. 784 (https://www.scstatehouse.gov/sess123_2019-2020/bills/784.htm).

9. See John Monk, "After 50 years, SC White Supremacists School Bus Riot Still Haunts Survivors," *The State*, March 8, 2020.

10. Alvin Heatley, "Eyewitnesses of the Civil Rights Movement," in person, USC Center for Civil Rights History and Research, Jerusalem Baptist Church, Hartsville, SC, March 3, 2023. In 1956, Heatley graduated from Butler High School, an equalization school in Darlington County. After earning his doctorate in

education, he returned to Darlington County as a coach and administrator in the public schools. The South Carolina House and Senate honored him with resolutions on May 26, 2015. South Carolina Senate, "A Senate Resolution to Honor Dr. Alvin T. Heatley of Darlington County for His Outstanding Accomplishments in the Field of Education and for His Dedicated Service to Butler Heritage Foundation as Its Chairman and to the State of South Carolina," S. 818, 121st Session (2015) (https://www.scstatehouse.gov/sess121_2015-2016/bills/818.htm); South Carolina House of Representatives, "A House Resolution to Honor Dr. Alvin T. Heatley" of Darlington County for His Outstanding Accomplishments in the Field of Education and for His Dedicated Service to Butler Heritage Foundation as Its Chairman and to the State of South Carolina," H. 4251, SC General Assembly, 121st Session (2015) (https://www.scstatehouse.gov/sess121_2015-2016/bills/4251.htm).

11. Robert Hammonds Jr., interview by Lakin Hanna, March 6, 2023. https://libguides.fmarion.edu/OralHistoryProj/RHammonds.

12. David Lunn, "Eyewitnesses of the Civil Rights Movement," in person, presented at the program Eyewitnesses: Memories of the South Carolina Civil Rights Movement, Spartanburg, SC, April 3, 2023. The author reports that there is no URL for this presentation.

13. American public support for school desegregation swelled from the 1950s to the 1970s. According to public polls, the percentage of Americans wanting integrated schools increased from forty-eight in 1956 to eighty-six in 1972. For more, see Erica Frankenberg and Rebecca Jacobsen, "Trends—School Integration Polls," *The Public Opinion Quarterly* 75, no. 4 (2011): 788–811.

14. Delia B. Allen, "The Forgotten *Brown* Case: *Briggs v. Elliot* and Its Legacy in South Carolina," *Peabody Journal of Education* 94, no. 4 (2019): 442–46.

15. Allen, "Forgotten *Brown* Case," 445.

16. Hammonds Jr., interview by Lakin Hanna.

17. Reverend G. T. Gillespie, "A Statement in Defense of the Principle of Racial Segregation," Reprint of speech given at the Synod of the Mississippi Presbyterian Church, November 4, 1954. Folder 285, Wallace Family Papers, South Caroliniana Library, University of South Carolina, Columbia [hereinafter cited as WFP]. The original text is available online (https://egrove.olemiss.edu/cgi/viewcontent.cgi?article=1000&context=citizens_pamph).

18. See, for example, Leah M. Bouchard, Sara Kye Price, and Laura E. T. Swan, "The Role of the Contemporary Christian Church in the Rural American South: Philosophical Approaches to Operationalizing Religion in Research," *Journal of the North American Association of Christians in Social Work* 47, no. 2 (2020): 47–64; David Goldfield, *Still Fighting the Civil War: The American South and Southern History* (Baton Rouge: Louisiana State University Press, 2013); and Robert B. Jones, *White Too Long: The Legacy of White Supremacy in American Christianity* (New York: Simon & Schuster, 2021).

19. US Congress (102nd). "The 'Southern Manifesto,'" 102 Cong. Rec. 4515–16 (1956).

20. Patricia Dillon, "Civil Rights and School Desegregation in Sanford," *The Florida Historical Quarterly* 76, no. 3 (1998)," 310–25.

21. Brown, "Busing," 24.

22. Dr. Carol Maurice McClain, interview by Alex Lietka and Erica Johnson, April 11, 2023. https://libguides.fmarion.edu/OralHistoryProj/CMcClain.

23. Better known as White Citizens Councils, these groups began in Indianola, Mississippi, after the *Brown* decision. They quickly spread from Mississippi into Texas, Arkansas, Alabama, and South Carolina, fighting against the integration of public spaces. See Harold C. Fleming, "Resistance Movements and Racial Desegregation," *The Annals of the American Academy of Political and Social Science* 304 (1956): 46–47.

24. William S. Milburn, "Some Problems of Integration," *The Citizen,* April 1966, 10.

25. Milburn, "Some Problems of Integration," 11.

26. Henry E. Garrett, *How Classroom Desegregation Will Work* (Richmond, VA: The Patrick Henry Press, 1965).

27. Jody Allen and Brian Daugherity, "Recovering a 'Lost' Story Using Oral History: The United States Supreme Court's Historic '*Green v. New Kent County, Virginia,*' Decision," *The Oral History Review* 33, no. 2 (2006) 41.

28. Anonymous quoted in McIlwain, "On the Overturning," 98.

29. Clarence Brunson, interview by Lakin Hanna.

30. Alabama Council on Human Relations, American Friends Service Committee, Delta Ministry of the National Council of Churches, NAACP Legal Defense and Education Fund, Inc., Southern Regional Council, and Washington Research Project, *It's Not Over in the South: School Desegregation in Forty-Three Southern Cities Eighteen Years after* Brown (Washington, DC, and Atlanta, GA: Southern Education Foundation and Urban Coalition, 1972) (https://files.eric.ed.gov/full text/ED065646.pdf).

31. Barbara Loomis Jackson, "Race, Education, and the Politics of Fear," *Educational Policy* 22, no. 1 (2008): 143.

32. See James E. Haney, "The Effects of the Brown Decision on Black Educators," *The Journal of Negro Education* 47, no. 1 (1978): 88–95; Linda C. Tilman, "(Un) Intended Consequences? The Impact of the Brown v. Board of Education Decision on Employment Status of Black Educators," *Education and Urban Society* 36, no. 3 (2004): 280–303; and Adam Fairclough, "The Costs of Brown: Black Teachers and School Integration," *Journal of American History* 91, no. 1 (2004): 43–55.

33. McClain, interview by Alex Lietka and Erica Johnson.

34. McIlwain, "On the Overturning," 98.

35. "Newspaper Clippings: 'Freedom of Choice' Opposes Integration Order" [newspaper clippings], Darlington County, SC: Lamar Riots Collection, Darlington Historical Commission and Museum [hereinafter cited as DHCM], n.d.

36. Jerry L. Allegood, "Watson Backs Protest," *Florence Morning News,* n.d., DHCM.

37. "Student Letter Critical of Decision," *Florence Morning News,* February 1, 1970, 3A.

38. "Darlington Attendance Up," *Florence Morning News,* February 26, 1970, 7B.

39. McIlwain, "On the Overturning," 99.

40. See Arthur W. Stanley, "White Violence—Lamar, SC," *The Crisis: A Record for the Darker Races* 77, no. 5 (1970): 200.

41. Stanley, "White Violence," 199.

42. McIlwain, "On the Overturning," 99.

43. Jon Nordheimer, "Gas Routs Whites Who Upset Buses at Carolina School," *New York Times*, March 4, 1970.

44. Quoted in Herb Frazier, "Lamar Riots," in *The South Carolina Encyclopedia*, Walter B. Edgar, ed. (University of South Carolina Institute for Southern Studies, June 8, 2014).

45. Jon Nordheimer, "27 Whites, Accused of Carolina School Riot, Lauded by Neighbors," *New York Times*, March 6, 1970 (https://www.nytimes.com/1970/03/06/archives/27-whites-accused-of-Carolina-school-riot-lauded-by-neighbors.html).

46. Richard T. Schaefer, "The Ku Klux Klan: Continuity and Change," *Phylon* 32, no. 2 (1971): 145.

47. For a useful history of Confederate memorials and their ideology, see Roger C. Hartley, *Monumental Harm: Reckoning with Jim Crow Era Confederate Monuments* (Columbia: University of South Carolina Press, 2021).

48. *State v Best*, 257 S.C. 361 (1972) (https://law.justia.com/cases/south-Carolina/supreme-court/1972/19343–1.html).

49. McIlwain, "On the Overturning," 100.

50. *State v Best*, 257 S.C. 361 (1972).

51. "Many of Lamar's Whites Seem Proud of Attack on Children," *The Afro-American*, March 17, 1970, DHCM.

52. Jon Nordheimer, "Lamar Gives Its Answer to the Courts," *New York Times*, March 8, 1970 (https://www.nytimes.com/1970/03/08/archives/lamar-gives-its-answer-to-the-courts.html).

53. Monk, "After 50 Years."

54. Brunson, interview by Lakin Hanna.

55. Brunson, interview by Lakin Hanna; Hammonds Jr., interview by Lakin Hanna.

56. "First, Education," Darlington County, SC: Lamar Riots Collection, DHCM, n.d.

57. "Lamar: 5 Years After," *Florence Morning News*, March 20, 1975.

58. Lunn, "Eyewitnesses."

59. "Transcript of Nixon's Statement on School Busing," *New York Times*, March 17, 1972, 22A (https://www.nytimes.com/1972/03/17/archives/transcript-of-nixons-statement-on-school-busing.html).

60. Brown, "Busing," 30.

61. Gloria J. Browne-Marshall, "Busing Ended 20 Years Ago. Today Our Schools Are Segregated Once Again," *Time*, September 11, 2019.

62. See, for example, Jaime Lovegrove, "SC Senate Policy Stakes: Graham Favors 'School Choice,' Harrison Backs Public Schools," *Post and Courier*, October 25, 2020; Lauren Camera, "DeVos Says School Choice Is Coming, like It or Not," *U.S. World News & World Report*, October 20, 2020; and David Marques, "Conservatives: 'School Choice' Will Punish Public Schools for Wokeness." *The New Republic*, January 27, 2023.

63. "Types of Private School Choice," in *The ABCs of School Choice* (Indianapolis, IN: EdChoice, 2023), 3 (https://files.eric.ed.gov/fulltext/ED628554.pdf).

64. In 1977, South Carolina passed the Education Finance Act, creating a formula for funding schools based on the numbers of students with and without special needs or services. The state passed the Education Improvement Act in

1984, creating a new sales tax to fund education. The state also has an education lottery. Beyond these state funds and some federally funded programs, school districts must provide thirty percent of education costs. See Allen, "Forgotten *Brown* Case," 447.

65. Mark Pearcy, "'The Most Insidious Legacy'—Teaching about Redlining and the Impact of Racial Residential Segregation," *The Geography Teacher* 17, no. 2 (2019): 44–55

66. Angela Simms and Elizabeth Talbert, "Racial Residential Segregation and School Choice," *Phylon* 56, no. 1 (2019)," 34.

67. Pearcy, "'The Most Insidious Legacy,'" 47.

68. Simms and Talbert, "Racial Residential Segregation and School Choice," 34.

69. See, for example, Ellen Goldring and Claire Smrekar, "Magnet Schools and the Pursuit of Racial Balance," *Education and Urban Society* 33, no. 1 (1998): 17–35; and Loretta F. Meeks, Wendell A. Meeks, and Claudia A. Warren, "Racial Desegregation: Magnet Schools, Vouchers, Privatization, and Home Schooling," *Education and Urban Society* 33, no. 1 (2000): 88–101.

70. Goldring and Smrekar, "Magnet Schools," 17.

71. Virginia Riel, Toby L. Parcel, Roslyn Arlin Mickelson, and Stephen Samuel Smith, "Do Magnet and Charter Schools Exacerbate or Ameliorate Inequality?" *Sociology Compass* 12, no. 9 (2018): 3.

72. Some schools include an on-site program. For instance, Darlington High School has an early college program. Other schools are full magnet schools, such as the Thornwell School for the Arts in Darlington. All seven magnet programs and schools are in the cities of Darlington or Hartsville. Darlington has a population of around sixty-one hundred, and Hartsville has a population of approximately seventy-five hundred. Neither of those populations qualify as urban, as they number less than ten thousand people (South Carolina Department of Education, Directory of Magnet Schools; https://ed.sc.gov/districts-schools/school-choice/school-choice/magnet-schools/).

WORKS CITED

"A Bad Day in Lamar." *Newsweek*, March 16, 1970, 26.

Alabama Council on Human Relations, American Friends Service Committee, Delta Ministry of the National Council of Churches, NAACP Legal Defense and Education Fund, Inc., Washington Research Project, and Southern Regional Council. *It's Not Over in the South: School Desegregation in Forty-Three Southern Cities Eighteen Years after* Brown. Washington, DC, and Atlanta, GA: Southern Education Foundation and Urban Coalition, 1972. https://files.eric.ed.gov/fulltext/ED065646.pdf.

Allegood, Jerry L. "Watson Backs Protest," *Florence Morning News*, n.d. Darlington County, SC: Darlington Historical Commission and Museum.

Allen, Delia B. "The Forgotten *Brown* Case: *Briggs v. Elliot* and Its Legacy in South Carolina." *Peabody Journal of Education* 94, no. 4 (2019): 442–46.

Allen, Jody, and Brian Daugherity. "Recovering a 'Lost' Story Using Oral History: The United States Supreme Court's Historic '*Green v. New Kent County,*

Virginia,' Decision." *The Oral History Review* 33, no. 2 (2006). https://www.jstor .org/stable/4495381.

Auchmutey, Jim. *The Class of '65: A Student, a Divided Town, and the Long Road to Forgiveness.* New York: PublicAffairs, 2015.

Bouchard, Leah M., Sara Kye Price, and Laura E. T. Swan. "The Role of the Contemporary Christian Church in the Rural American South: Philosophical Approaches to Operationalizing Religion in Research." *Journal of the North American Association of Christians in Social Work* 47, no. 2 (2020): 47–64.

Brown, Warren. "Busing: Bigots Battle to Keep Blacks Separate and Unequal." *Jet,* 42, no. 8, May 18, 1972. https://books.google.com/books?id=trEDAAAAMBAJ.

Browne-Marshall, Gloria J. "Busing Ended 20 Years Ago. Today Our Schools Are Segregated Once Again." *Time,* September 11, 2019. https://time.com/5673555/ busing-school-segregation/.

Camera, Lauren. "DeVos Says School Choice Is Coming, like It or Not." *U.S. World News & World Report,* October 20, 2020. https://www.usnews.com/news/ elections/articles/.

Chappell, David L. "Diversity within a Racial Group: White People in Little Rock, 1957–1959." *The Arkansas Historical Review* 66, no. 2 (2007): 181–93. https:// www.jstor.org/stable/40018698.

"Darlington Attendance Up," *Florence Morning News,* February 26, 1970, 7B.

Dillon, Patricia. "Civil Rights and School Desegregation in Sanford." *The Florida Historical Quarterly* 76, no. 3 (1998): 310–25. https://www.jstor.org/ stable/30148970.

"Directory of Magnet Schools." South Carolina Department of Education, n.d. https://ed.sc.gov/districts-schools/school-choice/school-choice/ magnet-schools/.

Fairclough, Adam. "The Costs of Brown: Black Teachers and School Integration." *Journal of American History* 91, no. 1 (2004): 43–55. https://www.umass .edu/legal/Hilbink/250/Adam%20Fairclough%20-%20The%20Costs%20of%20 Brown.pdf.

"First, Education." Darlington County, SC: Lamar Riots Collection, Darlington Historical Commission and Museum, n.d.

Fleming, Harold C. "Resistance Movements and Racial Desegregation." *The Annals of the American Academy of Political and Social Science* 304 (1956): 46–47. https:// www.jstor.org/stable/1032106.

Frankenberg, Erica, and Rebecca Jacobsen. "Trends—School Integration Polls." *The Public Opinion Quarterly* 75, no. 4 (2011): 788–811. https://www.jstor .org/stable/41288418.

Frazier, Herb. "Lamar Riots." In *The South Carolina Encyclopedia,* edited by Walter B. Edgar. University of South Carolina Institute for Southern Studies, June 8, 2014. https://www.scencyclopedia.org/sce/entries/lamar-riots/.

Garrett, Henry E. *How Classroom Desegregation Will Work.* Richmond, VA: The Patrick Henry Press, 1965.

Gillespie, Reverend G. T. "A Statement in Defense of the Principle of Racial Segregation." Reprint of speech given at Synod of the Mississippi Presbyterian Church, Folder 285, Wallace Family Papers, South Caroliniana Library.

November 4, 1954. Full text available at https://egrove.olemiss.edu/cgi/view content.cgi?article=1000&context=citizens_pamph.

Goldfield, David. *Still Fighting the Civil War: The American South and Southern History*. Baton Rouge: Louisiana State University Press, 2013.

Goldring, Ellen, and Claire Smrekar. "Magnet Schools and the Pursuit of Racial Balance." *Education and Urban Society* 33, no. 1 (1998): 17–35.

Grose, Philip G. *South Carolina on the Brink: Robert McNair and the Politics of Civil Rights*. Columbia: University of South Carolina Press, 2006.

Haney, James E. "The Effects of the Brown Decision on Black Educators." *The Journal of Negro Education* 47, no. 1 (1978): 88–95. https://www.jstor.org/stable/2967104.

Hartley, Roger C. *Monumental Harm: Reckoning with Jim Crow Era Confederate Monuments*. Columbia: University of South Carolina Press, 2021.

Hathorn, Billy B. "The Changing Politics of Race: Congressman Albert William Watson and the South Carolina Republican Party, 1965–1975." *South Carolina Historical Magazine*, 89, no. 4 (1988): 227–41. https://www.jstor.org/stable/27568058.

Heatley, Alvin T. "Eyewitnesses of the Civil Rights Movement." In person. Presented at the Eyewitnesses: Memories of the South Carolina Civil Rights Movement, March 3, 2023.

Jackson, Barbara Loomis. "Race, Education, and the Politics of Fear." *Educational Policy* 22, no. 1 (2008): 130–54.

Jones, Robert B. *White Too Long: The Legacy of White Supremacy in American Christianity*. New York: Simon & Schuster, 2021.

"Lamar: 5 Years After," *Florence Morning News*, March 20, 1975.

Lovegrove, Jaime. "SC Senate Policy Stakes: Graham Favors 'School Choice,' Harrison Backs Public Schools." *Post and Courier*, October 25, 2020. https://www.postandcourier.com/article_40cac610-1477-11eb-b1c3-afd330079cc0.html.

Lunn, David. "Eyewitnesses of the Civil Rights Movement." In person. Presented at the program Eyewitnesses: Memories of the South Carolina Civil Rights Movement, Spartanburg, SC, April 3, 2023.

"Many of Lamar's Whites Seem Proud of Attack on Children." *The Afro-American*, March 17, 1970. Darlington County, SC: Lamar Riots Collection, Darlington Historical Commission and Museum.

Marques, David. "Conservatives: 'School Choice' Will Punish Public Schools for Wokeness." *The New Republic*, January 27, 2023. https://newrepublic.com/article/170201/.

McIlwain, William F. "On the Overturning of the Two School Buses in Lamar, S. C." *Esquire*, January 1971, 98–103, 162–64.

Meeks, Loretta F., Wendell A. Meeks, and Claudia A. Warren. "Racial Desegregation: Magnet Schools, Vouchers, Privatization, and Home Schooling." *Education and Urban Society* 33, no. 1 (2000): 88–101.

Milburn, William S. "Some Problems of Integration." *The Citizen,* April 1966, 4–12. https://egrove.olemiss.edu/cgi/viewcontent.cgi?article=1071&context=citizens_news.

Minchin, Timothy J. "Making Best Use of the New Laws: The NAACP and the Fight for Civil Rights in the South, 1965–1975." *The Journal of Southern History* 74, no. 3 (2008): 669–70. https://www.jstor.org/stable/27650232.

Minow, Martha. "Confronting the Seduction of Choice: Law, Education, and American Pluralism." *The Yale Law Journal* 120, no. 4 (2011): 814–48. https://www.jstor.org/stable/41060152.

Moore, Winfred B., and Orville Vernon Burton, editors. *Toward the Meeting of the Waters: Currents in the Civil Rights Movement of South Carolina during the Twentieth Century.* Columbia: University of South Carolina Press, 2008.

"Newspaper Clippings: 'Freedom of Choice' Opposes Integration Order." Darlington County, SC: Lamar Riots Collection, Darlington Historical Commission and Museum, n.d.

Nordheimer, Jon. "Gas Routs Whites Who Upset Buses at Carolina School," *New York Times*, March 4, 1970. https://www.nytimes.com/1970/03/04/archives/.

Nordheimer, Jon. "Lamar Gives Its Answer to the Courts," *New York Times*, March 8, 1970. https://www.nytimes.com/1970/03/08/archives/.

Nordheimer, Jon. "27 Whites, Accused of Carolina School Riot, Lauded by Neighbors," *New York Times*, March 6, 1970. https://www.nytimes.com/1970/03/06/archives/.

Pearcy, Mark. "'The Most Insidious Legacy'—Teaching about Redlining and the Impact of Racial Residential Segregation." *The Geography Teacher* 17, no. 2 (2019): 44–55.

Riel, Virginia, Toby L. Parcel, Roslyn Arlin Mickelson, and Stephen Samuel Smith. "Do Magnet and Charter Schools Exacerbate or Ameliorate Inequality?" *Sociology Compass* 12, no. 9 (2018): e12617. doi.org/10.1111/soc4.12617.

Schaefer, Richard T. "The Ku Klux Klan: Continuity and Change." *Phylon* 32, no. 2 (1971): 143–157. https://www.jstor.org/stable/273999.

Simms, Angela, and Elizabeth Talbert. "Racial Residential Segregation and School Choice." *Phylon* 56, no. 1 (2019): 33–57. https://www.jstor.org/stable/26743830.

"South Carolina: Rebellion at Lamar." *Time*, March 16, 1970. https://content.time.com/time/subscriber/article/0,33009,909055,00.html.

South Carolina House of Representatives. "A House Resolution to Honor Dr. Alvin T. Heatley of Darlington County for His Outstanding Accomplishments in the Field of Education and for His Dedicated Service to Butler Heritage Foundation as Its Chairman and to the State of South Carolina," H. 4251, SC General Assembly, 121st Session (2015). https://www.scstatehouse.gov/sess121_2015-2016/bills/4251.htm.

South Carolina Senate. "A Senate Resolution to Honor Dr. Alvin T. Heatley of Darlington County for His Outstanding Accomplishments in the Field of Education and for His Dedicated Service to Butler Heritage Foundation as Its Chairman and to the State of South Carolina," S. 818, 121st Session (2015). https://www.scstatehouse.gov/sess121_2015-2016/bills/818.htm.

South Carolina Senate. "A Senate Resolution to Recognize an Incredible Group of South Carolina Citizens from Darlington County for Their Role in the Fight for Desegregation and for Their Outstanding Resiliency in the Face of Trauma,"

S. 784, 123rd Session (2019). https://www.scstatehouse.gov/sess123_2019-2020/bills/784.htm.

Stanley, Arthur W. "White Violence—Lamar, SC." *The Crisis: A Record for the Darker Races* 77, no. 5 (1970): 196–97. https://books.google.com/books?id=emuSKGogk4kC.

State v. Best, Supreme Court of South Carolina, 257 S.C. 351, 186 S.E.2d 272 (1972). https://law.justia.com/cases/south-Carolina/supreme-court/1972/19343-1.html.

"Student Letter Critical of Decision," *Florence Morning News*, February 1, 1970, 3A.

Sturkey, William. "The 1964 Mississippi Freedom Schools." *Mississippi History Now*, May 2016. https://www.mshistorynow.mdah.ms.gov/issue/The-1964-Mississippi-Freedom-Schools.

Tilman, Linda C. "(Un)Intended Consequences? The Impact of the Brown v. Board of Education Decision on Employment Status of Black Educators." *Education and Urban Society* 36, no. 3 (2004): 280–303.

"Transcript of Nixon's Statement on School Busing," *New York Times*, March 17, 1972, 22A. https://www.nytimes.com/1972/03/17/archives/transcript-of-nixons-statement-on-school-busing.html.

"Types of Private School Choice." In *The ABCs of School Choice*, 3. Indianapolis, IN: EdChoice, 2023. https://files.eric.ed.gov/fulltext/ED628554.pdf.

US Congress (102nd). The "Southern Manifesto," 102 Cong. Rec. 4515–4516 (1956).

Travels Down South

Stories of Asians and Asian Americans in South Carolina

Eli Kibler, Eva Kiser, and Kylie Fisher

More than a century ago, in 1898, the first Asian student came to Furman University by way of Southern Baptist missionary networks established in China. Since then, many more members of the Asian and Asian-American communities have shaped the cultures of the university and the surrounding South Carolina Upstate. Furman, a predominately white institution (PWI) and former member of the South Carolina Baptist Convention, has traditionally overlooked the experiences of institutionally marginalized groups on campus when narrating its history. For many years, Furman has framed its relationship with Asia—through its curricular offerings, study-abroad programs, and recruitment of international students and staff— in terms of avoiding the kinds of failures that marked the Vietnam War (1955–1975).[1] Indeed, there was public acknowledgment that the disastrous military involvement of the United States in Southeast Asia originated in a lack of understanding of the politics and identities of the people living there. Although this discourse may have motivated Furman faculty and administration to implement a new graduation requirement in 1968, making it mandatory for students to take one course related to Asian (or African) studies, our research demonstrates that Furman's connections with Asia extend beyond this narrow interest in Asian culture in the mid-twentieth century. Exploring Furman's relationship with Asia has also led to an examination of the presence and civic engagement of Asian immigrants in Greenville County during the same period to understand these individuals' journeys to the United States and their experiences in the American Southeast.[2] This study explores the contributions of the Asian and Asian-American communities at Furman and in Greenville over the past two centuries. It documents their experiences of attending a white (formerly) Baptist university and living in South Carolina and situates their stories within the broader cultural and demographic landscape of the region.

Our study contributes to recent scholarship on Asian populations in the American South.[3] Raymond A. Mohl, John E. Van Sant, and Chizuru Saeki's collection, *Far East, Down South: Asians in the American South* examines the Asian diaspora in Florida, Georgia, Louisiana, Mississippi, and North Carolina since the nineteenth century.[4] Although their text illuminates an overlooked part of the South's history, none of the nine chapters examines Asian or Asian-American experiences in South Carolina. Jigna Desai and Khyati Y. Joshi's *Asian Americans in Dixie: Race and Migration in the South* also expands our understanding of race relations and immigration history in the American South. Investigating the multifaceted identities, lived experiences, and perceptions of Asian Americans in the South, the collection challenges the thought that the South is untouched by global networks of cultural exchange.[5] Although immensely valuable, the essays do not focus specifically on South Carolina. Our research presents the stories of Asians and Asian Americans in two communities in northwestern South Carolina: Furman University and the city of Greenville. We work to reframe the narratives of these places by emphasizing the involvement of the Asian and Asian-American members of those communities.

Along with written accounts from the archives at Furman and Greenville, we make extensive use of oral histories.[6] We believe that it is critical to allow individuals to speak about their own experiences, especially when focusing on historically marginalized figures and groups whose stories have received little attention or have been inaccurately told. Without these voices, scholars may perpetuate already dominant, colonialist narratives that often whitewash records of history and cultural change. Oral histories enhance our understanding of our community members' actual experiences and cultivate a more diverse, just, and inclusive collective history of the local society.

At the same time, we acknowledge problems with treating individuals and familial descendants from Asia as a monolithic demographic and racialized category.[7] We use the generalizing terms *Asian* and *Asian American* to account for the multiplicity of Asian ethnicities and nationalities that exist in Greenville County. Doing so allows us to discuss broad trends in immigration from Asia to the American Southeast. US census data, although useful for understanding the generic ethnic and racial compositions of a given locale, do not represent those people whose identities may include more than one Asian nationality.[8] Thus, in striving for comprehensiveness and inclusivity, we use the categories "Asian" and "Asian American" to identify anyone whose place of origin is located on the mainland continent of Asia, surrounding islands in the Indian and Pacific Oceans, and the Hawaiian Islands before 1959 in addition to anyone of Asian descent who is a long-term resident of the United States.

"I Have Almost Forgotten That the Chinese Are of a Different Race"

Furman's activity in Asia, and particularly East Asia, began in the early nineteenth century when Southern Baptists participated in missions abroad. Since the sixteenth century, Europeans have embarked on missions to convert the Chinese to Christianity. However, these initial attempts were short lived, and by the eighteenth century, the Qing government expelled Catholic missionaries from the country. It was not until the following century that Protestant missionaries reached China. Southern Baptists traveled to East Asia by way of opium ships that landed at the Portuguese colony of Macao on China's southeastern coast, first in 1836.[9] Over the following decade, two Baptist missionary stations were established in Guangzhou—also referred to by its anglicized name, Canton—and Shanghai.[10] South Carolina missionaries, including those associated with Furman, helped to open up the region to the movement of cultures and people in the nineteenth century.

The first missionary affiliated with Furman to work in China was Issachar Roberts. An 1828 graduate from the Furman Theological Institute of South Carolina and a respected Baptist minister, Roberts journeyed to China in 1837 as an independent missionary with the profits he made from a real estate venture in Mississippi.[11] When he arrived in China, Roberts joined two other missionaries, William Dean and John Lewis Shuck, who, shortly before Roberts's arrival, were appointed to work in China by the Triennial Convention, the first national organization for Baptists in the United States.[12] Together, these men created a Baptist network in East Asia that grew over successive decades. By the early twentieth century, more than six hundred missionaries had conducted religious service in China, and Baptist membership among the Chinese peaked at one hundred twenty-three thousand.[13] Baptist missionaries continued to work in China until their expulsion by the country's communist leadership after its takeover in 1949.

Throughout the nineteenth and early twentieth centuries, several Furman alumni, faculty, and administrators participated in the transpacific journey to East Asia to spread Christianity across what they perceived to be—according to Gordon Poteat's account of his 1924 mission—the "strange, weird, and wonderful" land of China.[14] A 1910 graduate of Furman and son of former university president Edwin McNeill Poteat Sr., Gordon and his wife, Heather Anne Carruthers Poteat, set out for China in 1915 after Gordon earned his theological degree. Gordon and Heather Anne spent several years in Kaifeng as missionaries before traveling around the country, eventually relocating to Shanghai in 1921 when Gordon began teaching at the local university.[15] Gordon's brother, Edwin McNeill Jr., and father, Edwin McNeill Sr., joined Gordon and Heather Anne and also worked as missionaries. During this time, the number of churches sponsored by the American Baptist Foreign Mission Society increased ninefold, from eighteen around 1900 to one hundred sixty-four in 1927, the year in which Gordon and his family returned to the United States.[16] In the early twentieth century, strong communities of Chinese Baptists gradually formed in several cities such as Kaifeng, Guangzhou (Canton), and Shanghai. These networks encouraged young men and women from China and elsewhere in East Asia to study and practice Christianity in South Carolina.

In addition to his travel journal, Gordon and his family produced a photo album to document their years in China.[17] Furman University is fortunate to have this album as part of its Special Collections and Archives. The album consists of dozens of small photographs portraying the Poteats, their missionary friends and Chinese-language teachers, their house, and various landmarks and scenes of locals in the streets in China. Together, Gordon's writing and family photo album craft a mythology about the places and people he and his family encountered, emphasizing the foreign otherworldliness of Chinese culture. Similarly, many of Gordon's accounts poetically describe the landscape of the different regions he visited, highlighting the varied climates and wildlife he saw. Yet his texts are riddled with biases that juxtapose Euro-American Christian society with that of polytheistic China. During his travels from Shanghai to Beijing, Gordon spent time in Nanjing where "[b]eggars [were] a common sight along the streets, at the gates and temples, at the railroad stations where they cry along the trains [. . .] They say the Orient is the reverse of the Occident and this is another instance."[18] This passage from Gordon's writing indicates what American missionaries thought of the Chinese: They created and lived in a backward society.

Over time, as American missionaries converted more Chinese to Christianity, the perceived polarity between these two ethnic groups began to dissipate. In his journal, Gordon dedicated a chapter to celebrating Christmas in Kaifeng. He described the church services that his family and the local Chinese attended, highlighting his admiration for the choir of young children. Witnessing such of moments of shared faith between these two cultures prompted him to write: "I have almost forgotten that the Chinese are of a different race."[19] Like other missionaries in China, Gordon understood his role as a Baptist savior, who would help an uncultured and spiritually void Asian race grow morally through the adoption of Christianity.

Figure 8.1. Heather Anne Carruthers being carried by Chinese men, from *Poteat Family Scrapbook*, ca. 1921. Special Collections and Archives, James B. Duke Library, Furman University.

Figure 8.2. Heather Anne Carruthers with "Our 1st Chinese teachers," from *Poteat Family Scrapbook*, ca. 1921. Special Collections and Archives, James B. Duke Library, Furman University.

Figure 8.3. Heather Anne Carruthers and Gordon Poteat with their church teachers, from *Poteat Family Scrapbook*, ca. 1921. Special Collections and Archives, James B. Duke Library, Furman University.

"From the Far Away Land of Shrines and Temples"

Southern Baptists' characterization of the Chinese they met as the "exotic other" was a common trope applied to the Asian students at Furman in the earlier part of its history. In 1898, Chu Jung came to Furman as the school's first Asian student. Chu was from Guangzhou (Canton), which, along with Shanghai, was one of the original missionary stations in China. It is likely that Chu's exposure to Christianity through Baptist missionaries encouraged him to enroll in Furman's Preparatory School, which readied young men to matriculate as undergraduate students after two years of coursework in math, English, and civil government. In an article published by *The Baptist Courier* from November 1898, Chu was called "the offspring of the Celestial Kingdom," a common epithet for China that alluded to the Qing emperor's status as the "Son of Heaven."[20] The author commended Chu for his command of English, stating, "I am sure it would take me some years to learn as much of the impossible language of his fathers as he has learned of ours."[21] By referring to Cantonese as an "impossible language," the author emphasizes not only the differences between American and Chinese culture but also implies a complexity and peculiarity about Chu, perpetuating the Orientalist ideology of characterizing cultures in and individuals from the "East" as inferior to those of Europe and the United States.[22]

A little more than two decades after Chu studied at Furman University, the first degree-seeking Asian student attended the university. Charles Kilord Athen Wang from Kaifeng, China, enrolled at Furman in 1921 and graduated three years later.[23] In the 1924 Furman yearbook, each member of the graduating class received a brief biography to accompany their individual portraits. Charles's biography portrays him as the ethnic outlier on campus, stating that he came "from the far away land of shrines and temples . . . [and] desired the educational training of the western world."[24] Once again, Chinese culture is portrayed as exotic and perhaps inferior to American culture. Although singled out among his peers for his Chinese heritage, Charles's engagement at Furman matched that of his American classmates. His involvement in extracurricular activities and the leadership roles he held in various clubs, including secretary of the Tennis Club and vice president of the Student Volunteer Band, counter some popular assumptions about the social isolation that nonwhite students experienced at American colleges, especially in the early twentieth century.

It would be nearly three decades after Charles's arrival to Furman before the first female Asian undergraduate studied at the university. Gilda Cheng from Guangzhou (Canton) moved to Greenville in 1950. Although other Asian women would later join Gilda at Furman, she was the only Asian female student on campus during her initial year. Gilda had an active student life, participating in various organizations such as the Young Women's Christian Association and Chapel Choir. In 1953, she became the first Asian woman to graduate from Furman, earning a bachelor's degree in psychology. In her senior yearbook, Gilda's biography alludes to her good and selfless character, as well as also having a more humorous side to her personality.[25] These remarks suggest that, over time, Furman students began to recognize their Chinese peers as individuals rather than representations of the exotic.

By the mid-1960s, shortly after Gilda's time at Furman, Furman faculty approved a series of "non-Western" seminars in an effort to diversify the university's curriculum. The content of these courses initially focused on Communist China and were designed to shed light on the Asian Cold War. Then, in 1968, Furman added an Asian–African studies program to the general education curriculum with the goal of exposing students to cultures and histories outside of Europe and North America. During that same year, Furman hired its first Asian faculty member. The chemist, Dr. Paul Bien, traveled to Furman in January of 1968 to attend a seminar. Impressed by the caliber of faculty and students, who had "the proper curiosity blended with an inquisitive and critical mind," he joined the faculty later that year.[26] Although it may have been an easy decision for Bien to accept the offer to teach at Furman, his move from China was especially challenging. He escaped Shanghai just one week before Mao Zedong's troops took over the region. He came to the United States by way of Hong Kong when two of his close friends from his graduate career at Brown University helped him obtain a postdoctoral position at Indiana University.[27] Thanks to the Aid Refugee Chinese Intellectuals program, as Bien was an American-educated, Chinese-born person, his move to the United States was not included in the yearly quota established by the Asian Exclusion Act, which limited the number of Chinese immigrants to the country to one hundred.[28] After taking different posts in Indiana, Ohio, and Tennessee, Bien began his three-year teaching position at Furman in the Chemistry Department in the fall of 1968.[29]

A few years after Bien's start at Furman, the first Asian teacher with an academic specialization in Asian studies joined Furman's faculty. Dr. Lin Chen from China began his career in 1973 as an assistant professor of political science with an expertise in Asian politics. Chen's hire coincided with Furman's inaugural international study programs in Asia. Although study-abroad opportunities through Furman began in 1969 with a semester in England, by 1973, these learning experiences expanded to include countries outside of Europe, particularly Japan.[30] Alongside other faculty and administrators who were interested in creating study-abroad opportunities elsewhere in Asia, Chen developed a program in China. Because China was the second largest exporter of cotton textiles to the United States, Chen believed that American students in Greenville, a historic mill town, would benefit from studying the cultural, social, and economic relations between the two countries."[31]

Even though Furman continued to diversify its curricular offerings and faculty in the late twentieth century, its initial attention almost exclusively focused on East Asia, leaving out a number of other Asian cultures. It was not until the 1990s when Furman employed its first faculty member from South Asia. Dr. Kailash Khandke grew up in Mumbai, India. After receiving his doctorate, he taught at Santa Clara University and Middlebury College before joining Furman's economics department in 1995. Although initially apprehensive about moving to the American South because of the region's racial history, Khandke felt welcomed by his new communities at Furman and in Greenville.[32] Not long after he started teaching at Furman, Khandke helped to organize and then led Furman's first study-abroad program in India during the early 2000s. He later became the dean for Study Away and International Education, a position he held from 2007 to 2015. His personal and scholarly contributions as both a professor and leader of Furman's diversity efforts have since paved the way for the campus community to promote and prioritize intellectual curiosity about the world and inclusivity among its diverse members.

Furman University's growing commitment to creating a welcoming campus climate for its international population did not go unnoticed by its Asian undergraduates. In an interview, Su-Min Oon, who studied chemistry at Furman from 1975 to 1979, spoke fondly of his American college experience, recalling how his peers were willing to help him practice English and become accustomed to life in South Carolina.[33] Su-Min was born and raised in Malaya (now known as Peninsular Malaysia) and was the fourth member of his family to receive a degree from Furman: His father, Cheng Nan Wen; aunt, Beng Cheng Oon; and uncle, Seng Kok Oon, all studied at Furman in the early 1950s.[34] Cheng Nan first heard about Furman while attending St. John's University, a Jesuit institution in Shanghai. There, he met Baptist missionaries, who encouraged him to transfer to the South Carolina university. When Cheng Nan enrolled at St. John's after World War II, the Communist Party had recently secured control over China, creating an authoritarian state under Chairman Mao Zedong. This change in political power provided the impetus for Cheng Nan to return to Malaya. From there, he took a steamship to New York City before enrolling as a junior at Furman in 1950. A year later, Cheng Nan's younger sister, Beng Cheng, and brother, Seng Kok, came to Furman. As Su-Min explained, in the 1950s, it was very unusual for an Asian family to send their daughter to the United States for college, so Seng Kok accompanied his sister as a chaperone for their remaining years at Furman after their older brother graduated in 1952.

After finishing college, all three Oon siblings remained in the United States to pursue graduate studies. Beng Cheng and Seng Kok started their families abroad. Cheng Nan returned to Malaya where he later married Su-Min's mother. When he was growing up, Su-Min had no interest in attending college in America like his father. In fact, he had no plans to continue his postsecondary education and hoped to become an airplane mechanic. However, these professional ambitions changed when Su-Min saw his classmates applying to college abroad, mainly in North America, the United Kingdom, Australia, Singapore, and Taiwan. Su-Min followed suit and applied to universities in Taiwan and the United States, including Furman. Hearing about his relatives' successful educational careers in the states, he ultimately chose to accept his offer to one of South Carolina's premier liberal arts universities.

In the late 1970s, when Su-Min arrived at Furman, he was among very few students of color. He recalled that there were a handful of Black football players, two female students from Hong Kong, and a male student from Japan. Despite being part of a small demographic of nonwhite students, Su-Min did not feel alienated because of his nationality or race. Having arrived at Furman just after the conclusion of the Vietnam War, Su-Min was grateful that he neither witnessed nor was the victim of disparaging remarks toward Asians. He attributed his positive college experience to the welcoming attitude of his American peers and his supportive mentors in the chemistry department, particularly Dr. Donald Kubler, who helped him find a purpose and passion while at Furman. Su-Min's and his relatives' time at Furman represent one experience for Asian students at a Baptist PWI in the South during the twentieth century. It is worth emphasizing that not all Asian or Asian-American students at the university felt support and inclusivity from their white peers.

While Furman has made notable strides in growing its international students and staff and expanding multicultural appreciation, as Su-Min's story attests, the increase in ethnic and racial diversity on campus did not entirely overcome prejudice. For example, 1982 alumnus Henry Ho spoke about the racial profiling he experienced while at Furman.[35] As a Chinese American, Henry noticed how he was perceived to be part of a racial collective rather than an individual student. He recounted experiences on campus when he was mistaken for another non-Chinese Asian student solely on the basis of his appearance. In our conversations, Henry also emphasized that other students at Furman also experienced harmful biases. When Henry received his acceptance to Furman, he was excited to attend college with many of his friends from The Stony Brook School in New York, some of whom were Black. However, after arriving to Furman, the dynamic between the different racial groups on campus left him feeling torn, as he felt forced to choose to engage with either his Black or white peers.[36] Although Furman had been desegregated since 1965, racism, especially toward Black individuals, was prevalent. According to Henry, it was much easier for light-skinned Asian students to assimilate into to the predominately white student body. He felt comfortable participating in campus activities, such as the cheer team.[37]

Black students, on the other hand, were more hesitant to be part of campus life. Henry recounted feeling upset that he and his Black peers from high school were growing apart because of social pressure.

Not only students of color but also staff faced discrimination while at Furman and in Greenville. Dr. Shusuke Yagi, one of the founding members of the Asian studies department and professor of Japanese, anthropology, and film studies, recalled receiving threatening phone calls during his early years at Furman from students who interrogated him about his immigration status. Moreover, he remembered being followed and nearly hit by a van while walking in Greenville, seemingly targeted because of his race.[38] In spite of these challenges, Yagi has shared his knowledge of Japanese language and culture with Furman students, in Greenville and abroad, for more than three decades. When he joined the Furman faculty in 1989, he was hired as the university's first Japanese-language professor. Later, Yagi would go on to help establish the study-abroad exchange program at Waseda University in Tokyo, which began in 2013.

"Greenville [. . .] Gave Us a Sense of Belonging"

Exploring the experiences of Asian and Asian-American students, faculty and staff at Furman have revealed the way in which that community served as a microcosm of the surrounding region, not only in terms of local Asian immigration trends but also in terms of race relations and attitudes toward foreigners. According to the most recent census data, South Carolina's Asian, Asian-American, and Pacific Islander (AAPI) population has seen rapid growth over the past decades, increasing in size by approximately one hundred fifty percent.[39] Although there are many contributing factors for Asian immigration to the United States and the steady growth of the AAPI population in South Carolina, the impact of Southern Baptists in cultivating a place of belonging for Asian families in the region is undeniable.[40] The Baptist missionaries who arrived in East Asia in the nineteenth century initiated a network that enabled the movement of goods, culture, and people between Asia and North America over the next two centuries. Just as Furman's first Asian students were motivated to attend because of their Baptist connections, so too did others learn from missionaries about South Carolina as a place where they could achieve both spiritual and financial well-being.

The economic possibilities in the American Southeast also made the prospect of living abroad attractive, and starting in the second half of the nineteenth century, Asian immigrants made their transoceanic journeys.

At first, many of the jobs available to the immigrant workforce were in agriculture. During Reconstruction (1863–1877), southern plantations experienced upheaval when their formerly enslaved Black laborers left in search of better living conditions. This, in turn, created a labor shortage, prompting white southerners to hire Chinese workers.[41] In time, other types of work became available. The Chinese Immigration Convention held in Memphis in 1869 agreed to bring several thousand Chinese workers to the South for employment in railroad construction, sugar refining, and the production of cotton.[42] The arrival of Chinese laborers to the South at the mid-nineteenth century eventually led to other, nonindentured, Chinese to journey to the Atlantic coast in search of employment. In fact, some of the earliest Chinese immigrants to relocate to Charleston were entrepreneurs wanting to start family businesses, such as hand laundries, grocery stores, and produce markets.[43] The Chinese in Charleston found a particular niche in the laundry industry, and they continued to capitalize on this growing sector elsewhere in the state.

In the early twentieth century, more Asian immigrants transitioned from manual labor to entrepreneurship, as we see in the Upstate. Popularly dubbed the "textile center of the world," Greenville was home to lucrative mills that supplied textile products to the region and abroad. The first cotton manufactory in Greenville County opened in the early decades of the nineteenth century.[44] With the value of cotton at a historical high after the Civil War (1861–1865), cotton manufacturing became the principal method of restoring the economy in America's New South, ushering in the mill-building boom in the South Carolina Upstate.[45] Greenville's most profitable textile manufacturers drew acclaim from around the globe for their innovations in machinery and quality of product. In 1915, the Southern Textile Association held its first textile trade show in Greenville. The event was such a success that the association decided that Greenville would serve as the permanent site for the recurring exposition. As the number of exhibitors at the Greenville exposition increased, so did the number of attendees who traveled from around the world to witness the best of Greenville's textile industry. At the 1920 exposition, a group of Chinese financiers and manufacturers agreed to buy fifty million dollars' worth of machinery for factories in Shanghai.[46] Throughout the twentieth century, Greenville's reputation as a leader in the global textile industry continued to attract businesspeople from Asia.

Although the newly established Asian communities across South Carolina may have originally ventured to the United States in search of financial prosperity, what kept generations of Asian immigrants and their Asian-American descendants in the region was the perceived religious tolerance of Southern Baptists in the area. According to theological historian, Timothy Tseng, during the twentieth century, Southern Baptists were committed to growing and fostering new congregations. The institutional funds and support for establishing new churches appealed to Asian Christians and served as the catalyst for the formation of Asian-American congregations across the state.[47] As more and more Asian Christian immigrants moved to the United States, they found acceptance in the teachings and values of Southern Baptist churches. As Tseng explains, this was especially true for Chinese Christians who emigrated from Hong Kong.[48] With the closure of mainland China to Protestant missionaries at the mid-twentieth century, Hong Kong transitioned into a prominent Baptist missionary center.[49] The exposure of Hong Kong residents to Southern Baptist ideals undoubtedly inspired individuals and families to make personal and professional connections with Americans, which aided in their moving abroad.

Vivian and Thomas Wong, who came to South Carolina from Hong Kong in the mid-twentieth century, embody the Asian immigrant success story. The newlywed couple was working at a Hong Kong hotel when they learned of the opportunity to move to South Carolina. Greenville businessman and inventor of the first commercial rotisserie oven, Robert G. Wilson, sponsored the Wongs, who relocated to South Carolina in 1963, and hired them to staff his restaurant, Barbecue King. While working for Barbecue King, the couple dreamed of owning their own hotel in America, but they knew that starting their own restaurant was more feasible. In January of 1970, the Wongs opened Dragon Den, a Chinese restaurant located on Augusta Street. The success of Dragon Den led to the Wongs creating five other restaurants under the same franchise.[50]

While living and working in Greenville, Vivian and Thomas have defined what it means to be self-made entrepreneurs and philanthropists. After establishing their Chinese restaurant chain, they went on to run a silk flower business, became real estate investors, and donated to local charities and institutions, including Greenville Technical College and Prisma Health Children's Hospital.[51] In recognition of her outstanding service and philanthropy to the Greenville community, in 2002, Vivian received the Order of the Palmetto, the highest civilian honor that a South Carolinian can receive. In 2005, Vivian was also recognized as Ernst & Young's Entrepreneur of the Year in the Carolinas. For her success in business and investment in her local community, Vivian was also appointed as South Carolina's honorary trade ambassador by former governor Nikki Haley. These honors have earned Vivian the title of one of the fifty most influential people in the region by Greenville Business Magazine in 2018.[52] Over eight thousand miles away from their native Hong Kong, Vivian and Thomas Wong established a home in Greenville, which embraced their entrepreneurial spirit and altruistic attitude toward serving those around them.

Alongside the Wongs, other East Asian families immigrated to the United States at the mid-twentieth century in search of economic opportunities.[53] The Tsuzuki family from Nagoya, Japan, began their life in the Upstate in the late 1960s when Kiyohiro and his wife, Chigusa, moved to South Carolina to start their business, TNS (Tsuzuki New Spinning) Mills, a local supplier to the textile industry that produced cotton and synthetic fiber yarns. Greenville's long-standing reputation as a prosperous mill town encouraged the Tsuzukis to grow their company in South Carolina.[54] In addition to modernizing the textile industry in the region, the Tsuzukis have revitalized Greenville through their love of arts and culture. Among the family's most notable contributions to local civic life are donations to the Peace Center for the Performing Arts and the founding of Nippon Yagoto, the former Japanese cultural center in Greenville.

Since moving to Greenville, the Tsuzukis have shared their Japanese heritage and culture with their neighboring community. This desire ultimately inspired the family to donate their private Buddhist temple to Furman University. Now dubbed the Place of Peace, the reconstituted temple, which is now used as a secular space for teaching and independent reflection, is the first of its kind to be dismantled in Japan and subsequently reconstructed in the United States. Originally built in 1984, the intergenerational temple (Hei-Sei-Ji in Japanese) used to honor family milestones like births and funerals was once located on the Tsuzukis' property in Nagoya. However, by the early 2000s, the declining textile industry in Greenville prompted the Tsuzukis to sell some of their properties, including their home in Nagoya and give their former temple to Furman.[55]

The Place of Peace testifies to the Tsuzukis' gratitude to the Greenville community for its support of their family and serves as an invitation to teach locals about Japanese culture. Seiji Tsuzuki, son of Kiyohiro and Chigusa Tsuzuki, explains why his family gifted their temple to the city: "Greenville welcomed our family and gave us a sense of belonging. That is why it is so special to both my sister and me to have brought a piece of our Japanese heritage to Greenville."[56] Seiji has followed in his parent's footsteps and now works as president of Industria Textil Tsuzuki, a textile company based in

Figure 8.4. Place of Peace, Furman University, 2024. Photograph by Kylie Fisher.

Sao Paulo, Brazil, which specializes in producing fabrics, yarns, and protective apparel for agrotextile businesses. Seiji's sister, Yuri, still lives in Greenville where she is an internationally recognized artist, best known for her steel sculptures.[57] Both Seiji and Yuri credit their multicultural identity and interests to their upbringing in Japan and South Carolina.

Although many Asian immigrants in the late nineteenth and mid-twentieth centuries came to the American Southeast for employment, increasing US military intervention in Asia, which culminated in the Vietnam War, forced refugees from that part of the globe to flee in search of a safe haven abroad. Many of the men and women who held posts in the South Vietnamese government during the war were subsequently persecuted by the Communist regime after it gained control of the country. After the fall of Saigon in April 1975, Chi Tran, a former officer in the South Vietnamese army, was shipped off to a "re-education camp" in Hanoi where he spent five years imprisoned under brutal conditions. Chi and his wife, four sons, and one daughter were forced to work at a communal farm. The labor conditions were so horrific that his fifteen year-old daughter died at the camp. To escape their country's authoritarian government, the Tran family was among nearly forty thousand Vietnamese refugees who immigrated to the United States in 1995 in pursuit of civil and religious freedom.[58]

For most Vietnamese, including the Trans, their journey to North America began by boat across the Pacific Ocean from Southeast Asia to the US West Coast. From there, many moved to large metropolitan cities across the country. However, the Tran family settled in Greenville because they heard they could find steady work there.[59] In Travelers Rest, a city that borders Greenville to the north, several businesses were willing to hire these refugees. According to Joe Nettles, then-manager of Designer Ensembles in Travelers Rest, approximately eighty percent of the four hundred eighty employees at the plant were Vietnamese. One member on the staff was Chan Nguyen, who worked as a product manager. Chan escaped Vietnam in 1980 in a fourteen-foot wooden boat with sixty-five other refugees. He came to Greenville by way of Portland, Oregon, where he earned a degree in industrial drafting. Hearing from a Vietnamese friend already in Greenville that Designer Ensembles had hired a number of immigrants, Chan made his way to the Southeast in search of a more financially secure future. He began his employment at Designer Ensembles as a machine operator, but after quickly impressing his supervisors with his work ethic, he was promoted to product manager. According to Nettles, the Vietnamese employees at the plant had a higher production rate than other staff, and therefore, typically earned more than the average wage of seven dollars and fifty cents per hour.[60]

In addition to finding steady employment in Greenville, the Vietnamese who moved to the South Carolina Upstate cultivated a community in which they could openly practice their faith. Religious persecution in Communist Vietnam led to the closure of Christian churches and the imprisonment of numerous Christian priests and other practitioners.[61] Among them was Thai Nguyen, who received an eight-year prison sentence for his service as a chaplain in the South Vietnamese army during the war. When finally released from prison, Thai knew he had to leave Vietnam if he was to continue to practice Christianity, and thus, he joined the exodus of Vietnamese Christians to the United States. In the 1990s, Thai Nguyen served as one of three Vietnamese clerics at various Greenville churches and was responsible for ministering to the growing Vietnamese population in the area. As a church cleric, Thai has helped as many as one thousand Vietnamese in Greenville find work and a place to worship in their native language.[62] There are still several Vietnamese congregations across Greenville that are associated with different Christian denominations, including Vietnamese Blessing Baptist

Figure 8.5. Vietnamese Blessing Baptist Church, Greenville, SC, 2024. Photograph by Kylie Fisher.

Church on Poinsett Highway, Vietnamese Alliance Church on Rutherford Road, Greenville Vietnamese Baptist Church on Eisenhower Drive, and Faith Church on Ivydale Drive.

Conclusions and Implications

We live in a polarized society where our different social identities can make us targets of violence, racism, and other forms of systemic bias. In recent years, anti-Asian hate crimes have reached unprecedented levels, increasing over three hundred percent since 2020.[63] To combat such prejudices, we need ways to connect with one another, emphasizing our shared interests, values, and ways of life. This study offers readers stories of struggle, hope, and resilience to inspire compassion and a greater commitment to inclusive belonging. It also reminds us that we still have a long journey ahead to achieve a just and equitable society.

The authors of this article are all connected to Furman—a recent alumna, graduating senior, and professor—and they worked to uncover the Asian and Asian-American stories and experiences at their institution as a means to rewrite the university's narrative, which otherwise largely celebrates the efforts and accomplishments of white students, staff, faculty, and administrators. It is through this project that we aim not only to provide an opportunity for the Furman and Greenville communities to expand their appreciation and awareness of Asian and Asian-American experiences in white spaces but also to advance ongoing discourse about cultural and regional identity. Our reframed understandings of Greenville and Furman's respective ties to Asian people force us simultaneously to reconstruct both local and national histories to allow for more inclusive and comprehensive reflections of the past. Without the work of projects such as these, which center the voices and experiences of marginalized communities, the loss of such memories and stories would be truly devastating.

It is our sincere hope that our work will inform and instruct students, scholars, and others interested in learning about the history and relationship between Asia and the South Carolina Upstate. Furthermore, we anticipate that this project will not simply end where we left it but will be continued by others in the coming years.

Kylie Fisher is assistant professor of art history at Furman University. A supporter of the public humanities and diversity, equity, inclusion, and accessibility work, Kylie is enthusiastic about engaging diverse audiences in reflection on cultural heritage and history. Kylie's work on this article has allowed her to combine her fascination with travel accounts, all types of printed archival matter, and objects of various media with her goal of amplifying the stories of underrepresented peoples and cultures. As an educator of mixed heritage, including Japanese American, Kylie is proud to have authored this article in collaboration with her students.

Eli Kibler is a Charlotte, North Carolina, native who has spent most of his undergraduate career at Furman University examining various facets of literature, media, philosophy, history, and culture. These interests intersected through his majors in English and Asian studies and minor in film studies. With summer work experience in both academic archival research and professional, community-based journalism, Eli has always enjoyed using his skills as a writer and investigator to chronicle the ideas and narratives of others into a form that is cohesive, compelling, and accessible for readers. He finds great value in studying and discussing the important stories, both factual and fictitious, past, present, or future, that we as humans gravitate toward and identify with, a passion that he plans to follow into his professional career postgraduation.

Eva Kiser graduated from Furman University in 2023 with a double major in anthropology and Asian studies. As a student, she pursued academic and social projects that challenged and expanded people's perspectives on culture and world politics, and she became known in her department for both her research and leadership skills. She speaks openly about the importance of portraying culture authentically, and she is passionate about connecting different histories and telling stories through digital humanities and cultural heritage. Postgraduation, Eva now works as an archaeologist in the southeastern United States and hopes to continue finding ways to bring academic projects to accessible spaces.

NOTES

This article derives, in part, from our work on the digital humanities project, *Untold Journeys*, which began in summer 2022. Over the past two years, our work has been generously supported by multiple individuals and entities at Furman University. We conducted much of our research at Furman's Special Collections and Archives and are grateful to Julia Cowart, Jeffrey Makala, and Nashieli Marcano for making the university's archival records and Asian Artifacts Collections available to us. Research for this project also took place at the Greenville Public Library, and we appreciate the staff at the South Carolina Room for assisting us with gaining access to their holdings. We also thank a number of Furman colleagues, including Sarah Archino, Terri Bright, Alex Francis-Ratte, Sarah Gebbie, Lane Harris, Nadia Kanagawa, Kevin Kao, Kate Kaup, Kailash Khandke, Lisa Knight, Marta Lanier, Jim Leavell, Michael May, Ross McClain, Savita Nair, Katie Shamblin, David Shaner, Michele Speitz, and Shusuke Yagi, in addition to Furman alumni Henry Ho and Su-Min Oon. This project would not have been possible without generous grants from the Office of Undergraduate Research, Furman Humanities Center, and the Asian studies department. Last, we thank the editorial board of *Carolina Currents* and the reviewers for their insightful feedback and assistance with publishing this article. Eli dedicates this article to his family: Georgia, Ginger, and Chris Kibler. Eva dedicates this article to all Asian Furman University students, professors, and alumni/ae/x. Kylie dedicates this article to her obachan, Aiko Fisher. Together, the authors dedicate this article in memoriam to Dr. Savita Nair.

1. Jim Leavell, interview by Eli Kibler and Eva Kiser, July 25, 2022. Leavell explains that Furman's Asian-African graduation requirement in 1968 developed because of concerns over the Vietnam War and the growing anti-war movement. Moreover, an article published in *Furman Magazine* from June 1962 references the war's impact on curriculum development about Asia: "[W]e Americans until very recently have never given any serious thought to the study of Asia. Until a few years ago the cultures of Asia had no place in our public school system. . . . Our colleges and universities were equally remiss." See Dr. Paul H. Clyde, "Questions and Answers," *Furman Magazine* 11, no. 2 (1962): 7.

2. For additional information, see the digital humanities project, *Untold Journeys: Exploring Greenville and Furman's Connections with Asia*, produced by Eli Kibler, Eva Kiser, and Kylie Fisher, *Untold Journeys*. Furman University, July 29, 2022 (https://storymaps.arcgis.com/stories/4844f5d2a6a24ab497a01a465ce5e9c8).

3. The US Census Bureau defines the American South as the following: Texas; Oklahoma; Louisiana; Arkansas; Alabama; Kentucky; Tennessee; Mississippi; Delaware; Maryland; Washington, DC; Florida; Georgia; North Carolina; South Carolina; West Virginia; and Virginia. See US Census Bureau, "Geographic Terms," census.gov, 2021 (https://www.census.gov/programs-surveys/popest/about/glossary/geo-terms.html).

4. See Raymond A. Mohl, John E. Van Sant, and Chizuru Saeki, editors, *Far East, Down South: Asians in the American South* (Tuscaloosa: University of Alabama Press, 2016).

5. See, especially, Khyati Y Joshi and Jigna Desai, "Introduction," in *Asian Americans in Dixie: Race and Migration in the South* (Champaign: University of Illinois Press, 2013), 1–30.

6. To learn more about oral histories as a research methodology, especially for topics concerning marginalized identity groups, see Thalia M. Mulvihill and Raji Swaminathan, editors, *Oral History and Qualitative Methodologies: Educational Research for Social Justice* (New York: Routledge, 2022), 3–17. See also Patricia Leavy, *Oral History: Understanding Qualitative Research* (Oxford, England: Oxford University Press, 2011), 3–25.

7. Jigna Desai and Khyati Y. Joshi describe the common understanding of the terms "Asian" and "Asian American" in their work. See Desai and Joshi, "Introduction," in *Asian Americans in Dixie*, 14.

8. For an examination about how United States census categories impact the ability to track racial and ethnic inequality, see Hephzibah V. Strmic-Pawl, Brandon A. Jackson, and Steve Garner, "Race Counts: Racial and Ethnic Data on the U.S. Census and the Implications for Tracking Inequality," *Sociology of Race and Ethnicity* 4, no. 1 (2018): 1–13.

9. Albert W. Wardin, ed., *Baptists Around the World: A Comprehensive Handbook* (Nashville, TN: Broadman & Holman Publishers, 1995), 91.

10. See Li Li, "Diversifying the Operation: Southern Baptist Missions in China at the Turn of the Century 1890–1910." *Baptist History and Heritage* 34, no. 2 (1999): 167–68.

11. Yuan Chung Teng, "Reverend Issachar Jacox Roberts and the Taiping Rebellion," *The Journal of Asian Studies* 23, no. 1 (1963): 55–67." During his mission in China, Roberts became famous for introducing Christianity to Hong Xiuquan, the so-called "Heavenly King" and leader of the Taiping Rebellion, a civil war fought between the Manchu-led Qing dynasty and the Hakka, an ethnic subgroup of indigenous Han Chinese.

12. Wardin, *Baptists Around the World*, 91 and 99. For a lengthy study on Shuck and Roberts's missionary work in China, see Margaret M. Coughlin, "Strangers in the House: J. Lewis Shuck and Issachar Roberts, First American Baptist Missionaries to China" (PhD diss., University of Virginia, 1972). https://libraetd.lib.virginia.edu/public_view/sj1392079.

13. A total of 123,000 Baptist Chinese converts represented a tiny fraction of the population when considering that there were approximately five hundred forty million people in the country at midcentury. See A. J. Jowett, "The Growth of China's Population, 1949–1982," *The Geographical Journal* 150, no. 2 (1984): 1 56.

14. Gordon Poteat, *Home Letters from China: The Story of How a Missionary Found and Began His Life Work in the Heart of China.* New York: G. H. Doran, 1924, 9.

15. "Biographical Sketch," Special Collections and Archives: The Poteat Family Papers, Furman University (https://libguides.furman.edu/special-collections/poteat-family-papers/biography).

16. Wardin, *Baptists Around the World*, 92.

17. It is not certain when this photo album was compiled, or which members of the family compiled it.

18. Poteat, *Home Letters*, 14.

19. Poteat, *Home Letters*, 98.

20. "Class-Room Life at Furman," *The Baptist Courier*, Washington, DC: Library of Congress, 1898 (https://chroniclingamerica.loc.gov/lccn/sn82004649/1898-11–17/ed-1/seq-6/).

21. "Class-Room Life at Furman."

22. Edward Said coined the concept "Orientalism" to describe the Euro-American perception of the inferiority of countries and cultures that constitute the "East"; namely, Asia, the Middle East, and North Africa. In his seminal text, *Orientalism*, Said argued how academic and cultural narratives about the "Orient" have been inextricably associated with imperial activity. See Edward W. Said, *Orientalism* (New York: Pantheon Books, 1978).

23. Charles is listed as a student ("Wang Chas") in the Greenville City Directory from 1921. See "Greenville, S.C. City and Suburban Dictionary," *Greenville (S.C.) City Directories* XII (1921): 547 (https://cdm16821.contentdm.oclc.org/digital/collection/p16821coll26/id/546/rec/1).

24. Furman University, *Bonhomie Yearbook* (1924), 65.

25. Furman University, *Bonhomie Yearbook* (1953), 31.

26. "Foreign Professors Join Faculty," *The Furman Paladin*, October 4, 1968, 6, Furman University Student Newspapers Archives (https://cdm16821.contentdm.oclc.org/digital/collection/p16821coll21/id/27290/rec/160).

27. Claire Bien, *Hearing Voices, Living Fully* (Philadelphia: Jessica Kingsley Publishers, 2016), 29–30.

28. Madeline Y. Hsu, "Aid Refugee Chinese Intellectuals, Inc. and the Political Uses of Humanitarian Relief, 1952–1962," *Journal of Chinese Overseas* 10 (2014): 137–64."

29. Bien, *Hearing Voices*, 30–32.

30. Today, Furman offers three exchange programs in Japan through Waseda University, Kansai Gaidai University, and Seinan Gakuin University. These programs allow Furman students to spend a semester or year studying in Japan and Japanese college students to experience a year at Furman.

31. Robin Young, "Chen to Start China Studies," *The Furman Paladin* 65, no. 1 (1980): 5.

32. Kailash Khandke, "Kailash Khandke Oral History," interview by Eli Kibler, Eva Kiser, and Kylie Fisher, *Furman University Oral Histories*, Furman University, January 1, 2023 (https://scholarexchange.furman.edu/oral-histories/51/).

33. Kailash Khandke, interview by Eli Kibler, Eva Kiser, and Kylie Fisher, June 6, 2023. https://scholarexchange.furman.edu/oral-histories/51.

34. Eula Barton, "They Represent Nine Foreign Countries," *Furman Magazine*, 1, no. 1 (1951): 7, South Carolina Digital Library (https://cdm16821.contentdm.oclc.org/digital/collection/p16821coll5/id/27/rec/1).

35. Henry Ho, interview by Eli Kibler, Eva Kiser, and Kylie Fisher, November 28, 2022.

36. Raymond Mohl, John Van Sant, and Chizuru Saeki acknowledge how many Asians living in the American South were often characterized as "a third race," because they were neither Black nor white and did not fit into the traditional racial binary of the region. See Mohl, Van Sant, and Saeki, "Preface," in *Far East, Down South*, xiii.

37. University records suggest that Henry was the first Asian cheerleader at Furman.

38. Shusuke Yagi, "Shusuke Yagi Oral History," interview by Eli Kibler, Eva Kisner, and Kylie Fisher, Furman University Oral Histories, Furman University, January 1, 2023 (https://scholarexchange.furman.edu/oral-histories/49/).

39. Robert P. Fenton, "Asian American and Pacific Islanders in South Carolina: Diversity and Geographical Dispersion," *South Carolina Commission for Minority Affairs* 1, no. 3 (2022): 1–2.

40. See Timothy Tseng, "Polity, Theology, and Ethnicity: Three Factors in the History of Asian-American Baptists in Twentieth-Century America," In *Baptist History Celebration—2007: A Symposium on Our History, Theology, and Hymnody*, ed. Gary W. Long (Springfield, MO: Particular Baptist Press, 2008), 489–96."

41. Mohl, "Asian Immigration to Florida," in *Far East, Down South*, 74–79; and Desai and Joshi, "Introduction," in *Asian Americans in Dixie*, 8–9.

42. Jian Li, "A History of the Chinese in Charleston," *The South Carolina Historical Magazine* 99, no. 1 (1998): 36–37; and Peter Kung, "The Story of Asian Southern Baptists," *Baptist History and Heritage* 18, no. 3 (July 1983): 49.

43. In Charleston from the 1880s to the 1940s, Chinese families held a monopoly over hand laundries in the city. See Li, "A History of the Chinese in Charleston," 37 and 40–46.

44. Ray Belcher, *Greenville County, South Carolina: From Cotton Fields to Textile Center of the World* (Charleston, SC: The History Press, 2006), 15.

45. Belcher, *Greenville County*, 23.

46. Belcher, *Greenville County*, 63–65 and 73.

47. Tseng, "Polity, Theology, and Ethnicity," 493–95.

48. Tseng, "Polity, Theology, and Ethnicity," 494.

49. Wardin, *Baptists Around the World*, 90 and 99–100.

50. Abe Hardesty, "Thomas & Vivian Wong: Greenville fulfilled their dreams, so the Wongs are happy to return the favor." *City People*, February 23, 2000.

51. "Greenville entrepreneur Vivian Wong teams with Cérélia Group to donate one hundred thousand dollars to Prisma Health Children's Hospital," *Prisma Health*, September 15, 2021 (https://prismahealth.org/patients-and-guests/news/green ville-entrepreneur-vivian-wong-teams-with-cerelia-group-to-donate-$100,000 -to-prisma-health-chi).

52. Kathleen Maris, "50 Most Influential People of 2018," *Greenville Business Magazine*, December 28, 2018 (https://www.greenvillebusinessmag.com/2018/12/28/ 186169/50-most-influential-people-of-2018).

53. Mohl, Van Sant, and Saeki, "Preface," in *Far East, Down South*, xii–xiii.

54. "Kiyohiro Tsuzuki," *Spartanburg Herald-Journal*, January 19, 2005, https://www .goupstate.com/story/news/2005/01/19/kiyohiro-tsuzuki/29745031007/.

55. Scott Carlson, "A Southern University Embraces a Sacred Japanese Tradition," *The Chronicle of Higher Education* 54, no. 49 (2008): 612.

56. Leigh Gauthier Savage, "Place of Peace," *Furman Magazine* 51, no. 2 (2008): 6.

57. Yuri Tsuzuki, "About Me," https://www.yuritsuzuki.com/aboutme.

58. Ron Barnett, "Vietnamese find freedom in Greenville," *The Greenville News*, January 22, 1995, 1A.

59. Barnett, "Vietnamese find freedom," 1A.

60. Barnett, "Vietnamese find freedom," 3b.

61. See Peter C. Phan, "Vietnamese Catholics in the United States: Christian Identity between the Old and the New," *U.S. Catholic Historian* 18, no. 1 (2000): 19–35, especially 19–22; and Carl L. Bankston III, "Vietnamese-American Catholicism: Transplanted and Flourishing," *U.S. Catholic Historian* 18, no. 1 (2001): 36–53, especially 36 and 39–42.

62. Ron Barnett, "Vietnamese Refugee Escapes Communists, Leads local Church Group Now," *The Greenville News*, January 22, 1995, 3B.

63. Kimmy Yam, "Anti-Asian Hate Crimes increased 339 percent nationwide last year, report says," *NBC News*, January 31, 2022 (https://www.nbcnews.com/ news/asian-america/anti-asian-hate-crimes-increased-339-percent-nationwide -last-year-repo-rcna14282).

WORKS CITED

Bankston, Carl L. III. "Vietnamese-American Catholicism: Transplanted and Flourishing." *U.S. Catholic Historian* 18, no. 1 (2001): 36–53.

Barton, Eula. "They Represent Nine Foreign Countries." *Furman Magazine* 1, no. 1 (1951): 7. https://cdm16821.contentdm.oclc.org/digital/collection/p16821coll5/id/27/rec/1.

Belcher, Ray. *Greenville County, South Carolina: From Cotton Fields to Textile Center of the World.* Charleston, SC: The History Press, 2006.

Bien, Claire. *Hearing Voices, Living Fully.* Philadelphia: Jessica Kingsley Publishers, 2016.

"Biographical Sketch." Furman University Special Collections and Archives: Poteat Family Papers. Greenville, SC: Furman University, 2023. https://libguides.furman.edu/special-collections/poteat-family-papers/biography.

Carlson, Scott. "A Southern University Embraces a Sacred Japanese Tradition," *The Chronicle of Higher Education* 54, no. 49 (2008): 612.

Centers for Disease Control and Prevention. "Geographic Division or Region." Atlanta: Author, 2023. https://www.cdc.gov/nchs/hus/sources-definitions/geographic-region.htm#Figure.

"Class-Room Life at Furman." *The Baptist Courier.* Washington, DC: Library of Congress, 1898. https://chroniclingamerica.loc.gov/lccn/sn82004649/1898-11-17/ed-1/seq-6/.

Clyde, Paul H. "Questions and Answers," *Furman Magazine* 11, no. 2 (1962): 7.

Coughlin, Margaret M. "Strangers in the House: J. Lewis Shuck and Issachar Roberts, First American Baptist Missionaries to China." PhD dissertation, University of Virginia, 1972. https://libraetd.lib.virginia.edu/public_view/sj1392079.

Fenton, Robert P. "Asian American and Pacific Islanders in South Carolina: Diversity and Geographical Dispersion." *South Carolina Commission for Minority Affairs* 1, no. 3 (2022): 1–2.

"Foreign Professors Join Faculty," *The Furman Paladin,* October 4, 1968, 6. Furman University Student Newspapers Archives. https://cdm16821.contentdm.oclc.org/digital/collection/p16821coll21/id/27290/rec/160

Furman University. "Bonhomie Yearbook," Greenville, SC: South Carolina Digital Library, 1924, 31. https://cdm16821.contentdm.oclc.org/digital/collection/p16821coll4/id/11259/rec/54.

Furman University. "Bonhomie Yearbook," Greenville, SC: South Carolina Digital Library, 1924, 65. https://cdm16821.contentdm.oclc.org/digital/collection/p16821coll4/id/4133/rec/41.

"Greenville entrepreneur Vivian Wong teams with Cérélia Group to donate $100,000 to Prisma Health Children's Hospital." *Prisma Health,* September 15, 2021. https://prismahealth.org/patients-and-guests/news/greenville-entrepreneur-vivian-wong-teams-with-cerelia-group-to-donate-$100,000-to-prisma-health-chi.

"Greenville, S.C. City and Suburban Dictionary." *Greenville (S.C.) City Directories* XII (1921): 547. https://cdm16821.contentdm.oclc.org/digital/collection/p16821coll26/id/546/rec/1.

Hardesty, Abe. "Thomas & Vivian Wong: Greenville fulfilled their dreams, so the Wongs are happy to return the favor." *City People*, February 23, 2000.

Ho, Henry. Interview by Eli Kibler, Eva Kiser, and Kylie Fisher, November 28, 2022.

Hsu, Madeline Y. "Aid Refugee Chinese Intellectuals, Inc. And the Political Uses of Humanitarian Relief, 1952–1962." *Journal of Chinese Overseas* 10 (2014): 137–64.

Joshi, Khyati Y., and Jigna Desai. *Asian Americans in Dixie: Race and Migration in the South*. Champaign: University of Illinois Press, 2013.

Jowett, A. J. "The Growth of China's Population, 1949–1982." *The Geographical Journal* 150, no. 2 (1984): 155–70.

Khandke, Kailash. "Kailash Khandke Interview," Furman University Oral Histories, *Furman University*. Interview by Eli Kibler, Eva Kiser, and Kylie Fisher, January 1, 2023. https://scholarexchange.furman.edu/oral-histories/51/.

Kibler, Eli, Eva Kiser, and Kylie Fisher. "Untold Journeys: Exploring Greenville and Furman's Connections with Asia." Greenville, SC: Furman University, 2022. https://storymaps.arcgis.com/stories/4844f5d2a6a24ab497a01a465ce5e9c8.

"Kiyohiro Tsuzuki." *Spartanburg Herald-Journal*, January 19, 2005. https://www .goupstate.com/story/news/2005/01/19/kiyohiro-tsuzuki/29745031007/.

Kung, Peter. "The Story of Asian Southern Baptists." *Baptist History and Heritage*, 18, no. 3 (July 1983): 49.

Leavy, Patricia. *Oral History: Understanding Qualitative Research*. Oxford, England: Oxford University Press, 2011.

Li, Jian. "A History of the Chinese in Charleston." *The South Carolina Historical Magazine* 99, no. 1 (1998): 34–65. https://www.jstor.org/stable/27570280.

Li, Li. "Diversifying the Operation: Southern Baptist Missions in China at the Turn of the Century 1890–1910." *Baptist History and Heritage* 34, no. 2 (1999): 167–68.

Maris, Kathleen. "50 Most Influential People of 2018." *Greenville Business Magazine*, December 28, 2018. https://www.greenvillebusinessmag.com/2018/12/28/186169/50-most-influential-people-of-2018.

Mohl, Raymond A., John E. Van Sant, and Chizuru Saeki, eds. *Far East, Down South: Asians in the American South*. Tuscaloosa: University of Alabama Press, 2016.

Mulvihill, Thalia M., and Raji Swaminathan, eds. *Oral History and Qualitative Methodologies: Educational Research for Social Justice*. New York: Routledge, 2022.

Phan, Peter C. "Vietnamese Catholics in the United States: Christian Identity between the Old and the New." *U.S. Catholic Historian* 18, no. 1 (2000): 19–35.

Poteat, Gordon. *Home Letters from China: The Story of How a Missionary Found and Began His Life Work in the Heart of China*. New York: G. H. Doran, 1924.

Said, Edward W. *Orientalism*. New York: Pantheon Books, 1978.

Savage, Leigh Gauthier. "Place of Peace." *Furman Magazine* 51, no. 2 (2008): 6. https://scholarexchange.furman.edu/furman-magazine/vol51/iss2/4.

Strmic-Pawl, Hephzibah V., Brandon A. Jackson, and Steve Garner. "Race Counts: Racial and Ethnic Data on the U.S. Census and the Implications for Tracking Inequality." *Sociology of Race and Ethnicity* 4, no. 1 (2018): 1–13.

Teng, Yuan Chung. "Reverend Issachar Jacox Roberts and the Taiping Rebellion." *The Journal of Asian Studies* 23, no. 1 (1963): 55–67.

Tseng, Timothy. "Polity, Theology, and Ethnicity: Three Factors in the History of Asian-American Baptists in Twentieth-Century America." In *Baptist History Celebration—2007: A Symposium on Our History, Theology, and Hymnody*, edited by Gary W. Long (Springfield, MO: Particular Baptist Press, 2008), 489–96.

Tsuzuki, Yuri. "About Me." https://www.yuritsuzuki.com/aboutme.

US Census Bureau. "Geographic Terms and Definitions." census.gov, 2021. https://www.census.gov/programs-surveys/popest/about/glossary/geo-terms.html.

Wardin, Albert W., ed. *Baptists Around the World: A Comprehensive Handbook.* Nashville, TN: Broadman & Holman Publishers, 1995.

Yagi, Shusuke. "Shusuke Yagi Interview," Furman University Oral Histories. Interview by Eli Kibler, Eva Kiser, and Kylie Fisher, January 1, 2023. https://scholarexchange.furman.edu/oral-histories/49/.

Yam, Kimmy. "Anti-Asian hate crimes increased 339 percent nationwide last year, report says." *NBC News*, January 31, 2022. https://www.nbcnews.com/news/asian-america/anti-asian-hate-crimes-increased-339-percent-nationwide-last-year-repo-rcna14282.

Young, Robin. "Chen to Start China Studies." *The Furman Paladin* 65, no. 1 (1980): 5.

Review Essay

Who Are We? Where Are We?
Identity and Place Echo in Recent South Carolina Poetry Collections
Jo Angela Edwins

Jennifer Bartell, *Traveling Mercy* (Georgetown, KY: Finishing Line Press, 2023), 76 pp., paperback $22.99.

Evelyn Berry, *Grief Slut* (Knoxville, TN: Sundress Publications, 2024), 106 pp., paperback $12.99.

Willie Lee Kinard III, *Orders of Service: A Fugue* (New Gloucester, ME: Alice James Books, 2023), 100 pp., $18.95.

Len Lawson, *Negro Asylum for the Lunatic Insane* (Charlotte, NC: Main Street Rag, 2023), 92 pp., $15.00.

Ed Madden, *A pooka in Arkansas* (Washington, DC: Word Works, 2023), 99 pp., paperback $19.00.

Ed Madden, *A Story of the City: Poems Occasional and Otherwise* (Columbia, SC: Muddy Ford Press, 2023), 142 pp., $20.00.

Katherine Williams, *The Devil Cruises Pacific Coast Highway* (American Fork, UT: Kelsay Books, 2023), 112 pp., $23.00.

The year 2023 was anything but lean for poetry in South Carolina. So many books were published by South Carolinians this past year that this reviewer could not cover them all in this essay. Indeed, poetry lovers across the state have an embarrassment of riches to choose from if they wish to spend their free hours reading recent books by poets who call the Palmetto State home. Let us waste no time and begin our tour through recently published collections by six South Carolina poets.

University of South Carolina professor and former Columbia poet laureate Ed Madden, an Arkansas native, published two books of poetry in 2023, the first his Hillary Tham Capital Collection–winning book *A pooka in Arkansas*. The book's headnote from W. B. Yeats's 1888 volume *Fairy and Folk Tales of the Irish Peasantry* explains that a pooka is an animal spirit who may appear as any number of animals. Fittingly, the first poem in the collection, "When I was a young animal," describes a youngster growing up in the country, at one with the earth, and with its musks and textures. "On the farm, we were a pack,/the other cubs and me," the speaker declares, later describing how their mothers checked them for parasites. Later in the collection, "Carnivore" is structured around the images on a tin of animal crackers—bear, lion, tiger, buffalo—and twice in the poem the speaker declares, "Three of them would eat the other." The poem addresses an important theme in much of the collection, the speaker's struggle with his identity as a gay man in a family and community that cannot accept his identity: "For a long time I knew nothing/about what men do with men except//it was something I couldn't—." But at the end of "Carnivore," the mature speaker embraces his identity as the most powerful of all the animals in the circus or the zoo: "I am swallowing the animals one by one."

Another poem that addresses the pain of identity is the title poem, "A pooka in Arkansas," which describes the speaker walking a country road along the family land as his father lies dying. His mother warns him to be careful as there are "wolves/in the fields," but he must walk outside to call the man he loves, whom his family "refused to know,/a name they never used." Ahead of him as he walks, he sees a small dog, itself vulnerable and alone in a wild country. The poem ends on a note that highlights the similarities the speaker sees between the stray dog and himself, caught in hostile territory where even those meant to care for you cannot accept who you are. An interesting parallel poem to "A pooka in Arkansas" is "Fairy tale," in which the speaker explains, "What you thought was a wolf was not/a wolf. It was your father, mother, brother-/you did not remember what big teeth they had." The poem goes on to describe a boy groomed to participate in an attack on another boy, suggesting the complexities of victimhood, of guilt and innocence: "The wolf is in the mirror," the final stanza declares.

A long and powerful prose poem in A pooka in Arkansas, "Burning the fields" also grapples with the death of the speaker's father and the weight of the haunted landscapes of rural Arkansas. The poem begins with the speaker recalling the organized burning of husks in the fields at the end of the growing season, with a tinge of menace in the memory (one of the poem's most evocative lines): "A man stands, his head encased by a tiny church—as if the church were a vise, a mask, a hood." Threaded throughout the poem are ghosts of the past, in the image of abandoned farms, torn-down houses, and the specters of racism and homophobia. Late in the poem, Madden writes, "In 1848, Arkansas changed the penalty for sodomy for blacks. It remained 5–21 years for whites, but it was death for black men, free or slave. In 1873, the racial distinction was removed," although he does not tell us in favor of which penalty. Much of the poem grapples with the speaker's confused sense of identity after the death of his father, whom he both felt distanced from and mimics. "I am the son of a man now dead, who carried me low and long like a song sung off tune, then folded like a note into his wallet," the speaker declares, only to say two stanzas later, "I am the son of a man now dead. I carry him with me like a note in my wallet, wear him like a denim shirt." His family's refusal to accept him as a gay man complicates his mourning. The speaker states of his family, "What did they say when people asked after me?" Then he thinks of his mother, "My dad's gone now. Maybe they don't ask her anymore." He understands, however, that silence—so often the code of his family and his homeland—is erasure: "History is a finger on the lips, a hand over a mouth, a collar at the throat."

Madden's second book to appear in 2023 was his collection of poems written about Columbia during his time as poet laureate, *A Story of the City: Poems Occasional and Otherwise.* Some of the poems are, indeed, occasional, written in response to speeches or for events taking place in Columbia during his tenure as poet laureate, whereas others reflect Madden's responses to regional or national events during a turbulent time in American history. Poems such as "Body politic" blend the two inspirations. Written on the occasion of the January 31, 2017, state of the city address by then-mayor and current presidential advisor Stephen K. Benjamin, the poem begins with reference to the 2017 Women's March:

> When thousands of women with pink hats
> and placards fill the streets, think
> about how a city handles
> bodies, guides them down sidewalks
> and streets, between walls of stone
> and state, about the way a mass
> of bodies is a way of saying
> something.

Although the poem begins with an image of protest, it ends with images of unity, of a desire to work together to make the city, the body politic, better:

> Our city offers a hand, opens a door.
> Our city likes to talk.
> Our city would rather build a bridge than build a wall.
> Our city wants to hear your story.
> Our city leans in to listen.

Several other poems in *A Story of the City* blend the national and the local, the political and the personal. A good example of such an amalgamation is "Something to declare." The poem—dated July 11, 2018—begins by acknowledging that the news is focused on the president's overseas trip while the speaker's poetry camp students sit at small desks in a chilly classroom and try to write about what it means to live in their present moment. "Sachi talks about what it means/to declare something when you cross a border," the speaker says, and later, "Zoe describes her story as a scrap of paper swept/by the wind, litter snagged in a tree." The speaker cannot help but think about his dying cat waiting for him at home. The poem suggests that people with lives and loves and hopes and feelings cannot help but live in a world that leaders—some good, some dreadful, all far removed—can alter with the swipe of a pen. But the people with little power in the world, nevertheless, make their voices heard and use those voices to claim what power they can, as the last stanza illustrates: "This is only a little report from a summer arts camp,/where Makenna and Maya and Eva and Micah are writing/about their small, rich lives. We're here. You can find us here." Indeed, much of *A Story of the City* is about the power of the community and the individuals within it to stand against cruelty, greed, and evil intent.

Current Columbia poet laureate Jennifer Bartell is a native of the Bluefield area of Johnsonville, SC, a community that looms large in her debut collection *Traveling Mercy*. An African-American community that is home to Bartell's family and a wider circle of benevolent ancestors, Bluefield functions as both muse and chorus in Bartell's haunting poems. Bartell took it upon herself to perform an oral history of Bluefield, recording the wisdom and remembered stories of the women who shaped her generation of natives, and the notes to the collection illustrate the depth of the historical research that went into shaping the volume. Bartell's devotion to Bluefield's history emerges in the first poem the reader encounters: the collection's title poem, dedicated to the memory of three of those ancestors, as several of the poems in the collection are dedicated to the poet's elder guides. Immediately, the poet declares:

The Bluefield Griots plucked
me out of a jar before last breath
of prayer, buried me before birth:

This is how I time travel. I be seed
kept and passed, finger to palm,
planted and preserved for generations.

The poem, as does the entire collection, casts its gaze backward through history. The speaker of "Traveling Mercy" looks back across Jim Crow to the Middle Passage's nightmare transportation of captured African people across the ocean to slavery in America. As the poem draws to a close, the speaker imagines herself an okra seed in the hair of the "Jonah-woman" who first arrived in South Carolina and planted the seed that grew into the poet: "When fully grown, my yellow flower stretches/into green okra. Points its crooked finger to the sky."

Many of Bartell's poems are about such insistent survival, but many are also about loss and grief. One of the most powerful poems in the collection, "When you write your mother's obituary," is about exactly what the title says it is, a daunting task that the young Bartell—now a teacher in Richland County—did while working as a news reporter, one who sits in a county council meeting the next day while the thought of the obituary settles itself as "a seedling in your chest." The poet's mother, dying of cancer, dictates her final wishes to her daughter, who, after the death, fills out the obituary form and proceeds to "pick the last/dress she will ever wear." At the poem's end, the speaker realizes that the mother's obituary is her innocent self's "past obituary," as the seedling in her chest has grown to become a giant oak of grief.

Both the mother and the father of the poet are prominent figures in the book. They are the speaker's first dear loves and are direct outlets backward to the dearly held ancestors. They are also, of course, the speaker's literal reason for being. In "The Road to Being Born," we see the parents at odds after a second son is born, in a difficult labor leading to a caesarean section, over the mother's wish for a tubal ligation; the father wins the argument. Three years later, when the couple realizes they will give birth to a daughter—the poet—they both agree to have no more children. A few poems later in "Ars Poetica," the poet celebrates her role as emotional (not literal) truth teller, a role that her birth makes possible:

> I am the fisherman's daughter
> with net and oar.
> I am the poet
> in the mouth of the fish.
> I am the seamstress's daughter
> with my needle and thread.
> I am the design
> in her pattern.

The poet's birth allows her to tell the stories of her parents and the ancestors before them. She concludes "Ars Poetica" by reminding the reader, "I come with much work/and the light ain't long." But the shortness of life does not deter the poet, who concludes the volume with the short poem "The Okra," which echoes the opening title poem. Here, the speaker declares, "I was grown to be reborn," carrying with her "[s]eeds inside for next/generation's harvest."

Bartell, of course, is not the only writer concerned with history and legacy in her poetry. The latest collection from Newberry College professor and South Carolina native Len Lawson is his book *Negro Asylum for the Lunatic Insane*, an engrossing and heartbreaking collection that explores the lives of imagined characters committed to a fictional mental institution, a setting that, nonetheless, reflects the real cruelties inflicted on African-American mental patients in the era of segregation. Lawson dedicates the book to "patients of hospitals for 'insane Negroes' from the postbellum era to the mid-20th century" who suffered "mistreatment, racism, and cruelty more disturbing than these patients' minds were claimed to be." The collection depicts the lives of fictional men and women committed to the fictional John C. Calhoun Negro Asylum for the Lunatic Insane, which Lawson imagined to be dedicated at its 1950 opening by then-Governor Strom Thurmond. In the story Lawson's poems create, the asylum, named after a notorious advocate for slavery and dedicated by a staunch segregationist, is destined to become a site of further cruelties inflicted on African-American South Carolinians. Constructed on a former plantation that was lost by its gambling-addicted owner, the asylum becomes the site of a different sort of imprisonment for the African-American people housed there for decades beyond the Civil War.

Several individual poems tell the tragic stories of various inmates at the asylum. "Birdie" centers on a mother whose boyfriend, the father of her children, resents the children and the expenses they will cause, so Birdie strangles the children, hanging them from trees in a haunting gesture evocative of the horrific lynchings that were inflicted on African Americans throughout American history. "Birdie" is a villanelle, a poetic form that repeats two lines from the first stanza throughout subsequent stanzas, suggesting the cyclical nature of the subject matter, and one such repeated line describes the children as "strange" in a clear echo of the Abel Meeropol song "Strange Fruit," popularized by singer Billie Holiday in 1939. Lawson knows his cultural history, and the poems in this volume reflect those histories to provide context for the tragic events the collection describes.

"Ballad of Milton and Julia" uses the traditional ballad form and its common subject of doomed love to explain Milton's fifteen-year confinement to the asylum. Milton, unable to impregnate his beloved Julia, comes home early from work one day to discover a young minister named Stevenson in bed with his wife. Milton throws the minister from the room and castrates him with a boxcutter. It is Stevenson who convinces the state to commit Milton to the asylum instead of sentencing him to life in prison, a fate that the poem acknowledges may not have been a mercy:

> He would've preferred the chair and would have
>
> settled for the cell instead of seeing Stevenson
> once a week in front of his Calhoun chamber door
> begging for forgiveness and praying for their souls.

When, at last, Milton is released after fifteen years, he returns home to an empty house overtaken by snakes and rats, Julia having moved North to have children by two different fathers. The implication of betrayal haunting Milton is clear, as the line between wrongdoer and wronged in this poem is difficult to draw.

The central figure in Lawson's book and in the asylum is an inmate named Brock Bridges, who becomes a kind of folk hero to the other inmates. A gentle soul who loved butterflies and was committed after urinating on a woman who startled him in a Piggly Wiggly parking lot, Bridges gets a reputation after an orderly beats him up and Bridges retaliates by biting the orderly's neck so hard that he kills him. Bridges is treated, or punished, with electroshock therapy. In the poem "Shock Therapy," an employee of the asylum describes witnessing the treatment:

> Brock Bridges lay on a medical bed   two nurses held him down
> one at the head   one at the foot   Pushing my mop bucket past the
> cracked door sometimes I saw him vibrating in bed   Electric current
> flowing through that black body   under white sheets.

Much later in the collection, when Brock escapes the burning asylum, people speculate that he was the arsonist, though readers discover that the speculation is false. Still, Bridges—disappearing in the midst of the destruction of the infamous asylum—achieves hero status in his ability to survive and gain freedom after years of suffering at the hands of those meant to offer healing.

Indeed, Lawson's collection suggests that healing is never possible unless words are given to the truth and responsibility is taken for treating people inhumanely. Although the first goal might be accomplished poetically, much is yet to be done in our state and our culture to accomplish the second.

If Lawson's book shows how fictional scenarios echo lived history, Katherine Williams's *The Devil Cruises Pacific Coast Highway* shows how real life can take leaps into the fantastic. Williams, a native southerner who has lived in California and Virginia and currently resides in James Island, SC, pulls actual landscapes from across the world into her poems, some of which throb with the enchanting madness of a fever dream. The collection features poems in free verse and in a variety of forms—prose poems, sonnets, ghazals, pantoums, sestinas—all of which foreground Williams's luminous technical prowess. Many of the poems showcase sound brilliantly, and many resonate with multiple voices that create a kind of choral effect on the reader's/listener's ear. "The Summer of Nothing Moves" is a series of unrhymed tercets narrated by a speaker whose twelve-year-old niece is visiting for the summer, and the preteen's excited voice bursts through the first two stanzas, begging for permission to explore her precocious desires. Her pleas set a tone for a whirlwind summer that becomes an exercise in breathless motion. As is often the case in Williams's poems, there is a lovely musicality to the flow of the lines. After a tire blows on a trip to the Grand Canyon and the aunt teaches the niece how to put on a spare, the poem concludes, "Tires intact so far, we push through acetylene heat out to the edge,/ park the sedan, sit on a stone. Nothing moves before this great gash/in the Earth but the slow turning universe, our breathing bodies."

But it isn't just sound that weaves through Williams's verse, as these poems shimmer with color. Consider these gemlike images: "Men and maids upholstered in teal" ("Epithalamion"); "if i am a lunatic spelling the walls purple/then you are veins of garnet in a virgin rock-bed" ("Orthodoxy"); "Let your grimy little street's smoggy days/turn cerulean, and your moonless nights'/wild auroras burn green and purple" ("Blueaille"); "Red jaguar plays tug-o'-war with a purple lamb./Chartreuse gargoyle grooms yellow jackalope./Dragons witness their orangeness cast into the earth" ("On the Wing"). Still, of the kaleidoscope of hues featured in this collection, the dominant color is red, as is evidenced even just in the titles of poems such as "Red Side Blues," "The Red Terrance," and "Ode on Red." It's no accident either that blood as an image pulses throughout the collection. This adoration of scarlets is perhaps a reflection of the titular devil, who, in the book's title poem, fiddles with the radio in his '59 Chevy convertible while cruising the streets to find a woman to snatch and offer to share with God, to whom he declares, *"I'd be glad to pick up/a little blood on the way over. Amen"* ("The Devil Cruises PCH"). In "God Devil Ghazal," Satan mends fences with God before they attempt a world tour together, but God bores Lucifer with his tameness until they both agree to part ways once again.

Clearly, Williams's poetic toolbox is filled with dark humor, much of which, like the action in many of these poems, travels at the speed of light. Her *ars poetica*, "Termite Art," is a Shakespearean sonnet that features the muse as a drunken gangster/femme fatale forcing the poet to write at gunpoint. "Sonnet Comparing David Lehmans" is patterned after W. H. Auden's "In the Time of War, XII" and is written as a response to poet David Lehman's declaration that a *bouts-rimés* using the rhymes of any Auden sonnet would make a "great poem." The speaker of the *bouts-rimés*—landlady? lover?—discovers that the poet living under her roof has been running up the phone bill by calling phone sex lines. Subtle or direct or a little sad, the humor in Williams's poems is almost always there.

It should be noted that, as several poems already mentioned illustrate, many of the pieces in this collection highlight women's experience in varying degrees of humor and sadness. "San Quintín Harbor" beautifully describes—mostly from the woman's perspective—a couple in a strained relationship camping on a beach and speaking to each other of anything but their troubles. Two poems along, "Amicable Pre-Hearing Brunch" appears to feature the same couple comparing the restaurant dishware in front of them to memories of their almost-dead marriage (including the trip to San Quintín). "After Many Years Out West," a sonnet that may be the most linear narrative poem in the collection, describes a convenience store clerk's silent recognition of a boy she dated thirty-three years after the fact, in the face of a married and evidently well-off customer. She recalls herself as "the buoyant, licentious,/unwanted teen" and recalls him as afflicted with "the madonna/whore thing." Women—especially women's struggles with men, even if ironically distanced in narration—are a central theme of Williams's collection.

In a much different way, gender is at the center of Aiken County native Evelyn Berry's *Grief Slut*. In a collection that appeared just as 2023 was rolling into 2024, Berry, a transgender writer and editor now living in Columbia, examines the challenge and the beauty involved in growing up queer in the South. One of Berry's most shining talents is her ability to use the music of language to portray sensuality in everything—from sex to prayer, to computer coding, to mowing grass on a hot day—and it should be noted that anyone who has seen Berry perform her work at readings cannot help but hear the poems spoken in her lively voice. The opening poem of Part One, "queer the smear," is a poem whose title is created by inverting the homophobic name of playground football. It demonstrates well the sensual musicality and double entendre of Berry's poetry:

> behind
> the school,
> we scrum.
> we bum rush.
> we hum
> the slur,
> sing
> for brief
> carnage.

The poem's conclusion underscores the irony behind the homophobic name of an often homoerotic game:

> there is no other way
> boys may touch,
> may hold each other
> against the dirt.

Indeed, sensuality pervades in Berry's poetry, although what is sensed is not always pleasurable. As the title of the collection indicates, many of Berry's poems emerge from a common poetic wellspring, the poet's response to the agonies of grief. Berry tells us in the notes to her book that the "you" of many of the poems is her friend Abe, who committed suicide in 2020. Part Three of the four-part volume is dedicated to Abe, and several poems in the section are saturated with memories of the poet's lost friend. In the prose poem "coronation," the speaker recalls a visit to a Burger King with her friend on his thirtieth birthday, when he asks for a cardboard crown to wear, and for the rest of the night, the friends share the crown, growing soggy with their sweat. Months later, when the speaker unearths the tattered crown behind a bookcase after the friend's death, the memento triggers the speaker's grief again. In the poignant "ritual for remembering that one night you were still alive," the speaker uses a particularly acute image to illustrate the distortion that memory makes of a lost loved one's particularity: "a photograph deteriorates the more often it is touched." The challenge all poets face when writing about grief is how to translate the ineffable—love and loss—into words, something Berry addresses in "elegy," when she exclaims, "what is the use of words/if they only feed grief's appetite,/the use of any of this if I cannot keep you alive?" Berry's poems push us to acute feeling, whether that feeling is pleasure and joy or heartache and grief.

Another source of grief in Berry's book is the sadness evoked by hate crimes against the community of lesbian, gay, bisexual, transgender, queer/questioning, intersex, asexual/aromantic/agender individuals. In two poems titled "martyrdom of saint sebastian," the saint—whom, Berry explains in her notes, is "often revered as the gay saint"—suffers the kind of death too many queer people still suffer at the hands of the hateful, a reality emphasized in the second of these two poems, in which the saint's martyrdom is directly compared with the killing of Matthew Shepard in Wyoming in 1998. The powerful "controlled burn" describes a series of fires, including two arsons—the deadly 1973 burning of the UpStairs Lounge in New Orleans and a 2011 arson that killed two gay men in their Dallas apartment. In "on the question, 'wait, can trans women reclaim the word *faggot*?'" Berry explains that the origin of the epithet is the bundles of twigs "used in fires, which refers/to queer bodies used as/kindling." But although Berry gives powerful voice to the experience of the queer community facing life-threatening cruelties in a society still plagued by homophobia, *Grief Slut* does not portray only notes of sadness and horror. In "boyhood: revisions," Berry pays honor to her dead name and the life she lived as Derek, declaring, "i swear, i do not want to forget," and she explains in her notes to the poems that she does not want to "create a veil of shame around a name I used for the majority of my life, a past version of myself with whom I would like to cultivate a relationship of care and compassion." The final poem of the collection, "yes, i've seen the future & i promise i'm still alive," expresses the mixed emotions of living trans in such a culture but includes triumphant notes, as Berry declares:

> i am translated
> most simply
> as constellation
> cluster of stars
> with a name
> i've chosen myself.

Another poet whose work captures queer experience is Newberry native Willie Lee Kinard III, whose *Orders of Service* won the prestigious Alice James Award in 2022. Visually engaging, as might be expected from a poet who doubles as a graphic designer, the collection features some poems in traditional black print on a white background, some in white print on a black background, and several poems whose power derives in part from the shape of the poem on the page. The voices in the poems explore what it is like to be Black and queer and raised in the Christian South. The poems are complex works of art, which accounts for the collection's subtitle, "A Fugue." Kinard III writes poetry ripe with allusion, incorporating references from Greek mythology (such as Icarus, Adonis, the Minotaur, and the Gorgons), popular music (Beyoncé, Mariah Carey, Sam Cooke, SWV, and the Bee Gees), the Bible (Daniel, Jesus, and Pilate) and the animal kingdom (bees, crickets, and fish). Any single poem in the collection is packed with resonance, no doubt one of the reasons Kinard III labels their table of contents "epyllia," a series of narrative poems that carry the weight of epic in shorter form. Still, despite the rich diversity of metaphor and subject matter in the collection, a particularly important theme throughout is individual identity, including Kinard III's place in a family in which they share a name with male ancestors whose actions and attitudes do not always reflect the poet's. This is most evident in the poem "Labyrinth," in which Kinard III is figured as a Minotaur shackled by their own name, described as a "corn maze." The poet declares, "I will call my irons/Suffix," and later insists, "This yoke ain't easy. I pull my father/behind me, slosh through stubborn puddles/of his absence." It is clear in this collection that the father's failures become a harder burden to bear when the child carries his name: "I will be frank:/it is exhaustive. Willie is usually diminutive." Later in the collection, "Frostbite" depicts the anger of a child disciplined and criticized by an often absent father who does not bother to support his family enough to keep them out of the cold, literally and figuratively.

Another aspect of family identity important in the collection is Black identity and the burden of legacies of slavery and racism in the South, as is most clearly illustrated in "When My Family Says We Were the Regulars There." The poem describes the often unspoken intersections between descendants of the enslavers and the enslaved, including "the name of their family the name of our family stretching the span/of this place's origins & everybody knows it." The poem calls out what is often unsayable in a still racially divided South: "my mother/likely knew our enslavers, in our neck of the woods, one does/their best by not reminding them of it." Indeed, many of the poems in Kinard III's collection attempt to speak truths people often try to keep quiet for a variety of reasons.

One recurring poem in the collection that uses graying-out of text to speak such hidden truths is "Automation," whose various iterations have different subtitles. The poem's first appearance, titled "Automation: Flight or Exit Interview with Holy Woman," is structured in a question-and-answer format, with italicized questions aimed at the audience's psychology—for example, *"If you trying to escape so bad, why you keep moving the same way?"* and *"How long it's been since you last made stars with your smile?"*—and the "answers," which appear to be excerpts from an explanation of the sexual roles of queen bees. Later iterations of the poem gray out text that is not meant to be read, to create erasure poems out of the original, until the final poem, "Automation: I," leaves to be read only one question and two small words as an answer. The poem "shrinks" as it goes along, suggesting that the answers to questions of identity, perhaps especially queer identity, cannot easily be answered, even with an elaborate natural metaphor.

Of course, as "Automation" alludes, a major issue of identity at work in the collection is queer identity, and several poems give voice to their speakers' search for love and understanding in a confusing and often hostile world. "Return Policy" is a beautiful erotic poem set among the trappings of a luscious breakfast. The various "Hymn" poems in the collection reflect the experience of online dating in queer communities; for example, "Hymn: Chainsweat" is a raucously sensual depiction of online hook-up culture in which the speaker describes Summer, "the most glorious cicada," about whom is declared, "I haven't wanted to be someone else's as much as I do now." Arguably, the most epic of the epyllia in Kinard III's collection, "How Deep Is Your Love" is a twenty-eight-sectioned centerpiece that, according to the poet's notes, "alludes to the myths (& deaths) of Icarus & Adonis in an attempt to explode or dissect the sonnet." Indeed, Icarus and Adonis bleed through this poem, but one additional influence that Kinard III does not mention in their notes appears to be Walt Whitman, as "How Deep Is Your Love" contains echoes of Whitman's epic "Out of the Cradle Endlessly Rocking." Birds—a robin, a lark, a thrush—become prominent figures in the poem, as they lift the boy to the sky (Icarus, yes, but also the poet born of his encounter with the birds?), only to drop him into the sea, which is held by a yard bathed in heat that claims the birds, as the boy "eats the sea" and "joins the birds." In time, the speaker finds his lover dead but does not wish to admit it: "Give me another word than that./I will not call him *dead*." Like the mockingbird in Whitman's poem whose mate will not answer him, the speaker's lover does not respond to his calls: "He will not call back./There is nothing left to answer to." The speaker/poet declares in section twenty-seven, "There is nothing left to sing about./There is nothing to brag about," but being a poet, the speaker cannot go silent, instead returning in the final section twenty-eight to demand, "Give me another word." "How Deep Is Your Love," like the whole of Kinard III's collection, is a complex hymn to love, loss, and the difficulties of being a poet/singer whose identities the world often refuses to embrace.

Every so often, as happened most recently in late 2022 in a much-maligned *New York Times* opinion piece, someone insists that poetry is dead. Don't believe it. Anyone who says so does not read much contemporary poetry, which expresses ideas and emotions in richer diversity today than ever before. And if any South Carolina readers of such poppycock are inclined to believe those lamentations, they need only turn to the "South Carolina Authors" bookshelves of their local bookstore to see that, indeed, poetry is alive and well, waiting for readers to let the poems sing in their ears.

Jo Angela Edwins is professor of English and Trustees' Research Scholar at Francis Marion University. A widely published poet, she currently serves as the poet laureate of the Pee Dee. Her recent collection, *A Dangerous Heaven*, was published in 2023.

Reviews

Patricia Causey Nichols, *Voices of Our Ancestors: Language Contact in Early South Carolina* (Columbia: University of South Carolina Press, 2009), 196 pp., paperback $32.99 (2022), ebook $32.99 (2022).

Patricia Causey Nichols makes it easy to anthropomorphize language in *Voices of Our Ancestors: Language Contact in Early South Carolina*. In her well-researched and lucid account, languages are born, develop, mature, and grow. Sometimes languages encounter other languages, which can result in changes to either or both. Languages can merge and diverge, conquer or be conquered, and they can die, never to be heard again. Nichols reminds us that the history of language is necessarily the history of people, and patterns of change and continuity in the lives of people and their communities affect the languages they speak and hear as well. She takes the reader on a deep but highly readable excursion through seventeenth-century South Carolina that effortlessly blends insights from history and sociology, as well as linguistics. Nichols's thoughtful analysis demonstrates how the European conquest of North America catalyzed both the invention of racial categories and change in and development of languages. The racial categories invented by colonists, she asserts, then stimulated the development of new, racialized identities to replace older, "tribal" ones. New languages and dialects created by South Carolinians helped create, sustain, and transmit those identities. *Voices of Our Ancestors* is an effective book that manages to document and explain the effects of decades of profound changes on people, places, communities, and languages without getting mired in excessive historical detail or cumbersome theory.

A main contribution of Nichols's work is to shine a spotlight on the role that European aggression played in a sociological and political transition in the minds of Natives, colonists, and African people "[f]rom tribes to race." European settlers, she claims, long had seen themselves as members of groupings such as Scots, Welsh, or Castilian much more than they possessed national identities such as "British" or "Spanish," let alone racial identities such as "White" or "European." Similarly, the indigenous Carolinians sorted themselves and others into a diverse variety of tribal and kinship groups, from the extensive and organized Cofitachequi chiefdom to many smaller and less centralized bands such as the Edisto or Stono. Enslaved Africans were brought to South Carolina first by the Spanish, then later in large numbers by English settlers. Many were brought from rice-growing regions in West Africa, others were brought from the Niger River delta area, and yet more were brought from Angola and even more distant parts of Africa where they possessed well-established tribal identities such as Yoruba, Wolof, Ewe, and others. Those traditional groupings would suffer threats to their centripetal force in colonial South Carolina.

The dislocations and tensions caused by European settlement spurred the development first of racial categories and later, identities. Within existing groups, European expansion facilitated the blurring of long-held differences in religion, culture, lifestyle, and language. Around Charleston and Georgetown, Native Carolinians were pushed south and west, where increased contact with existing tribes eroded long-standing differences. Outnumbered by both the indigenous population and the African-descended population they imported, European colonizers found reason to elide their own differences in identity, culture, habits, and faith, whereas the English language provided a convenient *lingua franca* to link the European settlers of Carolina. Similarly, African people were torn from their own rich webs of culture and imported with little regard to any consideration other than economic. In the Carolinas, enslaved Africans were compelled to make what connections they could among themselves, simultaneously trying to preserve and pass on their own identities while absorbing influences from other Africans, Native Carolinians, and their European enslavers. Differences in physical appearance, usually ascribed by white settlers, reinforced the emerging groupings and contributed to the development of new, racialized identities.

Voices of Our Ancestors is ultimately a book about language, particularly speech patterns in the English spoken in eastern South Carolina. To that end, Nichols charts three particular linguistic developments: the variety of English often called "Gullah" or "Geechee" by African Americans, the English spoken by the Lumbee Indians residing along the border of North and South Carolina, and a "southern" dialect common to the broader region. Similarities far outweigh differences, she tells us, although native Carolinians are able to parse subtle differences that reveal variation on the basis of ethnicity, region (low or upcountry), and class. Here, Nichols blends historical research with her own extensive fieldwork, demonstrating how patterns of migration and contact influenced the development of the three dialects, all eventually informing the English spoken in various parts of eastern South Carolina today. The development of the Gullah–Geechee language receives particular attention, with emphasis on the degree to which the speech of South Carolina's early inhabitants exerts a continuing influence on the current population.

Nichols tells us that, "Like politics, all language is local." South Carolina's linguistic history reflects influences from the array of cultures and languages that streamed into South Carolina from the 1500s onward. Contact between and among Native, European, and African/African-American people blurred boundaries that previously divided the various "tribes," whereas perceived visible differences facilitated the drawing of new, racial lines between groups. However, constrained by geography, South Carolinians developed a common culture and way of speaking that is representative of its unique history and development. *Voices of Our Ancestors: Language Contact in Early South Carolina* effectively blends primary source information with extensive fieldwork to highlight the relationships between movement, contact, and communication. Written for a professional audience, but readily accessible to the public, Nichols's book is worthwhile both as a readable and lucid history of early migration into South Carolina and also as an effective primer on language development and change. I recommend it for undergraduate courses in linguistics, history, and South Carolina studies, and to the interested public.

Richard A. Almeida, Francis Marion University

Robert Green II and Tyler D. Parry (eds.), *Invisible No More: The African American Experience at the University of South Carolina* (Columbia: University of South Carolina Press, 2021), 268 pp., cloth $49.99, paperback $24.99, ebook $24.99.

Did you know South Carolina College (now the University of South Carolina [USC]) enslaved people of African descent? How about the fact that it desegregated twice? Were you aware that a Black faculty member taught Black students at USC in the 1870s? *Invisible No More* documents the African-American experience at USC from 1801 to the present, seeking to answer the question, "What does it mean to be an African American at the flagship institution located in the capital city of the seedbed of the Confederacy?" Through a series of chronologically organized chapters, the book shows how Black individuals actively "molded the university into something greater than the sum of its parts." Instead of focusing on a particular time period, this ambitious volume purposefully connects over two hundred years of Black agency against the consistent and evolving efforts of oppression. In doing so, it shows the "centrality of African Americans to the history of the University of South Carolina."

The book opens with a foreword by Valinda W. Littlefield, who recounts the origins of this volume, which grew out of fiftieth-anniversary commemorations of the second desegregation (1963) at USC when Robert Anderson, Henrie Monteith, and James Solomon enrolled. Graham Duncan then reveals the connections between USC and slavery before the Union's victory in the Civil War. Duncan's meticulous combing of archival documents shows that the university hired enslaved individuals to help build the campus and care for its students and faculty by cooking, cleaning, and performing other essential tasks. On occasion, the university itself enslaved individuals such as Jack, who aided professors in their laboratories. Jack's mysterious death after university president Thomas Cooper's request and authorization to "direct proper punishment to be inflicted upon him" reminds us of the backlash to even the smallest gains of autonomy for Black individuals.

In chapter two, Tyler D. Parry recounts the first desegregation of USC with Henry E. Hayne's enrollment and the brief moment in which a university "irrespective of race or color" existed during Reconstruction. As Parry argues, "the university not only disproved racist generalizations of Black intellectual inferiority but also rebuked the belief that the races could not amicably coexist in the same space." New scholarships provided opportunities to Black students and poor white students, thus challenging the socioeconomic hierarchy of the state. Women attending the Normal School located at the university also benefited from this intellectual environment and went on to become educational leaders across the country. This progress came to a screeching halt when Wade Hampton III assumed the governorship and embarked on his plan to "starve out the University . . . and reopen it as a school for white youth exclusively."

The next two chapters are biographical in nature and highlight largely forgotten figures of USC's history. In chapter three, Christian K. Anderson and Jason C. Darby focus on the remarkable life and legacy of Richard T. Greener, a Black professor, librarian, and student at USC during Reconstruction. Highlighting the extraordinary accomplishments of Greener and his fellow colleagues and students, the chapter leaves us wondering what could have been. Meanwhile, Evan A. Kutzler uses a cache of letters to piece together the little-discussed life of Simon Peter Smith, an enslaved man forced to labor at South Carolina College who eventually earned degrees from Howard University and Chicago Theological Seminary before embarking on a theological career.

In chapter five, Brian A. Robinson zooms out to situate the events at USC within the educational developments across South Carolina. The reconstruction government's push for educational opportunity, regardless of race or class, was ultimately undermined in the 1880s. Using racial fears to divide the populace, wealthy politicians successfully undermined public education in hopes of restoring the antebellum racial and social class hierarchy.

Attention then shifts to putting the efforts of desegregation into context. Robert Greene II details how two separate and unsuccessful attempts to desegregate USC in the 1930s and '40s ultimately contributed to the downfall of segregation. Although USC remained an all-white institution, these attempts at integration engendered court decisions that led to the creation of a law school for Black students at South Carolina State. Ironically, this new school created to satisfy the "separate but equal" clause would soon produce the lawyers who ultimately dismantled segregation in the state.

The last third of the book centers around the experiences of Black students in the latter half of the twentieth century. In chapter seven, Marcia G. Synnott explores the experiences of the Black students who desegregated USC a second time in 1963. Although legal barriers fell, these students continued to face prejudice and had to carry on the fight for equality that their predecessors began. In chapter eight, Ramon M. Jackson looks at how students and faculty pushed for change during the Black Campus Movement at USC, and in doing so, brought new intellectual ideas and programs to the university.

The last two chapters explore the power of symbolism and memory. In chapter nine, Holly Genovese focuses on Black students' efforts to protest the playing of "Dixie" and the display of the Confederate battle flag. The racist response of some white students highlights how entrenched white supremist ideology was on the campus. Finally, Katharine Thompson Allen and Lydia Mattice Brandt recount the challenges of commemorating African-American history at USC using the creation of historical markers and a statue for Richard T. Greener as examples. Their measured prose remind us that true reconciliation requires meaningful introspection and structural change. Acknowledgment is only the beginning. In an afterword bringing the volume to a close, Henri Monteith Treadwell, one of the students who desegregated the school in 1963, provides a candid and inspiring recollection of her time at USC and a call to action as many of the indignities that she endured in the 1960s persist.

As with most edited collections, there is uneven coverage of certain time periods and subjects, but the editors and authors beautifully used the threads of agency and resistance to stitch together a cohesive and accessible volume. As Greene and Parry remind us, "the process of desegregation should be thought of as *ongoing*," and the "memory of the past cannot, by itself, be a substitute for genuine change in the present." In keeping with that spirit, this is a book every USC student must read and every South Carolinian should read.

Joshua Casmir Catalano, Clemson University

Ralph C. Muldrow, *Charleston Renaissance Man: The Architectural Legacy of Albert Simons in the Holy City* (Columbia: University of South Carolina Press, 2022), 188 pp., cloth $49.99, ebook $49.99.

In his classic history of the American preservation movement, Charles B. Hosmer Jr. wrote, "It might not be an exaggeration to say that the whole historic district of Charleston emerged as a grand design from the drawing board of Albert Simons."[1] As an architect working in Charleston and almost exclusively in South Carolina, Simons designed "background buildings," writes Ralph Muldrow, "understated yet fine designs in the traditional styles, mostly Colonial Revival . . . that still serve to create continuity with the buildings of the more distant past without offering unnecessary competition to the existing built environment." Context and compatibility were the hallmarks of the architectural career of Albert Simons, but as significant, and directly related, were his contributions to historic preservation. As author Muldrow notes, "Simons played a key role in creating the first historic district in the United States, which became the model for hundreds of local historic districts across the country." As an exemplary civil servant, Simons was willing "to serve on and with many national and local committees and organizations mak[ing] him an exemplar for architects in the service of their hometown." In sum, writes Muldrow, Simons "saw the fields of architecture, preservation, planning, and art as inextricably linked," and this breadth of view prompts the accolade that Albert Simons was a modern-day "Charleston Renaissance man."

As Witold Rybezynski notes in his foreword, citing Robert Stern, Albert Simons was part of the "lost generation" of American architects whose traditional design inclinations "did not fit the evolutionary model espoused by historians of modernism." It was an artistic generation who learned how to draw in beaux-arts schools and who illustrated the *art* of architecture with accomplished travel sketches, student studies, and finished renderings of medieval and classical buildings, then similarly rendered their own projects in beautiful watercolor, pen and ink, and pencil drawings. Indeed, one of the merits of Muldrow's book is its color reproductions of Simons's student drawings and professional etchings, paintings, and measured drawings of historical buildings preserved in the Special Collections at the College of Charleston and the South Carolina Historical Society. These drawings are reproduced as full-page and half-page illustrations in the large nine-inch by twelve-inch Simons monograph.

After studying one year (1906–7) at the College of Charleston, Simons entered the architecture program at the University of Pennsylvania, where he, like Atlanta's Francis Palmer Smith before him, studied with beaux arts–trained Paul Philippe Cret. Cret's focus for his students was the art of architecture, assigning exercises aimed at developing an eye for harmonious proportions, balanced scale, classical ornamental detail, and the preservation and reproduction of traditional stylistic forms and decoration. Indeed, in the respective archives of Albert Simons and Francis Smith are drawings of the same historical buildings such as the chapel at the Chateau of Amboise and the Chateau of Azay-le-Rideau, as well as ancient column capitals and other classical details, whose careful study was encouraged by Cret. Smith graduated in 1908 and carried Penn's beaux-arts curriculum to Georgia Tech, where he was head of architecture from 1909 to 1922; Simons earned his bachelor of science degree in 1911 and his master of science degree in 1912, and after a year in Baltimore, he returned to Charleston in 1914 to begin a career as a beaux arts–trained architect in a traditionalist city whose citizens valued their architectural history. Both Cret students had major impacts on their respective communities. Initially, however, when he returned to Charleston, there was little work for Simons, so he spent twelve months measuring and drawing old houses in Charleston for the book by Alice Ravenel Huger Smith and Daniel Elliott Huger Smith titled *The Dwelling Houses of Charleston*. It would be a significant postgraduate training ground for Charleston's most noted restoration architect.

Charleston Renaissance Man: The Architectural Legacy of Albert Simons in the Holy City is organized in seven chapters. As one might expect of a Charleston study, chapter one establishes pedigree and describes the family roots of both Albert and his wife, Harriett Porcher Simons, as being "descended from old Charleston families." Chapter two establishes young Albert's initial exposure to beaux arts classical architecture evidenced at the South Carolina Inter-State and West Indian Exposition (1902), whose staff (plaster) buildings styled in classical forms looked back to the 1895 Cotton States Exposition in Atlanta, and to the Columbian Exposition in Chicago in 1893. Muldrow then addresses Simons' education at the College of Charleston and at the University of Pennsylvania, as well as his travels in Europe from 1912 to 1913. His emerging restrained classical design predilections were influenced not only by Cret but also by native South Carolina architect Robert Mills. A brief chapter describing Simons's early professional experiences and activities during World War I is then followed by chapters five and six on the 1920s and 1930s, during which Simons's reputation was made as a traditional Charleston architect, planner, and preservationist. The final chapter addresses Simons's postwar encounter with modernism, when he designed his only genuinely modern building—Charleston's airport terminal—and when he continued his leadership as a city planner in Charleston. Two appendices offer significant contributions in describing "Albert Simons' Service to the American Institute of Architects" and in publishing a *catalogue raisonné* of the work of Simons and Lapham, including over a hundred projects in Charleston alone.

For preservationists, Albert Simons is best known for his pioneering work in the creation of Charleston's Old and Historic District with distinct boundaries and a board of architectural review, which became models for countless other preservation strategies nationwide. His survey of historic homes on the peninsula, which ultimately led to the book *This is Charleston* (1944) by Samuel G. Stoney, established a list of criteria for judging the merits of historic buildings and a system repeated by subsequent preservationists. Each building was ranked in one of five categories: (1) national importance, (2) valuable to the city, (3) valuable, (4) notable, and (5) worthy of mention. Helen McCormick of the South Carolina Historical Society worked on the survey; and judges included Albert Simons, John Mead Howells, Alice Revenel Huger Smith, and Sam Stoney, author with Simons of *Plantations of the Low Country* (1938). John Mead Howells, a prominent architect (Chicago Tribune Building, 1922–25, and Daily News Building, NY, 1928–30), was also author of several noted books of architectural history: *Lost Examples of Colonial Architecture* (1931), *The Architectural Heritage of the Piscataqua: Houses and Gardens of The Portsmouth District in Maine* (1937), and *The Architectural Heritage of the Merrimack: Early Homes and Gardens* (1941). Howells was a New Englander who owned Charleston's 1772 John Stuart House as a second home, and he became a longtime friend of Albert Simons. With Simons, Howells, Smith, and Stone, the survey of Charleston's historic buildings had a formidable panel of judges who helped guide the city's awareness of its past.

Although preservation is a significant subject and focus for a monograph on Simons, readers might rightfully expect a more thorough discussion of Simons's original design work as a practicing architect and restoration architect. Muldrow provides information in text, drawings, and photographs on the saving of the Heyward Washington House, for which Simons provided restoration architectural drawings and specification, but few of Simons's other works as an architect and/or restorationist are treated in detail. Several projects are mentioned with drawings and photographs published, but they lack in-depth analyses of the contextual merits of Simons's original, but compatible, Colonial Revival designs. Also lacking are practical discussions of his transferable restoration and planning strategies beneficial to maintaining a town's historic character and ambiance as a place (*genius locii*). Such critical assessment and discussion of the interaction of restoration and original design would serve two purposes. First, it would attract architect readers who struggle with similar issues of design compatibility and contextual sensitivity in today's architectural practices. Second, it could beneficially inform planning efforts impacting historic towns and urban neighborhoods elsewhere. Nonetheless, Muldrow's book is handsomely produced, rich in imagery, important as an introduction to the career of one of America's most significant pioneer preservationists, and accessible to both professional and general readers.

Robert M. Craig, Georgia Institute of Technology

NOTE

1. Charles B. Hosmer Jr., *Preservation Comes of Age: From Williamsburg to the National Trust, 1926–1949* (Charlottesville: University Press of Virginia, 1981), 240.

Jill Beute Koverman, and Jane Przybysz (eds.), *The Words and Wares of David Drake: Revisiting "I Made This Jar" and the Legacy of Edgefield Pottery* (Columbia: University of South Carolina Press, 2024), 228 pp., paperback $34.99, ebook $34.99.

There was once a prolific master potter who turned pots in the Edgefield district of South Carolina. His name was Dave. He was also enslaved. Between 1829 and 1864, Dave produced various pottery forms, some of which were of mammoth scale, holding over twenty gallons. We know all this because he often signed and dated his pots. On numerous occasions, he even scribed original rhyming verses into the surface of clay. The book, *The Words and Wares of David Drake: Revisiting "I Made This Jar" and the Legacy of Edgefield Pottery*, edited by Jill Beute Koverman and Jane Przybysz, is a collection of essays, all tasked with the same purpose: to illuminate the identity and legacy of David Drake, master potter, poet, and emancipated man.

Through a series of essays, each with its own perspective and theme, the book paints a faceted portrait of Drake. The scant documentation of his existence comes mostly from family estate plans and sales documents, wherein he was listed as property to be sold, traded, and inherited. Additional information about his life comes from direct examination of the wares he produced and the dates, marks, and verses he wrote on the clay. Absent more firsthand documentation, researchers explore the physical condition of the potteries in which he worked and the societal conditions through which he navigated daily life. To this end, each essay tackles a specific element of his identity. The result is a mosaic approach to understanding David Drake, what he accomplished, and what his legacy means to contemporary art and culture.

The book is presented in two parts. The first part of the book is a reprint of the exhibition catalog produced to accompany the exhibition "I Made This Jar: The Life and Works of Enslaved African American Potter, Dave." Originally published in 1998, the catalog is a collection of well-researched essays that attempt to answer some of the crucial questions about Drake's life. Questions about his birth and death, the origins of his literacy, and his evolving skill as a master potter are all explored. Occasionally, the essayists shift focus from Drake to the physical and societal environment in which he lived. One such essay takes a historical look at the Edgefield district, noting the commercial and political constraints that prevailed during his lifetime. Another essay reveals archaeological information related to the pottery sites where Drake worked. Still other essays focus on his writing, linking his verse to early African-American poets and placing it in the larger tradition of pottery poetry from elsewhere in the United States and Europe. The final essay in part one returns our focus to Drake and looks directly at the verses he scribed, asserting his familiarity with social satire, the Bible, the larger world, and his place in it.

Compiled some twenty years later, the essays in the second half of the book attempt to pick up where the first publication left off. Although the essays in this portion of the book seem a bit disjointed, they do represent the diverse research that has occurred. As a ceramics educator, I was particularly fascinated by the archaeological evidence regarding the kilns used at several Edgefield potteries where Drake worked. Unlike the kilns commonly found in South Carolina, the Edgefield kilns were up to three times larger, and aspects of their construction resembled kiln designs from Europe and Asia. Additionally, as pottery forms and shards attributed to Drake have been categorized by date, aesthetic attributes, and scribed verse, interesting patterns arise, revealing glimpses into which days of his workweek were most labor intensive and which years his pots went unsigned or undated, his voice inexplicably silenced. Analysis of the wares produced at these potteries provides evidence as to where Drake worked and how his work evolved as he was transferred from one owner to the next. Ongoing research in this area means additional pots continue to be discovered and attributed to Drake, thus broadening his oeuvre and our understanding of it.

Not all the essays in the book, however, focus on artifacts and accounts of the past. Two essays in the second section examine the ways in which Drake's work has influenced and inspired contemporary Black artists such as Jonathan Green, Carrie Mae Weems, and Theaster Gates. Each of these artists produced artwork inspired by, and reflective of, Drake's life and experience. Consequently, these artists are presented as cultural historians, promoting global awareness of Drake by illuminating details of his life and planting his legacy firmly within the context of contemporary culture.

These essays are paralleled by the final essay in the book, written by a descendant of one of the families that owned Drake. This essay pulls us back into the past once more and, while providing additional information, it highlights the book's limitation—that to know more about David Drake, we must rely on adjacent accounts of his life and station—and therein lies the book's greatest challenge. Absent accounts directly from Drake or his descendants, his identity remains tantalizingly incomplete. More research is needed.

The book concludes with a fascinating series of appendices that stand as the culminating record, to date, of the documented data on Drake's life and work. An attempt is made to document all the African-American potters and associated laborers working in the Edgefield District during Drake's lifetime. There is also a chronological listing of all known inscriptions incised by or attributed to David Drake, as well as an inventory of his dated vessels listed chronologically with museum affiliation should one want to see an example of his work in person.

The authors and editors present a fascinating and multifaceted portrait based on what is currently known. However, if the purpose of the book is to reveal his identity, this reader is left craving more. The available research has begun to clarify several specific dates, events, and aspects of his life, but many of the larger questions raised within the book remain unanswered. For example, what was the extent of his liberties, and how did his obvious skill, talent, and education affect his status? In such a punitive environment, it seems radical, this act of rebellion with words, to write on pots and boldly sign his name. One also wonders: Who was the intended audience for his verse? Were his words solely an expression of identity and independence, or were they more of a signal to other enslaved people, or possibly a tool used for the education of others? Much remains to be confirmed about his personal life, his motives, and his tribulations. Perhaps in another twenty years, yet another update to the publication will provide answers to these questions and more. In the meantime, this text is an excellent culmination of existing research and opinions concerning the life and identity of David Drake. As awareness of David Drake grows, the opportunity for new discoveries, connections, and conjecture will surely continue to expand in pace.

Douglas E. Gray, Francis Marion University

Karen Hess, *The Carolina Rice Kitchen: The African Connection,* 2nd ed. (Columbia: University of South Carolina Press, 2022), 328 pp., paperback $26.99, ebook $26.99.

According to culinary historian Karen Hess, this volume is quite simply "a hymn of praise for Carolina rice," based on the concept of a rice kitchen, a household where "rice appears on the table every day and is treated with due respect as one of our oldest and most prized grains." Hess, who died in

2007, is well known for having annotated and edited historic recipe collections and cookbooks by people such as Martha Washington (unpublished until 1981), Mary Randolph (1824), Amelia Simmons (1796), Abby Fisher (1881), and Hannah Glassie (1805), which she introduced with thoroughly researched historical analyses. In some respects, *Carolina Rice Kitchen* follows that same formula in that it includes a facsimile of a collection of two hundred thirty-seven recipes compiled by Mrs. Samuel G. Stoney under the title *Carolina Rice Book*, which was offered as a twenty-five-cent souvenir for the not-particularly successful South Carolina Interstate and West Indian Exposition of 1901–02. However, unlike her other works, in *Carolina Rice Kitchen*, the historic cookbook is almost an afterthought. Instead of an introductory essay, Hess devotes a full one hundred fifty-five pages to describing the history of rice in South Carolina, discussing its preparation and use in pilau, casseroles, Hoppin' John, soups, breads, desserts, and medicines. In this book, she takes a folkloric approach, using, as food writer John Martin Taylor notes in his foreword to this new edition, "linguistics, demographics, geology, geography, climate, politics, religion, botany, agriculture, and kitchen gardens . . . in her efforts to define the Carolina rice kitchen." Hess freely admits that she delves into areas of speculation as she attempts to trace the origins of Carolina rice dishes but asserts, "my hypotheses hold up from every point of view, culinary, historical, and linguistic, but there is an element of conjecture, hence possibility of error." She fills her investigations with recipes from across cultures and time, adding personal asides. She documents her chapters with footnotes (after thanking an impressive list of people in her acknowledgements), but she also introduces "a great deal of material into my text in a parenthetical manner," often involving digressions she feels are "illuminating in some way," because, as she explains, "I have learned . . . that few people read the notes." The result is that *Carolina Rice Kitchen* reads more as a conversation than an academic study, as Hess escorts the reader on her personal pilgrimage through Lowcountry rice culture.

One theme that runs throughout *Carolina Rice Kitchen* is the importance of the roles played by African and African-American women, "who created the celebrated rice kitchen of the South Carolina Low Country," even though "save for an occasional slave name, such as Maum Sarah, their names are forgotten." Indeed, Hess argues that "most of the peculiarly South Carolina culinary splendors were Asian and African in origin, and African American in execution."

As she explores the origins of different Lowcountry rice dishes, Hess devotes most of her time in discussing pilau, "the most characteristic dish of the Carolina rice kitchen." She investigates its origins in Persian cuisine, traces its movement to France, and its transition through the hands of African-American cooks into a uniquely Carolina experience, declaring, "The classic pilau is not so much a receipt as a culinary concept." She posits that pilau arrived in seventeenth-century South Carolina thanks to French Huguenots from Provence, who moved to the colony seeking relief from Catholic persecution. After discussing various incarnations of pilau, she moves onto related dishes such as jambalaya and Jewish saffron rice and devotes an entirely separate chapter to the evolution of Hoppin' John in its diverse forms.

Carolina Rice Kitchen is an engaging and entertaining study, but one cannot help but think there was a missed opportunity here. Although the University of South Carolina Press published this as a second edition, it is simply a reprint of the original with the addition of John Martin Taylor's brief foreword. Many scholars have conducted excellent research on rice culture over the thirty years since the book first appeared in 1992. Taylor himself was involved with the Carolina Gold Rice Foundation, an organization that helped lead to the restoration of the famous strain as a viable crop. Scientists have mapped the DNA of varieties of rice from Africa and Asia, allowing for new explorations of the origins of rice in South Carolina. Also, there are any number of recent studies greatly expanding knowledge about enslaved people and their vital history in the development of South Carolina and rice culture. Were she still alive, Hess undoubtedly would have revised and updated many of her original themes and ideas. It is a shame that another writer did not do that for her. It would have been an appropriate tribute to this champion of "one of our oldest and most prized grains"—rice.

Christopher E. Hendricks, Georgia Southern University

Robert Maynor, *The Big Game Is Every Night* (Spartanburg, SC: Hub City Press, 2023), 264 pp., paperback $16.95, ebook $9.99.

The Big Game Is Every Night won Hub City Press's 2022 South Carolina Novel Series and was published in 2023. The novel follows high schooler Grady Hayes's tumultuous coming of age in rural South Carolina. After suffering a brutal injury during a football game, Grady works toward a difficult physical recovery only to discover that it's his relationships and his understanding of himself that's truly in need of healing.

I was looking forward to seeing Hub City's announcement of the latest novel series winner, but I'll be honest. I felt a sink of disappointment when I learned they'd chosen "a football book." Growing up in rural Texas, there are few things more important than high school football, which is great if you play and not so great when you don't. I've served a youth's sentence of Friday pep rallies and small-town player privilege, and I thought I'd had my fill of clapping for high school athletes. And maybe I have, but Grady is more than a football player, as asserted by his mother, who says, "I didn't give you a number. I gave you a name."

But for Grady, football is football, but football can also be an awakening. Playing in a Friday night football game is "like being born. Opening new eyes to a world I'd never known." Although not all readers will have experienced putting on a jersey and a helmet and heading out onto the field, they will understand what it's like to see the world anew, to want a stadium full of people to know that you are "strong enough, fast enough, good enough, tough enough." Sure, Maynor is writing about football, and as far as I can tell, he does that well in terms of technicalities. But more important, Maynor is doing what all good writers and artists do: using the particular to reach out to something larger, something shared by those outside the specific experience.

And he entertains us, too, makes us laugh with dialogue so familiar I found myself reading out loud. On a visit to his grandmother's to celebrate her birthday, Grady's cousin Marcus says, "You ain't supposed to be cooking." Meemaw responds, "I know. I just couldn't help it." Grady puts a hand on his grandmother's back. Like a teenager, he asks, "How's it feel to be so old?" Meemaw answers, "Useless really." These moments are as accurate as a blade's edge. They are humorous and poignant. Like so many of our grandmothers, Meemaw can't stop cooking, and like so many of our grandmothers, Meemaw really does feel a certain kind of futility. Grady might not see it yet, but most of the novel is about *his* finding some sort of purpose.

Along the way, Grady learns to navigate the complex relationship he has with his mother. At one point in the narrative, Grady's mother says, "Feels like we haven't talked in forever." This is a point, and there are many, when Maynor's choice of the first-person point of view is vital, because we see that Grady is thinking about his mother, that he is trying to communicate. He talks about the upcoming game, that the coach thinks it will be tough. His mom responds by telling him she's proud of him like, Grady thinks, "she hadn't heard me at all." This is one of the most powerful exchanges in the novel. Here and elsewhere, the first-person perspective is essential to bridge the dissonance between what Grady is thinking and what he says and does. From the dialogue, we understand that Grady's mother believes that her son is quiet and doesn't want to talk to her, but the novel's point of view shows us that Grady feels like his mother isn't listening.

The turbulence in their relationship escalates as the narrative continues to unfold. On receiving some upsetting news about his mother, Grady storms out of the house. In this moment, he wants to escape everyone and everything, but because of the novel's perspective, Maynor gives the reader permission to be right there with him. We see more than an angry teenager heading into the woods and sitting on a fallen log. We have access to Grady's thoughts, that what we're actually witnessing are his attempts to "calm myself by not thinking any thoughts . . . I wished I was a snake . . . I could shed my skin. Have a whole new hide, itching with possibility."

Animals figure heavily into the book. It is set in rural South Carolina after all, and you might be surprised to learn that the cover of the book doesn't feature a football or a field or a helmet, but an owl. I can't say more than that. You'll have to read the book to find out why.

With *The Big Game Is Every Night*, Maynor opens a door into a teenage boy's world, and through this door, you, like me, might be a little startled to find a mirror, with familiar reflections—what it means to grow up, to try to heal the things that are really broken. With careful writing and thoughtful construction, Maynor develops a meaningful relationship between his main character and even this initially reluctant but at last deeply satisfied reader.

Landon Houle, Francis Marion University

Michael S. Martin, *Appalachian Pastoral: Mountain Excursions, Aesthetic Vision, and the Antebellum Travel Narrative* (Clemson, SC: Clemson University Press, 2022), 208 pp., cloth $130.00, ebook $130.00.

In this compelling, accessible study, Michael S. Martin surveys nineteenth-century depictions of southern Appalachia. For many readers, the authors and texts he considers will be unfamiliar. In fact, many of the primary texts are out of print. This is unfortunate. Martin's cogent readings of these works demonstrate their importance not only in terms of literary history, but also regional identity. Even fictionalized travel guides, he ably demonstrates, have defined southern environments and culture.

Martin builds his argument on a strong theoretical foundation that combines ideas from the Myth and Symbol School of American studies (notably R. W. B. Lewis's *The American Adam* and Leo Marx's *The Machine in the Garden*) with those of ecocriticism, which considers how the "real-world mountain space" shaped "poeticized prose portrayals." More specifically, he shows that antebellum understandings of Appalachia reflect a collision between the visceral experience of the mountains themselves and the shaping influence of British landscape aesthetics. Pastoralism becomes a "framing device" that allows writers to confront "an unknown landscape through a literary trope familiar to Northern readers."

There were also, of course, nonliterary forces that influenced perceptions of Appalachia. These include eighteenth- and nineteenth-century maps, which were "created for furthering commercial and national interests," understandings of the "land mass and topography" inherited from "native populations," and the "forces of westward expansion and development that informed American nationalism as a whole during the nineteenth century." For writers such as Caroline Howard Gilman, whose *Poetry of Travelling in the United States* provides vivid sketches of antebellum Charleston as well as the southern highlands, these cultural dynamics made Appalachia both familiar and inexplicable. Literary tradition, particularly pastoralism, provided a way of bridging the gap between actual terrain and readers' expectations.

Martin's point comes into particularly sharp focus through his discussions of Philip Pendleton Kennedy's *Blackwater Chronicle* (1853) and David Hunter Strother's *Virginia Illustrated* (1857). Both writers juxtaposed "real-life, scientific observations" with "fictional narratives." They did so to appeal to an "upper-class readership" that was already familiar with literary traditions. At the same time, their use of the pastoral, notably the claims that Appalachia constituted a new Arcadia, defined the region as an escape from the busyness of urban life. *The Blackwater Chronicle*, in fact, offers "a type of cultural tourism or voyeurism for the Northern reader into both the culture and natural world of the 'undiscovered' Appalachian Mountains." Strother, who provided illustrations for Kennedy's work and *Harper's Magazine*, continues the mythology, showing land cleared for farming but without the presence of tools or people. Even cultivated spaces appear inviting because they remain unscarred. The Appalachian Mountains thus become a kind of "natural paradise" or "perpetual Arcadia that nullifies, or at least ameliorates, the overarching conflict between nature and culture."

To a large degree, the texts Martin explicates promoted tourism, an enterprise that values both the unique and the familiar. Travelers long to see something unusual but without the inconveniences of the foreign. Henry Colton's *Mountain Scenery: The Scenery of the Mountains of Western North Carolina and Northwestern South Carolina* (1859) and Strother's *Virginia Illustrated* sought to balance these desires through their application of picturesque traditions, their depictions of social class, and their appeals to nostalgia. Colton's descriptions of such "memorable scenes" as Caesar's Head and Table Rock, which he imagines "rising in stern grandeur," demonstrate his ability to use the picturesque evocatively. At the same time, he makes the region "known" through his assurances that upper-class visitors will find "luxuriantly adorned" accommodations in Asheville.

Beautiful scenery, of course, makes up only part of the mountains' visual appeal. There is also the sublime—that overwhelming, sometimes terrifying, sense of greatness that leads the viewer toward the ineffable. In the mid-eighteenth century, the British philosopher Edmund Burke provided an influential treatise on the sublime, *A Philosophical Enquiry into the Origin of Our Ideas of the Sublime and Beautiful* (1757), which, Martin demonstrates, influenced American travel writers. In a particularly compelling discussion, Martin contrasts William Gilmore Simms's depictions of coastal South Carolina, notably in his novel *The Yemassee* (1835), with his portrayals of the Appalachian Mountains in such works as *Southward Ho! A Spell of Sunshine* (1834). Although both texts celebrate the natural world, they do so for different purposes. The Lowcountry embodies the beautiful, whereas the mountains evoke the sublime; the former offering reassurance and comfort, and the latter, a sense of the majestic. In this way, Simms's descriptions of the Carolinas separate the various "regions according to Burke's model of landscape features."

In his final chapter, Martin uses the interdisciplinary approaches associated with rural studies to examine idealistic understandings of Appalachia hinted at in the various travelogues he studies. Writers, he reveals, understood rural areas "dialectically in relation to developed land and urban areas." In doing so, they often extended the sort of valorization of agrarianism found in Thomas Jefferson's writings. In Philip Pendleton Kennedy's works, recurring references to railroads join "the natural and the technological" in ways that promise to preserve the mountains' "pure wilderness" while promoting accessibility and comfort. Ann Newport Royall offers a more ambivalent understanding. For her, the landscape contributes to some of the least laudable characteristics of the inhabitants, including many of the caustic stereotypes still applied to rural populations. At the same time, Royall, like her contemporaries, imagines an ideal country life without cities, an Appalachia of "workable farmlands" cultivating the "crops best suited for that particular ecosystem." Elisha Mitchell—the minister, geologist and professor for whom the highest peak east of the Mississippi is named—offers a similar vision. His responses to his beloved mountains speak to his aesthetic, spiritual, and scientific interests. At the same time, he imagines "a restorative component to the natural realm and an improvement in farming practices in Appalachia." Martin concludes his study with a brief epilogue that urges Appalachian Studies scholars to "look backwards and gain historical grounding before moving forward." He notes that understandings of Appalachian culture remain too centered on the twentieth century, almost as if the region was invented by the 1965 mapping project of the Appalachian Regional Commission. As Martin skillfully shows throughout his study, Appalachian culture existed during the antebellum period and grew out of European and regional traditions, some of which predate the nation.

Michael S. Martin has done important work in this study. He demonstrates how many long-forgotten, quasifictional texts have shaped understandings of a vitally important region. He also reveals the complicated interactions between imaginative constructions—particularly, British pastoralism—and the actual environments in which writers find themselves. This clearly written, carefully argued, and handsomely illustrated study will be of great interest not only to historians and literary scholars but also to those who feel the irresistible draw of our beautiful southern mountains.

Christopher D. Johnson, Francis Marion University

Peter N. Moore, *Carolina's Lost Colony: Stuarts Town and the Struggle for Survival in Early South Carolina* (Columbia: University of South Carolina Press, 2022), 196 pp., cloth $98.99, paperback $32.99, ebook $32.99.

Peter N. Moore weaves a narrative of imperial and Indigenous rivalries in the colonial southeast through the lens of a raid on Santa Catalina de Afuica in March 1785. With the support of their Scottish partners, Yamasee warriors attacked the Spanish mission for the Timucua in central Florida, raiding for captives to enslave and sell. The Scottish–Yamasee partnership that facilitated the raid "marked a turning point in the history of the colonial southeast." Moore stresses that this moment was far from inevitable; indeed, it was contingent on "local circumstances, personal rivalries, unexpected opportunities, and shifting conditions." Although it took place within the context of a transition from Spanish to British colonization from 1660 to 1690, Indigenous peoples held the power in the region.

His prologue details the Indigenous South Carolina before and during their encounters with Spanish colonizers. Coastal Indians maintained seven autonomous towns, which they occupied seasonally. Autonomy was sacred to coastal Indians as "their values and practices, their very separateness itself, had a spiritual source and a religious dimension, and they were reflected in myth and ritual." The Spanish established a settlement at Saint Helena, a location strategically determined by the Orista. Moore explains that the Orista did not trust the Spanish, so they "steered" them "to a location that marginalized the Spaniards while prioritizing their own economic, territorial, and defense needs." However, when the coastal Indians could not control the Spanish in their region politically and economically, they turned to warfare. When Spanish Ensign Hernando Moyano disrupted an Escamaçu religious feast in 1576, the coastal Indians slaughtered Moyano and twenty of his men. The Guale joined the Escamaçu in fighting the Spanish, and soon the Escamaçu War became a "regional conflict that united Natives all along the southeastern coast." The pan-Indian alliance proved fragile, and the Spanish abandoned Saint Elena in 1587.

Moore skips ahead to the 1660s in the first chapter, with English colonization and the Westo invasion. He titles it "Maneaters," because Indians around the English settlement at Charles Town reported that the Westo were cannibals. Moore claims the Westo invasion brought about the collapse of the coastal peoples and "opened the door to Scottish and Yamasee colonization of Port Royal." The Yamasee did not come into existence until around 1663. They were one of the "southeast's coalescent societies," a loose confederation of previously separate groups forced together through the instability brought on by European colonization. As the Westo moved into the area, coastal Indians allied with the English for protection. Moore challenges traditional historiography in his interpretation of the Westo War. Although other scholars have viewed it through an Anglocentric perspective, he argues that the Westo were not "English puppets" and that they were asserting their power in the region with violence and captive-taking.

Moore provides a trans-Atlantic history of Scottish desire to create an empire in the Americas in the 1680s in the second chapter. The Church of Scotland embraced Presbyterianism, which rejected a state-controlled church, and many members, called Covenanters, took an oath to defend it. When Charles Stuart took the thrones of England, Scotland, and Ireland in 1625, his adherence to the episcopal system of the Church of England threatened Scottish Presbyterianism. Furthermore, the English Parliament passed the Navigation Acts, forbidding the Scottish from trading with England's colony. In 1681, the Scots were able to establish a colony at Port Royal within England's territory in South Carolina. In 1682, Scots, led by Covenanters, founded a joint-stock company, the Carolina Company. As the Scottish government fiercely persecuted Covenanters in Scotland, "the colonial scheme took a greater sense of urgency," and Stuarts Town was born out of this apocalyptic moment." Moore's discussion of the convict trade will prove problematic for some readers, as he claims that "in Carolina, they were treated like slaves." In his notes, he explains how he follows "John Donoghue's lead in seeing indentured servitude and chattel slavery as two varieties of enslavement rather than two completely distinct labor systems." However, this downplays the racial ideologies that perpetuated the enslavement of Indigenous and African peoples in the Americas for centuries.

In the third chapter, cleverly titled "Unsettling Port Royal," Moore details the demographic chaos of the colony in 1684. Coastal Indians, Scottish religious refugees, Yamasee, and fugitives from Spanish missions in Florida came to populate Port Royal. Through separate treaties, nine coastal Indian towns ceded their lands to the Lords Proprietors of South Carolina. Although this was supposed to ensure their protection from enslavement, colonial authorities defied agreements with the Lords Proprietors. The demographics were not balanced. By 1685, there were as many as two thousand Indians living at Port Royal but only around sixty Scots. Nonetheless, "the Scots had big dreams for Stuarts Town, envisioning it as the seat of a Scottish empire." This might have been possible through their alliance with the Yamasee.

Moore turns up the heat in chapter four, "Consuming Fire." By the end of 1684, the Lord Proprietors outlawed Carolina's Indian slave trade and placed restrictions on the export of Indigenous peoples for enslavement. However, the Scottish settlers and Yamasee "reignited the trade." In the raid on Santa Catalina de Afuica in March 1785, the Yamasee took twenty-eight captives. The Yamasee kept only two of them, and the Scots sold the rest in South Carolina and the West Indies. The raid was "a clear assertion of

Scottish empire," as well as a signal of Yamasee power. The Scots also began to seek enslaved Africans to work in their colony. The Spanish, Timucua, and Apalachee exacted revenge by sacking a Yamasee settlement at Santa Catalina de Guale and leaving Stuarts Town in ruins.

Moore's epilogue traces the aftermath. He explains that "the timing for a new colony was all wrong; in some sense, it was doomed to fail from its inception." He also discusses Scottish settler William Dunlop's paradoxical history with slavery. He went to South Carolina "as a missionary to Native people but ended up enslaving them." Dunlop went on to write a document that seems to be proslavery and antislavery at the same time. Intriguingly, the Yamasee were able to establish communities at Port Royal without the Scots until the English began to encroach on their lands in the early 1700s. Moore's concise monograph is a quick read. Because significant portions of it have been published elsewhere, the chapters stand alone well and could quite easily be assigned to more advanced students individually.

Erica Johnson, Francis Marion University

Courtney L. Tollison Hartness, *"Our Country First, Then Greenville": A New South City During the Progressive Era and World War I* (Columbia: University of South Carolina Press, 2023), 328 pp., cloth $104.99, paperback $34.99, ebook $34.99.

Local histories can provide a microcosm of broader state, regional, national, and even international events, something Courtney Hartness had done exceptionally well in her book, *"Our Country First, Then Greenville."* Indeed, Hartness' history of Greenville is arguably one microcosm within another, for her interest is not the entire history of that city but only the years of World War I. She demonstrates that at a time of domestic reform and international strife, Greenville simultaneously was forward-looking yet unable to escape its past.

In writing her monograph, Hartness mined a wide array of sources, ranging from more than a dozen archives both within and outside South Carolina to numerous newspapers, government documents, books, and articles. She found that Greenville's leaders adopted the ideas both of the "New South," years before use of that term, and the Progressive movement that had appeared by the late 1800s. Like the proponents of the New South, the city had begun to industrialize and seek to end post-Civil War animosities. Like the Progressives, Greenvillians touted their efforts at beautification, restricting alcohol, enhancing educational standards, and improving their local and regional transportation infrastructure.

Yet for all of its efforts to highlight its modern and progressive credentials, Greenville could not escape its past. For all their talk of social justice, Progressives nationally gave little attention to African-American rights. Such was the case in Greenville, which, like many other southern municipalities, remained a segregated city. Similarly, calls for suffrage for women found a largely cold reception among the political elite in both South Carolina and Greenville. "Whether Greenvillians were or were not progressive," writes Hartness, "is debatable; whether Greenville's leaders wanted to be progressive and saw themselves as such is not."

World War I, which underlies the majority of the chapters in the book, did little to change these trends. Before and during America's entrance into that conflict, Greenville's white population joined broader homefront initiatives, such as raising money and conserving food. The city's leaders sought to become the site of a military training camp, believing it would be economically beneficial. They were pleased to learn in 1917 that they would be the site of Camp Sevier. Indeed, the US government put many of these training camps in the South to break down still simmering post-Civil War divisions and "imbue those communities and their soldiers with a heightened state of nationalism." Women did their part, providing support for the troops at Camp Sevier, raising money, taking the jobs of men who left to fight, and joining the Progressives' effort to combat prostitution—the last of which became a growing problem once Port Sevier opened. African Americans in the community sought to help as well, raising funds and offering to combat enemy forces abroad.

Still, Greenville remained stuck in the past. Both at a national and local level, suffragists hoped that women's support for the war effort would lead to them winning the right to vote, yet local and state leaders remained opposed to granting them that right. Indeed, despite the fact that the Nineteenth Amendment, passed in 1920, granted suffrage to women, South Carolina itself did not ratify it until 1969.

Nor did life change significantly for African Americans. About nine hundred Blacks from Greenville served in the war, but, as was the case for others who joined the armed forces, they found a military that discriminated against them, whether it be at Camp Sevier or in Europe, and a reluctance to allow them in combat. At home, President Woodrow Wilson showed little interest in protecting African Americans' rights. The War Department touted that its collegiate Student Army Training Corps (SATC) program would not make "distinctions . . . in race, color or creed." Yet because college administrators oversaw the SATC, southern institutions of higher education, including Furman, adhered to their segregationist policies. It is understandable, therefore, why many southern Blacks, including a significant number from Greenville, left the South and headed north, where they hoped to find better jobs and greater acceptance.

Hartness is careful to note that there were exceptions to the rule. The fighting prowess of African Americans, when given the chance to fight, impressed their white comrades. When the Spanish flu epidemic hit Greenville in 1918, the need for medical personnel gave African-American nurses an opportunity to offer their services, which meant working alongside white nurses at camps like Sevier. Despite resistance among white nurses to work hand in hand with Black peers, the latter received praise from their superiors for the quality of their work. The fact remained, however, that African Americans, who had hoped their service during World War I might lead to an improvement in their socioeconomic status, found that little had changed afterward, whether it be at the national or, in the case of Greenville, the local level. Greenville's leaders continued to point to their city's progressive credentials, but "white citizens found the community far more attractive than African Americans did."

Hartness ends the book with a poignant epilogue that attests to the struggles Americans continue to face as they confront their national, state, and local histories. Using the theme of memorialization, she points out that it took decades for Greenvillians to recognize the contributions of the local African-American community to their city's history. One example was the founding in 2022 of a new public space called Unity Park. Yet a mile away stands a memorial honoring those who fought the Union during the Civil War. Hence, even today, Greenville, like so many other towns and cities, continues to struggle with its past.

Scott Kaufman, Francis Marion University

June Manning Thomas, *Struggling to Learn: An Intimate History of School Desegregation in South Carolina* (Columbia: University of South Carolina Press, 2022), 320 pp., cloth $44.99, paperback $22.99 (2024), ebook $22.99.

Struggling to Learn offers a tragic, hopeful history of public school integration in South Carolina. Combining history and memoir, Thomas creates a narrative in which resilient African Americans and a few white actors worked tirelessly to improve educational opportunities. These brave individuals faced considerable resistance and danger as they sought "to build an egalitarian society." In telling her history, Thomas counters the proposition that South Carolina, in contrast to other southern states, earned a "reputation for peaceful transition" toward integration. Although her arguments are compelling and well documented, a similarly comprehensive investigation of other Deep South states, particularly Mississippi, might challenge her claim.

Thomas depicts the various obstacles Black families confronted while striving for advancement. As she confirms, the events of the postslavery period are critical for understanding South Carolina's later civil rights struggles. Both the state's 1895 constitution and the infamous 1896 *Plessy v. Ferguson* ruling segregated the state's public schools and effectively erased whatever progress had been made during Reconstruction. "By 1916," Thomas argues, "South Carolina, ignoring the 'separate but equal' principle mandated in *Plessy v. Ferguson*, spent 9.4 times more per white student than per Black." Racial disparities between rural schools and urban schools were even sharper. In 1920, South Carolina provided the lowest expenditure per student nationally.

Black families had to adapt while persevering. In Orangeburg, the Rosenwald School Program exemplified Black people's dedication to education. The program, funded by John D. Rockefeller Sr. and other northern philanthropists, provided construction funds "to support programs that used the Hampton-Tuskegee model of industrial education," but Black citizens still had to put forward matching monies "to get schools built." According to Thomas, "Black people had to deed their own money, land, and labor to local public-school systems." By 1932, Orangeburg residents helped build eighteen schoolhouses with Rosenwald support.

Thomas addresses other triumphs that coincided with hurdles. For example, the National Association for the Advancement of Colored People

(NAACP) and Thurgood Marshall achieved equal teacher pay, but South Carolina legislators prevented many Black teachers from overcoming the "step" standards required for pay increases. At the same time, South Carolina civil rights advocates fought provisions that ensured all white teachers in Black schools. Thomas details the courageous Black citizens of Clarendon County who risked their livelihoods and lives to combat the egregious separate and unequal public school policies, especially the district's failure to provide bus transportation for Black students.

Still, Black children experienced profound inequities as is evidenced in *Briggs v. Elliott*, which originated in Clarendon County. *Briggs* became the most decisive of the five cases that resulted in the landmark 1954 *Brown v. Board of Education of Topeka, Kansas* ruling, the most momentous legal breakthrough to assault Jim Crow segregation. Thomas provides a nuanced description of *Brown*'s consequences. In particular, she addresses local white resistance and efforts by the state's leadership to preserve Jim Crow. "Looking at the civil rights era merely as a time of heroic action," Thomas contends, "overlooks the tenacity of segregationists and leaves us unprepared to understand contemporary racism." As Thomas confirms, "all the [*Briggs*] petitioners suffered, losing jobs, having long-term debts called in for repayment, and being unable to obtain supplies or equipment to carry out their trades or till their soil," and one plaintiff participant died mysteriously. Unsurprisingly, the *Brown* decision resulted in many southern whites harassing Black advocates of integration. Public school employees could lose their jobs if they joined the NAACP. Even white advocates, including Chester Travelstead, the dean of education at the University of South Carolina, found out the danger of speaking out on behalf of public school integration. His advocacy resulted in his dismissal from the university.

In 1956, Thomas's family moved to Orangeburg and thrust themselves into the local civil rights movement. "Black activism," Thomas affirms, "was not the product of 'outside agitators,'" even though national notables, including Dr. Martin Luther King Jr., visited Trinity Church in Orangeburg and met with Thomas's father, who served as president of Claflin University. Thomas remembers King as the most striking of the civil rights leaders: "I remember the power of his delivery, the fevered pitch of his crescendos, and most impressively the ecstasy with which the packed audience shouted in enthusiastic assent."

King's presence was indicative of the shifting social and political climate of the 1960s. The forces perpetuating segregation would soon confront the fiercest storm of those frustrated with the slow pace of change. In 1963, the breakthrough matriculation of Harvey Gantt into Clemson University, followed by that of Henri Monteith and two other Black students at the University of South Carolina, created a ripple effect that quickly reached Orangeburg. At the height of the civil rights transformation, Thomas's parents bravely enrolled her in Orangeburg High School, where she became one of only thirteen Black students. Although Orangeburg High School provided superior educational opportunities, most Black parents were hesitant to involve their children in the "harsh racial realities" that could arise with integration.

Thomas hoped for a new beginning at Orangeburg High School, but she soon faced raw, vicious racial discrimination. As she recalls, "my fledgling hopes for friendship or at least tolerance immediately died. . . . The students' response to our presence seemed to be an organized effort to resist by harassing us in whatever way was possible, using such means as catcalls, mocking and twisted faces, racial epithets, spitballs, and other creative mechanisms." The only positive aspects came from Orangeburg's high academic standards and three supportive teachers.

Thomas found some solace when she enrolled at Furman University. As a grassroots civil rights participant in Orangeburg, she had merely endured. At Furman, she could thrive, or so she hoped. The private university had recently integrated, and, despite its "pro-slavery roots," Furman embraced "relative liberalism." Still, barriers existed. White students "were not hostile," but they "were not particularly friendly, and very few reached out" to Black students. While at Furman, Thomas limited her activism to styling her hair in a "natural Afro," reading voraciously, and congregating with other Black students, especially the campus's first three Black female students.

In 1968, the Orangeburg Massacre and the assassination of Dr. King convinced Thomas to transfer to Michigan State University. After seeing King's casket in Atlanta, Thomas told her parents that she would "rather drop out of college than stay in the South." Now a participant in the Great Migration, she left her home state to attend a university that promised greater tolerance and offered a "major in something that I cared about."

Struggling to Learn tells a story of the passionate perseverance for Black education. It provides a detailed account of the "destructive and constructive forces" that formed South Carolina's present-day public educational institutions. In doing so, the book advocates for racial cooperation, harmony, justice and acceptance in the spirit of the Baha'i Faith, which Thomas first embraced at Furman. Thomas affirms that dire circumstances remain for Black South Carolina students, but her concluding message looks toward a time when "enough people support change not only in structures but also in their hearts." For Thomas, the struggle for educational and racial equality persists.

Jason Kirby, Francis Marion University

Elizabeth J. West, *Finding Francis: One Family's Journey from Slavery to Freedom* (Columbia: University of South Carolina Press, 2022), 204 pp., cloth $98.99, paperback $29.99, ebook $29.99.

Francis Sistrunk is not a name found in most history books; she is well known to neither experts nor the lay reader. But Elizabeth West weaves Francis, her story, and her descendants into the historical fabric of America in this deeply researched study.

Rather than titling it after the Sistrunk family or after the regions of the south—South Carolina, Georgia, Alabama, and Mississippi—that the family lived and farmed in, West deliberately focuses on the person of Francis Sistrunk, who lived from 1827 until sometime in the last decades of the nineteenth century. At the start of the book, West emphasizes that genealogies and other historical accounts frequently omit the enslaved. They were not permitted to write accounts of their own lives, and when they are included in records, they are often listed as nameless property. So they must be *found*, and within the pages of this book, West names Francis Sistrunk and reminds us that "without explicit records noting the names, date of birth, parents' names, and other personal-individual evidence of existence, the presumption is that we cannot know them." West turns that assumption on its head by "layering the antebellum records with samplings of post-emancipation records and archives" to tell Francis's story.

In reading this book, one will certainly learn a lot about Francis, her six children, and the generations that followed her (West herself is a sixth-generation descendant). Tracing the family's movement across the southern states, West's impressive research reveals details about land holdings, financial transactions, church foundings, and census records. But this book is at its most engaging when these details are linked to larger societal issues of both yesterday and today. For instance, West discusses the fear of African Americans after the Civil War, challenging any notion that freedom meant safety. She writes, "Francis had to instill in her children an awareness of situations that could be put their lives and fates in the hands of whites who had the full force of the law to wield against them." This "heightened state" is, of course, still heightened, many generations later, as noted in recent books by Ta-Nehisi Coates and Kiese Laymon.[1] The "talk" that Black families have with their children has a long, painful history. Thinking about this through Francis's position as a formerly enslaved mother and recognizing that it's a conversation happening right now in our country is both sobering and deeply troubling.

Another thread that West traces back to Francis is the act of naming. Although it is easy to look at a mother naming a child after a relative or ancestor as a straightforward move to respect or honor that familial tie, West reveals that in Francis's case, it is much more. She writes, "The lasting imprint of Francis's connection with Shadrack II is in the name of their son. By naming her son Shadrack, Francis created a family and kinship line for her son and for future generations," further reminding us that "enslaved people often conferred names to children to help them maintain knowledge of their family connections and origins, especially considering the probability that they may be separated."

It is surely interesting to read about the life of Francis and the details of her familial history. But what's moving and engaging about this book is how West uses Francis's life to teach us so much more about enslavement and the deliberate steps that women such as Francis made to forge community and build families after the Civil War.

Meredith A. Love, Francis Marion University

NOTE

1. Ta-Nehisi Coates, *Between the World and Me* (London: Oneworld Publications, 2015); Kiese Laymon, *Heavy: An American Memoir* (New York: Scribner Books, 2018).

Jo Angela Edwins, *A Dangerous Heaven* (Norman, AR: Gnashing Teeth Publishing, 2023), 112 pp., paperback $15.00.

In *A Dangerous Heaven*, Jo Angela Edwins explores the precarious relationships between womanhood and religion. Edwins takes her reader on an intricate, beautifully scripted poetic journey that blends historic literature, scientific beauty, and the emotional depth and breadth of being a woman confronting the large, often overwhelming, details of life. Scattered throughout the collection are poems that focus on biblical women. In "Eve," "Magdalene," "Bathsheba," "Mary," and "Leah, Rachel, and Dinah," Edwins rips through the fabric of the patriarchal system so well documented in the Bible. Each poem poignantly exposes the underbelly of Christianity and the prescribed roles of subservient, silent women. Edwins recasts these women and gives them a voice where none previously exists. With that voice comes power, and readers can better see how women have an impact in this "beautifully flawed world."

Although representations of biblical women tether the collection together, there are also poems that explore the modern woman's relationship with religion. One of the most notable is "An American Woman Steps Inside an 800-Year-Old Church." Here, Edwins masterfully depicts the discomfort of a woman visiting a church that she knows was not built for her to visit. The vibrant descriptions of the church, with its "smells of beeswax/and moldering Latin" and "chalky holy water," allow the reader to immerse themselves into the scene. By triggering our senses, Edwins allows us to truly feel what the woman in the poem feels—unease, "like a minor demon," with a deep sense of grief.

Edwins plays on our emotions throughout her collection, and not just with grief. Pain, loss, anger, joy, forgiveness, acceptance—Edwins explores them all. "Parents" navigates the loss of mothers and fathers and the depth of emotion that comes with those experiences. In "For Newton, For Townville" and "Calhoun," Edwins exposes the tragedy of American gun violence as she explores not only school shootings but also the Mother Emanuel Church killings in Charleston. She speaks on war and violence against children in "The Children Have Stopped Crying." She navigates the hurt we feel when betrayed by those we love the most in "That Hurt." With each of these poems, Edwins helps us understand the complicated feelings that arise from the real-world situations to which many of us have become unwittingly apathetic. She brings it all to the forefront and does so in a spiritual, self-reflective way. Although many of these poems do not explicitly refer to religion, there is an undercurrent of the fragility of faith throughout each.

In "This Year," an especially powerful poem, Edwins discusses both the sexualization of women and the violence enacted on them—a crude Halloween decoration, women being murdered, a grandmother "hunched in a ditch," the "sunken in shallow graves" of brutalized women, a woman decaying in a field. After documenting these atrocities, Edwins writes, "And people wonder still/why we tell sad women's stories." These stories need to be told because of everything exposed in this collection. The sad stories will continue until society truly invests in the safety and security of women. Meanwhile, women can only do what Edwins advises: "Ask the people to sit down" and listen to our stories. The hope is that empathy will follow. Although, as Edwins reveals, empathy seems quite difficult to come by, especially when combining religious practice with women's human rights.

In *A Dangerous Heaven,* Jo Angela Edwins demonstrates a masterful control of language and poetic form. She illustrates the experiences of women and affects the reader's heart, causing them to contemplate not only the complex structures that drive the daily narratives of power, grief, misogyny, and self-worth but also the myriad ways women respond to these structures. Although the themes offered in the collection can be heavy to the heart, the ways in which Edwins presents them are breathtaking and powerful. With this collection, Edwins herself stands as a truly remarkable example of why women's voices are both strong and needed.

Natalie S. Mahaffey, Central Carolina Technical College

Patrick D. McMillan, Richard D. Porcher Jr., Douglas A. Rayner, and David B. White, *A Guide to the Wildflowers of South Carolina,* revised and expanded ed. (Columbia: University of South Carolina Press, 2022), cloth $119.99, paperback $39.99, ebook $39.99.

I love a longleaf pine savanna, specifically of the mesic variety. The more mesic the better. Imagine a canopy of towering longleaf pines (*Pinus palustris*) acting as the sentry of an expansive habitat. Amid shallow pools, emerald green pitcher plants (*Sarracenia flava*) rise from the ground like elegant trumpets. Although small, the dwarf sundews (*Drosera brevifolia*) dot the ground with anthocyanin rich splotches. These carnivorous plants glisten with droplets of dew that act as sweet and deadly bait for small insects. In the midst of summer, an observer may be greeted by the striking, vibrant orange of a pine lily (*Lilium catesbyi*) flower or the more muted, but no less beautiful, yellow of a fringeless orchid (*Platanthera integra*). In this same scene, a keen observer will also notice dozens of other distinct plant species, some of which may be missing flowers, or fruits, or even leaves. So, how does one determine what they are looking at without the answer being whispered into their ear? A trusty field guide is an age-old classic, and for good reason. This guide is organized primarily into physiogeographic region and secondarily by a collection of plants expected in that region, ranked alphabetically by common name. Each entry has a nice description, photograph, and overview of the species's known distribution in South Carolina. The guide does not serve as a replacement for a taxonomic key. Instead, I would encourage a user to research a site they may visit, decide its most likely physiogeographic region (a brief guide exists in the book for this task), and then spend some time studying which plant species one might expect to find at such a site.

There is always an outstanding question with these kinds of reference materials: Are they for use in the field or are they better served left at home and used as a reference later? I say leave a reference like this at home and take many pictures and notes while out in the field. Why? First, this book weighs over three pounds and beautifully describes one thousand twenty-two of the approximately three thousand vascular plant species found in South Carolina. The thousand or so species highlighted in this text are well chosen, representing the showiest (i.e., most noticeable), most abundant (*i.e.* most common), and most notable (i.e., most interesting) plant species the state has to offer, but it is not exhaustive and does not claim to be. Second, simply because of the format of the book, included plant species have a main entry under one physiogeographic region only, even though they may well appear in multiple habitat types. Third, and finally, phenotypic variation can be difficult to account for in guides like this. This is not a flaw in the book, just a necessity because of space limitations. The persistent trillium (*Trillium persistens*), for example, displays a staggering amount of variation in its petal color with age, ranging from white to pink, or even purple. To the credit of the diligent authors, this guide includes exemplars of the extreme colors and a description of the color changing process. Certainly, the photography is one of the highlights of the book. One of my favorite photographs in this work is of the beautiful large marsh rose-pink (*Sabatia dodecandra*) with two side-by-side flowers, one with white petals and one with pink petals. It is interesting that, although the trillium petal color is dictated by age, petal color in the marsh rose-pink is a polymorphic genetic trait with flowers ranging from pink, to purple, to blue, to white. Again, I call attention to the phenotypic diversity found within species only to highlight what a difficult job it is to create an informative guide with an appropriate amount of resolution without being impossibly long and cumbersome.

Furthermore, competent photography for a guide like this is about more than an artistic endeavor, the experience of the photographic direction is key. An example of this executed well would be the attention to detail given to the ladies' tress orchid (*Spiranthes laciniata*). A photograph of the orchid's flowering stalk is provided in two resolutions: one that highlights the arrangement of the flowers along the flowering spike and a second, at greater magnification, that draws attention to the very fine hairs that line the flowering spike—an important diagnostic characteristic for this particular species.

As the authors point out, "No one can expect to learn the flora of a state, or even the flora of a region, in a few sessions. Wildflower identification is a lifelong commitment." Indeed, I echo this sentiment and encourage the use of multiple tools as you study the world around you—including this one. I have had, and used, a version of this book for the eight years I have lived in South Carolina, and I will continue to keep a copy on hand. This is certainly an excellent resource for entering the world of botany as a hobby, but even a seasoned field botanist will find the reference incredibly useful.

Jeremy D. Rentsch, Francis Marion University

Mary Martha Greene, *The Cheese Biscuit Queen Tells All: Southern Recipes, Sweet Remembrances, and a Little Rambunctious Behavior* (Columbia: University of South Carolina Press, 2021), 248 pp., paperback $24.99, ebook $24.99.

I am no cook. I know this. My family knows this. But I am a southerner, a food lover, a storyteller, and—after reading Mary Martha Greene's *The Cheese Biscuit Queen Tells All: Southern Recipes, Sweet Remembrances, and a Little Rambunctious Behavior*—a believer in the idea that every southern recipe comes with several fantastic stories behind it.

Pairing each recipe with a story is what makes Greene's text so much more than a cookbook. These snapshots of various moments help to give the dishes deeper sentimental meanings while inviting the reader into Greene's past and personality. Throughout its pages, the reader is introduced to family members and friends while being exposed to recipes that leave lasting impressions in the mouth and on the heart. As pages turn, we learn about her Aunt Mimi's shocking similarity to Queen Elizabeth II, a crawfish mission gone awry, and their family's 2008 voting "scandal," among many other memorable tales. The different stories in the cookbook are vivid and endearing and are just right in length when thinking about reading a quick vignette before cooking.

The people in the stories add warmth to the food behind the tale, and readers are able to develop an association between the dish and its past while adding their own stories and memories after the recipe is created. Furthermore, dishes are not just general dishes; rather, they hold a certain allure because of the stories and those affiliated with them. Several of them even include their namesakes in their titles such as "Dessie's Blueberry Cobbler" and "Aunt Lou's Famous Chocolate Roll." Greene's tribute to each person, each recipe is evident from start to finish, and her compilation ranges in topic and emotion and is created with the perfect mixture of family and culture, including a pinch of humor, a dash of drama, and a cup of love.

The organization of the cookbook categorizes the food in familiar ways, making items easy to locate. Its eight sections cover a wide variety of food, including, but not limited to, "Breakfast Baking," "Hors d'Oeuvres," "Meats and Poultry," "Seafood," and "Libations." Perhaps my side-dish-loving, sweet-tooth self was most engulfed by the side dishes and baked treats listed.

Greene includes images of people and of pictures of handwritten recipes to add to the aesthetics and includes tips and tricks to offer enticing and useful alternatives. Although most relate to substitutions or variations in the actual recipe (something that I am sure helps when cooking), my favorite tip is mentioned in the story connected to her "Smoked Salmon Cheesecake" recipe, when she suggests to "pick a favorite charity and give your next party a purpose." Such a statement stresses the author's generous nature while highlighting how food can bring communities together.

The Cheese Biscuit Queen Tells All is filled with oldies and goodies and gives some classic dishes new twists. I can imagine this text being a go-to favorite in kitchens, especially in a South Carolinian's kitchen with all its cultural and regional extensions. Moreover, I suspect that this text could help even the worst cook pass for a decent cook, and I personally cannot wait to try some recipes such as "Chicken and White Bean Chili," "Key Lime Chicken Strips," and "Jane's Slow Cooker Pulled Pork" to name just a few. Regardless of its ability to convert me into a cook, this book is filled with recipes one will return to and stories one will remember.

Rachel N. Spear, Francis Marion University

TAKE ON THE
SOUTH

USC
1801

Take on the South explores the complexity of
the United States' most distinctive region through
conversations with those who think, write, teach,
and reflect on the South, both historically and
today.

Our rotating panel of hosts takes a deep dive on
the meaning of the South in the 21st century by
inviting guests to offer their take on that same
South. Join us as we ... Take on the South!

https://linktr.ee/sostatusc

Take on the South is a podcast produced by the
Institute for Southern Studies at the
University of South Carolina.